Also by John Francis, Ph.D.

Planetwalker: 22 Years of Walking. 17 Years of Silence.

THE
RAGGED
EDGE
OF
SILENCE

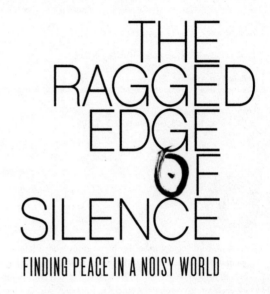

THE RAGGED EDGE OF SILENCE

FINDING PEACE IN A NOISY WORLD

JOHN FRANCIS, PH.D.

NATIONAL GEOGRAPHIC

WASHINGTON, D.C.

For our Fathers

Published by the National Geographic Society
1145 17th Street N.W., Washington, D.C. 20036
Copyright © 2011 John Francis. All rights reserved. Reproduction of the whole
or any part of the contents without written permission from the publisher is prohibited.

All illustrations by John Francis.

Library of Congress Cataloging-in-Publication Data

Francis, John, 1946 Feb. 23-
The ragged edge of silence : finding peace in a noisy world / John Francis.
    p. cm.
ISBN 978-1-4262-0723-5
1. Silence. 2. Francis, John, 1946 Feb. 23- I. Title.
BJ1499.S5F73 2011
814'.6--dc22
                        2010050497

The National Geographic Society is one of the world's largest nonprofit scientific and educational
organizations. Founded in 1888 to "increase and diffuse geographic knowledge," the Society
works to inspire people to care about the planet. It reaches more than 375 million people worldwide each month through its official journal, *National Geographic,* and other magazines; National
Geographic Channel; television documentaries; music; radio; films; books; DVDs; maps; exhi-
bitions; live events; school publishing programs; interactive media; and merchandise. National
Geographic has funded more than 9,200 scientific research, conservation, and exploration projects and supports an education program promoting geographic literacy.

For more information, please call 1-800-NGS LINE (647-5463) or write to the following address:

National Geographic Society
1145 17th Street N.W.
Washington, D.C. 20036-4688 U.S.A.

Visit us online at www.nationalgeographic.com

For information about special discounts for bulk purchases, please contact
National Geographic Books Special Sales: ngspecsales@ngs.org

For rights or permissions inquiries, please contact National Geographic Books
Subsidiary Rights: ngbookrights@ngs.org

Interior design: Cameron Zotter

Printed in the United States of America

11/QGF-CML/1

CONTENTS

INTRODUCTION

Amid the clamor of day and the quietude of night,
it waits for discovery. Like the wilderness beside an asphalt road,
in a vacant city lot or park, silence is the refuge and the void
to which we are both drawn and repelled. At its edge
all creation begins and ends.

When I told my friends that I was going to write a book on silence, there were of course a few suggestions that I turn in a blank manuscript. I am sure this would have impressed my editor, at least as much as it could make him laugh. But in the end he would undoubtedly have asked me to write some explanatory text on top of the blank pages to help readers better understand the pages of silence.

So to satisfy my editor, myself, and a few other curious minds, I have added a few illustrations and words of explanation to the blank pages, in my small attempt to describe what is, in reality, ineffable. At most I hope to be able to point toward the experience of silence and the boundary from where our existence springs—that is, the Ragged Edge of Silence.

The Ragged Edge of Silence digs deeply into the phenomenology of silence and the practice of listening. As in *Planetwalker: 22 Years of Walking, 17 Years of Silence,* I followed a methodology that recognizes the importance of personal documents, explanations, and interpretations of silence. This story, then, is my personal account and interpretation of silence as I experienced it. Several of the episodes included in this book also appeared in *Planetwalker.*

In most instances I tell these stories for the sake of continuity and a better or deeper understanding of events that I may not have been able to illuminate in *Planetwalker*. Others stories are new, but they shed light on the subject of silence and listening.

This book also touches on the history of our awareness of silence as a phenomenon, a religious experience for purification, and an ontological study. It is not, however, about dissuading you from your religious beliefs or faith, nor is it written to turn you toward the religious life. Regardless of my own beliefs, which you may glean from my writings, I have written this book in the hopes that silence can be made more accessible for people of any denomination, and that you will be able to enhance your life and discover or rediscover who it is you really are—in essence, to find your place on the planet.

This is an attempt to make silence more accessible to all of us, not only the spiritual or contemplative warrior, although you may find that in the process you are one or the other, or both. As you read the stories, you should come to understand that reading is another way of listening. And listening is so important, because without listening we can recognize neither silence nor each other.

To help you in your own search to find the Ragged Edge of Silence, after each chapter I have placed an exercise based on my own experience or on consultation with others. In the last exercise you will read a koan told to me by Father Robert Kennedy, who shares the distinction of being a Buddhist *roshi* and a Jesuit priest. Kennedy teaches ecumenical theology and Japanese at St. Peter's College in Jersey City. You will also find references to the teachings of Irv Rose, who was hired by the U.S. Coast Guard to instruct a bunch of us project managers, engineers, and attorneys on how to brief the admirals on oil pollution regulations in light of the *Exxon Valdez* spill in Alaska.

Irv looked the same as he had 20 years earlier, except the black hair had turned to white, making him seem a bit like Patch Adams. He was still excited about communication, especially in how listening plays a big part.

"You ask people who have been divorced," said Irv, "and inevitably they will say their spouse didn't listen to them. So now it is a major issue, because we just don't do it; we just don't listen."

I asked Irv to give me a good exercise to teach the importance of listening. You'll find his answer on page 219.

When I was a young man it never occurred to me how important listening was. To me it was more important to talk—to use words to get the things I wanted, to hide my true self from myself and others, to pretend to be the person I was not (but thought I wanted to be), for competition, telling, often shouting. As the basis for any relationship, this was poison.

When I first stopped speaking, it was a way to avoid arguments. That first step was the gift that was given to both my community and myself, as we all need the opportunity to listen and to be heard.

In college and graduate school it was listening that elevated my time from pedestrian to enlightening. I learned as much from listening to my colleagues, their questions, and their conversations as I did from the instructors and texts. It was at least an acknowledgment of the interconnectedness we share that carried through to teaching at the University of Montana, where my silence allowed students to find their own voices, and listening to them was the education I could have missed.

In communities across the country I came in silence to listen and to learn; I was welcomed into the homes of those I had not known before. As I walked, newspaper and television reporters sought me out to listen with their hearts to the story that I had to tell. Then I came upon an editor of a local Pennsylvania newspaper who explained that he wasn't interested in doing a story because, the way he saw it, all kinds of people walked, skateboarded, or some such thing through town every few weeks.

I appreciated the editor's explanation at least for entertainment's sake, as in my mind I saw a troupe of travelers skateboarding, pogo sticking, and hopscotching down the highway right into his office. It was I who had to listen. It made me smile, but my rule was to make myself available to reporters and the media, not to convince them to report on my journey. If I needed to convince anyone of anything, it would have been more like coercion, and then who knows what would have been reported? I was quickly out the door, soon to meet a different attitude among the editors and news reporters who wanted to listen.

After 17 years on the ragged edge of silence, I knew how profoundly being the listener affected my relationships with others and myself. As I lived this quiet life, friends and strangers sought me out, and they were eager to share their lives with me because they accepted my silence as a sign that I would listen. And after they filled me with the words that were often of their sorrow, I would play the banjo and turn their misery, which had become ours, into light.

Sometimes we would smile together, or I would let their tears fall on me as I kept the secret of their agony. Listening had brought me to this place of quietude, stillness, and vision even in the busy world around me. It had helped me find myself.

Without listening we can receive neither what is unknown in each other nor the silence that contains us. Our challenge is to experience the moment of silence while we are living in the world.

So I thanked Irv Rose once again and shared his exercise with my wife in the hope that we could learn to be even better listeners. We are now planning our second honeymoon.

All these exercises are here to assist you in your own discovery just like they assisted me in mine. Take them a little at a time; some, you will notice, may be similar to previous ones; however, the slightly altered details may be monumental in terms of what you experience as you practice.

For those of you who are new to experiencing silence this way, these exercises may not on first glance seem very difficult; however, you should know that being still and silent for even five minutes can seem like a long time for a new practitioner. Just remember to do the best you can and to be gentle with yourself. If it is too hard when you first try, wait a day and try again. Eventually you will succeed.

As you turn these pages, remember that they are blank, save for the words and images of explanation that have been placed upon them, grounded in the experience of silence to point in the direction from where they themselves are grounded.

Enjoy the journey.

—*John Francis, Ph.D.*
West Cape May, New Jersey

BEGINNING

It was a cold and foggy February night when I was pulled from my mother's womb at Temple University Hospital in North Philadelphia. She took me in her arms and eyed me carefully.

"This isn't my baby," she said. "My baby is dead." She handed me back to the nurse and started crying.

A year earlier, my sister had died three weeks after her birth. No one had come up with a cause, except that things like that just happened.

My mother sank into a depression so deep that it changed her usually sunny outlook to one of worry and foreboding. She believed that I had died as well, and that, fearing another depression, my father (in cahoots with the hospital) had switched me with someone else's baby.

My dad told me this story as a way to help me understand my mother's feeling toward me, or maybe it was to help him understand his own feelings. In the years that followed, it helped me understand why they were so protective and why they seemed to hold on to me so fiercely.

Very early in our relationship my mother and I developed an unusually close bond. There is a nonverbal connection between a mother and her child. Of course it may have been simple biology, but it was also something deeper; it was what eventually connects us all.

Over the last 300 years of research in physics, scientists have proposed the existence of what Albert Einstein called the unified field, which would allow all the identified forces and particles that are usually considered separate and fundamental to be understood as a single field. There is still no accepted unified field theory, as it remains open to research and speculation.

In the realm of consciousness, however, there also exists a unified field theory that states that everything is energy and there is no singularity or oneness, for everything exists in a unified field that is the source of all creation. It is the silence from which all else arises. But in trying to explain fully the deep connection between my mother and me, I lean on the words of American civil rights leader Dr. Martin Luther King, Jr., who said, "Occasionally in life there are those moments of unutterable fulfillment which cannot be completely explained by those symbols called words. Their meanings can only be articulated by the inaudible language of the heart."

Still, however short-lived my mother's initial fears, there seemed to be a ghost that haunted her; it was the sadness of having lost her first child.

This closeness, later in life, allowed my mother to accept more easily my difference in the world of conformity. My father, however, saw conformity as a strength, as a way to blend in and not to be noticed.

My father was born in Panama, where his Antiguan parents, along with two sisters and a brother, had gone to find work building the canal. He immigrated to the United States with his folks while he was still a little boy.

My mother, La Java Kirby, was from a Philadelphia family of 11 children. She could trace her roots to American Indians and North Carolina slaves.

Born February 23, 1946, I was named after my father. I was a talkative child. In the process of learning to speak, I found that each new word I uttered brought great joy to my parents. Each time a new expression, whether correctly spoken or not, brought smiles and laughter—often more laughter when incorrectly spoken. My parents would clap at my efforts, and I grew to crave this attention to my verbal calisthenics.

What was true did not seem to matter. What mattered is that I spoke, and as I spoke I became more like my parents and like the world around me. When I was a child it was especially important to be part of the world shared not only by the adults in my life, but also by other children.

I was full of stories and had an imagination that spilled over into a little boy's reality. Sometimes I swept up my family into my make-believe world. There was the time I had become an elephant boy, but I was without my elephant, my turban, and my loincloth. I wanted to ride my elephant in the New Year's Day parade. In the evening before bed, my parents would wrap a towel around my head. They would promise that a loincloth would follow in the morning, and that the following week they would get the elephant. But by that time the towel had fallen off, and I was a cowboy in search of his pony.

We lived in the North Philadelphia neighborhood of Nicetown. Our street was lined with tall elms, broad-leafed maples, and syca-more trees. In the summer the trees made wonderful shade. In front of my house an old elm tree with massive roots buckled the con-crete sidewalk. Somewhere among the branches, fat gray squirrels lived. My parents let me put peanuts on the roof of our porch, and I would watch from the bedroom window until the squirrels came and packed the nuts into their cheeks.

To me the city was a paradise. Just a few blocks away was Hunt-ing Park, where the squirrels would take the peanuts right out of your hand. There was a merry-go-round, too, and a large swimming lake made of concrete and stone. The streetlights were jets of mantled gas that illuminated the sidewalks with a warm green-yellow glow.

The two-story brick row houses had been built in the 1920s. Each had a small front lawn, usually decorated with beds of roses, tulips, and other flowers. Watering the lawn in the cool of a summer eve-ning was a welcomed social event. On Saturday mornings my mother and the other mothers would scrub their front steps and the marble tiled vestibules, at least until their kids were old enough to earn a 50-cent-a-week allowance. Each house had a wooden porch with outdoor furniture, metal gliders, and green-striped canvas awnings with fringed edges.

At night I would fall asleep while listening to the sounds of traffic grumbling over the cobblestone streets and the Number 23 trolley with steel wheels that glided on ribbons of steel track.

I was surrounded warm and soft by the love of parents, grandparents, aunts, uncles, cousins, and family friends. Most lived within a few blocks of one another. So ensconced in daily life and the care given by relatives, I was nearly grown and out of my parents' home before I realized that for a time my mother worked during the days as a maid and house cleaner, and nights on an electronics assembly line for RCA.

When I was still very young but old enough to leave her and our city nest, La Java would take me on the train to spend the summers with Aunt Sadie and Uncle Luke in the little hamlet of Harmony Village, Virginia. It served as the foundation for my appreciation of the physical environment. But as I was away from the frenetic sounds of the city, it also planted the seeds of quietude and silence that came from the unamplified sounds of nature.

My aunt and uncle lived on the shores of the Rappahannock River where it emptied into the Chesapeake Bay, in a small wooden house at the end of a sandy dirt road. Fields on three sides and woods on the back surrounded it.

There was no electricity, and the water came from a hand-dug well in the yard. The well wall, made of stone, was taller than me. I had to stand on a little bench to look down at the water, and then only when Sadie or Luke was around to watch me. I would shout and listen to the echo. Above the well was a little peaked roof from which hung the cast-iron pulley, the wooden bucket, and the rope. I was not strong enough to pull up the bucket once it had filled with water.

Our food came from the fields of sandy soil, the garden, and the river that stretched out into oyster beds and upside-down reflections of spiky pine forests in cerulean blue skies. Melons, tomatoes, squash, and all kinds of beans and greens, damp with beads of dew, could make me smile. I did not like the idea of eating oysters, however, much to the displeasure of Aunt Sadie. Oyster loaf was her specialty, but to me there was something otherworldly about their scrappy shells and slimy soft bodies.

On some Sundays the congregation of the Baptist church we attended gathered down by the river. The preacher dipped its new members with their white robes into the brackish water to wash their sins away. Then everyone would sing, "Wade in de wata chillin." The men sang in deep, resonant voices that made me listen in awe, while everyone swayed to the gospel beat. The little girls would giggle and talk about how the crabs nibbled at their toes.

In the afternoon Uncle Luke would catch a few chickens, tie their legs together, and cut off their heads with a small hatchet. Blood spurted and the headless chickens flapped about, to my horror and to the delight of my year-older cousin Eddie, who laughed and teased me. Aunt Sadie, a round, squat woman with graying black hair, would toss the carcasses in boiling water for a few minutes and then, with whomever was on hand, pluck the birds clean. I grew to love Aunt Sadie's fried chicken. Everybody did. They came from miles around for Sadie's fried chicken dinner. Most everyone in Harmony Village walked, but some of the teenagers rode mules. The preacher showed up driving a dusty black car.

As I grew older, however, things were not as idyllic as they may have seemed. Life was unsettled in Philadelphia as it was all around the country; we were at war in Vietnam, and I was embroiled in a world of palpable racism, which was made all the more prominent with my first unsuccessful attempt at attending college at LaSalle. There was a revolution going on, both in the country and in my soul. I needed to go to the front lines.

In 1969 I left my city home in Philadelphia to find the revolution in California. Like many of my generation, I was drawn to the music, reports and images of the Summer of Love, and a back-to-the-earth movement that seemed to promise a more natural and peaceful life.

I moved to the small, bucolic village of Inverness, where I lived with my girlfriend, Jean Lohman, a Standard Oil heiress, on the shores of

Tomales Bay at the edge of the San Andreas Fault. Downtown Inverness consisted of half a dozen clapboard buildings of various shapes and dimensions along a pitted asphalt road. On the bay side were the grocery store, library, and Chevron gas station. The library was a narrow, one-room shack, barely wide enough to fit the librarian's desk. At the center of the room was a little table, usually piled high with the books that could not fit on the shelves. On one side of the library, the Inverness store spread itself wide, plain, and square with the only bit of sidewalk in town. Painted in big red letters on each of the picture windows facing the street were the words "Vegetables and Meats."

Just off to the side and to the rear of the parking lot, a little dock reached out over shallow Tomales Bay. It was a place to sit and look out over the water, but at low tide it stood above the mud. Across the street, the post office, which was a little bigger than the library, was squeezed between a real estate office and an art gallery.

Scattered about were other houses and cottages, tucked away here and there among the trees and on the mesa. Most lay empty over the winter. Further down the road, a motel and a few cottages clung to the shore. Beyond them were a dairy ranch or two, the Point Reyes Lighthouse, and Great Beach, a ten-mile stretch of Pacific Ocean, sand, and solitude. The beach is where I would go when the walls of our cottage seemed too close.

It is open country, the Point Reyes Peninsula. Shrouded in fog, wild and tame all at once, it is an "island in time" on the western side of the San Andreas Fault. It slips a few centimeters north each year. Strong, clean, and bracing, it is a long, long way from where I began.

Again, life seemed idyllic, but only on the surface. I continued to pursue happiness in the most physical ways. I imagined that if I had the right car, the perfect girl, the dream house, and the recognition of my peers, I would have it all. But I also thought I needed to add something to the world, not merely to take something away. I knew I had a calling in my life. I may have been in the right place, may have been with the right people, but I had yet to find out what exactly I was being called on to do.

Then, in the early morning hours of January 17, 1971, shrouded by fog and night's darkness, two oil tankers collided beneath the Golden Gate Bridge. About 840,000 gallons of crude spilled out of the *Arizona Standard* and the *Oregon Standard* into the choppy waters of San Francisco Bay.

The incoming tidal flow was nearly over when the collision occurred. As a result, the oil reached only four and a half miles into the bay, and then it slowly drifted seven miles to sea before it flooded back onto the coast. The fog that gathered close for a few hours hid the dying birds, fish, and seals whose bodies cluttered the sandy beaches and rocky shores. Their mouths and lungs were filled with black, iridescent tar.

The sickly sweet smell of oil hidden in the morning fog drifted up from the water. My head swam, and my stomach churned as it had when I was a kid squeezed between two fat Philadelphia relatives in the backseat of a hot summer car—air conditioner failing, windows barely open. My stomach had sagged, and my body had bounced at each dip and pothole.

Within hours, and without being asked, thousands of volunteers swarmed along the beaches to rescue stranded waterfowl and to help with the cleanup. Schools dismissed their students, and offices shut down early or never opened. In marinas around the bay, people feverishly hauled boats out of the water to protect the finish of their hulls from the oil.

In Bolinas, north of San Francisco along Highway 1, knots of residents worked frantically to prevent the contamination of one section of beach, and when that failed, they sought to protect another. They gathered dead seabirds in a pile and carried others, still clinging to life, to an animal rescue center in a dreadful sort of triage.

Painful snapshots captured the seemingly fruitless effort. At the edge of the Bolinas lagoon, a young woman with waist-length hair waded neck deep in the dark water to capture distressed birds. Attempting to escape her grasp, they flapped their sodden wings and slipped farther beneath the surface.

On the shore, armed with shovels and pitchforks, workers collected straw that helicopters and small craft had dropped onto the oil. Kneeling in the sand, a grown man cried as a blackened grebe died in his hands.

Back in Inverness the stench of oil and the images of dying birds gathered close. They hung in the air like shreds of fog and Spanish moss in the tall, gnarly bishop pines that crest the Inverness ridge. It surprised me that I tried to fight back the tears but not the need to cry.

As a result of the spill, my life took a drastic turn. I was so disturbed by the environmental impact of the spill that I gave up driving and riding in all motorized vehicles and started walking instead. It wasn't an immediate reaction. It took a few months for me to sit with the decision, but a friend's death convinced me that we only have right now, this moment. There was no guarantee that tomorrow was going to come, that whatever conditions we were waiting for would ever happen. We only have this moment.

And so to me it seemed quite logical. I no longer wanted to contribute to what had caused this great environmental disaster, and I felt that, as long as I kept driving, my hands were dirty. So after making a 20-mile walk to celebrate my friend's death, I handed my girlfriend the car keys and proceeded on foot.

I would remain on foot for the next 22 years.

Repercussions were quick. First, I lost my job as manager of a local avant-garde jazz band. I assured them that there was a lot of work I could do over the phone, but as I was no longer able to conduct all the group's business without driving, they felt they had to let me go. Next, I was demoted from firefighter to dispatcher at the volunteer fire department because I wouldn't ride the fire truck, and, as the chief said, my running alongside the fire truck would not engender confidence—even if, in some cases, I knew the local trails that could get me to the fires before the truck could arrive.

Relegated to society's fringe, I found myself arguing with my friends and neighbors about whether one person walking could make a difference in the world.

During the long, solitary walks from one town to the next, my head would be full. In an attempt to prove to myself that I was right, I replayed real and imagined conversations. I did not like the anger I felt; it ate into my gut. I realize now that I had taken a stand that challenged a way of life, a way of seeing things. It is no wonder that people challenged me. I was challenging myself.

I felt frustrated because though it was clear to me, I was unable to articulate why I had decided to walk, beyond the simple phrase, "I like to walk." It was even more difficult for me to understand the burgeoning feeling of something spiritual and sacred in the ordinary act of walking. I started to feel that each step I took was part of an invisible journey, for which there was no map and few road signs. I was not sure I was prepared, and the discomfort both frightened and excited me.

One day I was just outside town when a person stopped me. He bore a familiar, mustached face, but I had yet to attach a name to it. The gravel crunched beneath the tires of his car as he pulled onto the shoulder of the road. Rolling down the window, he smiled and asked if I wanted a ride. I thanked him and said I wanted to walk.

"Why don't you want a ride?" he asked. His eyes narrowed. The smile disappeared from his face, and I could tell he wanted to hear more than just the usual "I like to walk." But he didn't wait for my answer.

"I heard about you," he said with a snicker. "You don't want to ride because you think you're better than me. Isn't that right?"

I shook my head and tried to explain about the oil spills and automotive pollution, but that made little difference.

"Maybe if you had seen the dying birds you would feel differently," I offered.

"Oh, yeah, well, I like birds too. Are you trying to make me feel bad?"

I found myself standing beside the road and yelling at this man who was yelling at me while trying to make a point. I could soon see that nothing I said, short of accepting his offer of a ride to town, would make any difference. He told me he viewed my decision not to ride in cars as a personal attack.

I was more than relieved when a friend walked up and defused the situation by making some enthusiastic remarks about living in a free country. I ended up leaving them there as I continued on to Point Reyes Station.

Usually, after an altercation of this sort, I would partake in an alcoholic drink or a controlled substance to relax and quiet my mind. But after I started walking, I soon gave up drinking alcohol and smoking marijuana. The most I did to assuage my troubled mind was to sit and paint in the sketchbook journal that I now carried with me.

My mind was filled with chatter and what seemed like a hundred conversations and arguments as I tried to navigate myself into a place of understanding. The only thing left for me to do was to call home. I knew my mother would understand.

It was night when I found myself in the roadside phone booth ten miles from Inverness. My mother was still home in Philadelphia, and I was looking forward to telling her about my decision to walk. She accepted my collect call, and for a few minutes we talked about relatives and family. I casually mentioned that I had stopped riding in cars.

She laughed wryly and added, more for herself than for me, "Don't worry, you'll be riding in cars again. This is only a phase you're going through."

I explained about the oil spill and how I wanted to make a difference. My dad was sitting nearby and caught the drift of our conversation, and he asked why I didn't do this when I was 16 (the age when I could get a driver's license). My mother, mostly playing along, asked how I was going to visit them in Philadelphia. "I would have to walk," I answered, not sure if such a thing was possible, and then, "but I am really happy."

"Well, that's very nice, Johnny," she said. "But when a person is really happy they don't have to tell people about it. It just shows."

The phone call was over, and I was back out onto the road to walk the rest of the way home, through the big redwoods of Sam Taylor Park, with my mother's words replaying in my head.

Embarking on such a journey made me anything but happy, and my mother knew me well enough—even though I was 3,000 miles away, with my voice transmuted through the telephone speaker—to sense that I was anything but happy. The chorus of voices in my head became so much louder that I had difficulty thinking.

It was in the midst of one of my walks to town, as I was engrossed in inner conversations, that I first noticed Charles, red-tipped cane in hand, clinging precariously to the embankment as he felt his way along the Inverness road just outside of town. Flinching at the passing of each vehicle, he walked directly toward the traffic.

I stopped to say hello and asked if he needed any help.

"No," he said, a little surprised at hearing a voice amid the cacophony of the road. He continued alone. It was painful for me to watch.

A week later, at the request of a neighbor, I found myself sitting in Charles's living room and sharing a meal that he had prepared. We were talking about walking and the things I saw. I soon discovered that Charles, despite being blind from birth, must have been an individual of strong will and determination to live beyond the boundaries of his sightlessness. He was not satisfied with merely hearing me recount stories of my journey; he wanted to walk the rocky trails and the narrow brushy paths up and down the hills all the way to the sea. He asked me if I would be his eyes. With Charles, my walking took on a new dimension. I moved more slowly, and I learned it was best for him to hold onto my arm. I also learned not to grab his arm as he tested and read the ground, his feet negotiating what seemed like a path of obstacles, even as I gave direction. I soon began to see the world around me more clearly just from the urgency of the questions he asked.

Weeks went by as we walked the back trails together. One day we were following the dirt road outside Charles's cottage to the saddle on top of Inverness Ridge.

"Do you hear it?" Charles asked.

I turned from him and looked out over the rolling hills and forest of bishop pines, through the milky blue distance to the sea.

A California blue jay swooped low, squawked, and landed on a nearby limb. I described what I saw, especially how it glided down, below the limb, with wings outstretched and then lifted itself upward to land ever so softly, but his mind was on something else.

"You don't hear the plane, do you?"

I tilted my head and cupped my hand around my right ear as I listened for the growl of an engine. "I don't hear it," I said. "Is it a plane?"

He nodded his head and said that he had heard it just a moment ago, and that if we continued to listen we would hear it again. In a few moments, we heard the low groan of a small prop plane that passed over the spot where we were standing. Charles explained that the sound of the engine as it reached us was not uniform. "You may think that the sound reaches us uniformly as if we were in a smooth sphere." He waved his hand in a circle above his head. "It doesn't, because of the wind and maybe some other atmospheric conditions. The result is that we can hear the sound sporadically as the plane approaches until those conditions have minimal effect. It's like a ragged edge," he offered triumphantly.

"Yes, I see," I said with a nod. I was still puzzled, but like a Buddhist koan, I thought about it the rest of the day and into the week. I contemplated Charles's words during my solitary walks until finally they made sense. I concluded that the "ragged edge" plays an important part not only in how sound comes into our awareness—haltingly at first—but also in how life works as a whole and how we learn and practice.

We're all connected, everything, from the world that we can see right before our eyes—the cup of coffee we hold in our hand and the newspaper laid out before us—to the world just at the fringe of our perception—the truck rolling by and the air conditioner humming in the background—to the world at the very jagged edge—the child of poverty sitting on a mother's lap and the freedom fighters eating breakfast in their bunkers.

All of it. All we have to do is to be still and listen, to focus, to be in the moment and to listen like Charles told me.

"It's the same way with smell," said Charles. He took a big sniff of air. Holding his breath, he seemed to be in deep thought. "Pine trees and then the ocean, and the damp fragrance of the soil. That's what I smell, but first the soil, and then there is an acrid smell of dry grass."

We had already climbed to the top of Inverness Ridge. I took a deep breath through my nose, and as I looked out past all that I could smell and hear, all I could see was the horizon, and beyond that, the ineffable and divine.

Slowly the dynamic of our walks evolved, and Charles wanted to listen more and rely less on my descriptions. I was surprised when Charles's voice took on a new tone. Like others in my community, he felt that my giving up motorized vehicles was a little crazy, even if it had brought us together. "One person walking is not going to make any difference," he argued. Besides, he found it annoying that I would not drive him anywhere.

Personally, however, I was enjoying the silence of our walks and the luxury of not having to defend myself. I had begun drawing each day in a small, blank bound book—the sights, landscapes, trees, insects, flowers, and birds. These were meditations that put me more in touch with my world, with the life around me, from the life I could directly lay my hands on, to the perceptions at the fringe of my reach, to the very jagged edge of existence.

I can clearly remember one particular meditation that began in the morning. I was in someone's garden by a still pond, and a bamboo fence kept the noise and the hustle of the road away. There was a quiet rustle, and within a soft "swoosh" there was a promise of something deeper. I thought about the next day, when I would turn 27.

The numbers ran through my head. Three nines. Three nines make 27. I thought three and nine might have some mystical powers. Or maybe it was just the line in a Beatles song—"number nine, number nine, number nine"—that made me fixate on what must be in part the math of the universe.

No matter. For some reason I felt that this birthday was special and that some great change would occur. I wondered how I would commemorate the day. I could walk into San Francisco to see my cousin, have a special meal with my girlfriend, Jean, or spend it as I often spent New Year's Eve, in reflection.

I had already changed my life as dramatically and as drastically as I could imagine. I had walked hundreds of miles throughout three counties and even to San Francisco, but somehow it didn't seem like enough. Something in the way I spoke, argued, and defended my walking was troubling.

I slept out on the Inverness mesa a little way up from the house. Stars were still shining in a partly cloudy sky. Later the predawn quiet was interrupted by the sound of rain. I felt the first few drops on my face, and in the dark I reached automatically for the protection of the plastic tarp beside me before returning to the edge of bamboo dreams, the rustle of bamboo leaves. I was not surprised that my dreams were filled with bamboo's soothing sounds; the two realities of waking and dreaming sometimes overlap.

In the morning the rain stopped, and large, resplendent drops hung from slick, green pine needles. The air was alive with moist smells. Beside me I heard the bamboo rustle. It was my 27th birthday, and to commemorate its passing I was struck with the idea of remaining silent for the day. It would be a birthday gift to my friends, who had to put up with my arguments and chatter.

This idea of giving gifts to others on one's birthday came from J. R. R. Tolkien's *The Hobbit,* and in the silence I smiled to myself as a vision of a furry-footed hobbit scurried across a dreamscape of bamboo and disappeared into soft, thick leaves. The specialness of this day and my introspective state of mind led to my decision to have a day of silence. It was something I had never done before. I wondered how it might change my life. There *was* magic on the mesa, as I waited for the ragged edge.

I never suspected I would be silent for the next decade.

Lesson in Silence: Listening for the Ragged Edge
Objective: Experiencing the edge of silence and sound

After reading about the life-changing story of Charles and how I learned to listen for the ragged edge of sound, you might want to try this exercise yourself to see if you can hear it. First, find a quiet place. If you are lucky enough to be in a wilderness area or a national park where there is the kind of quiet that few of us get to experience, that would be great. But for many of us a city park will do, or even a bench out on a quiet street. Now, close your eyes and listen for all the sounds that you can easily hear and identify.

Next, listen for the sounds that become faint, and then more faint, until you can no longer hear them. Do they fade in and out before they are completely gone? That is the ragged edge.

Now listen for the sounds that are coming to you. They will fade in and out before the sound is sustained. When the sound is fading in and out, you are in effect listening not only to the sound, but also to the silence, the ground on which the sound is built. From here we can reflect and contemplate phenomena.

BEFORE

During the first century A.D., a Greek teacher and philosopher, Apollonius of Tyana, embarked on a silent journey, which reportedly lasted for five years. While some consider him the first person to use silence as a discipline, given the breadth of human history, that distinction may be difficult to believe. Nevertheless, he at least gained some notoriety as he wandered about the empire. People said he communicated very well without words through his eyes, nods of the head, and his whole being. In his writings, Philostratus reported that Apollonius quelled riots with only a glance, thus bringing peace where words and reason failed.

Philostratus wrote that whenever Apollonius came into a city that was engaged in some low-level civil conflict—for example, a disagreement about the way a ceremony or dance should be performed—he would identify the arguing factions and settle the dispute by nonverbal means. By this time Apollonius had gained some stature not only because he didn't speak, but also because people saw him as a standup guy with high morals. So when Apollonius became involved, people simply came to their senses.

However, when Apollonius went to Aspendus in Pamphylia, built on the River Eurymendon, he found nothing but vetch on sale in the market, and the citizens were feeding upon this crop and anything else they could get. It turned out that the rich men had shut up all the corn and were holding it up for export from the country.

A riot had ensued, and the people were lighting a fire to burn the governor alive. When Apollonius arrived, the governor was clinging to a statue of the emperor. Such statues were located throughout the empire and were even more inviolable than the statue of Zeus at Olympia.

Apollonius made his way through the crowd and went straight up to the governor.

"Dear man, what is the matter?" Apollonius conveyed with signs of his hand. He touched the governor gently on his shoulder, and Apollonius's face took on the visage of both questioning and listening.

"Oh, Apollonius, I am glad to see you," the governor answered. His voice was filled with apprehension and relief. "I have done no wrong, but indeed I am being wronged quite as much as the populace, and I feel that if I do not get a hearing this day I will perish along with them."

The crowd gathered close, for Apollonius was considered a miracle worker at about the same time as the man who would be called Jesus the Christ. Apollonius then turned to the bystanders and beckoned to them that they must listen. They not only held their tongues from wonderment at him, but also laid the fire they had kindled on the nearby altars.

The governor then plucked up his courage and named those who "are to blame for the famine which has arisen; for they have taken away the corn and are keeping it, one in one part of the country and another in another."

The inhabitants of Aspendus thereupon passed the word to one another to make for these men's estates, but Apollonius, using his head, signed that they should do no such thing, but rather should summon those who were to blame and obtain the corn from them with their consent.

When, after a little time, the guilty parties arrived, Apollonius very nearly broke out in speech against them, so much was he affected by the tears of the crowd. The children and women had all flocked together, and the old men were groaning and moaning as if they were on the point of starvation.

Apollonius respected his vow of silence, however, and instead of speaking he used a writing board to communicate his indictment of the offenders. He handed it to the governor to read aloud.

"Apollonius to the corn-dealers of Aspendus," the governor read. "The earth is mother of us all, for she is just; but you are unjust because you have pretended that she is your mother alone; and if you do not stop, I will not permit you to remain upon her."

The corn dealers were so terrified by these words that they filled the marketplace with corn, and the city revived.

More recently, in 1925, Meher Baba (Compassionate Father), a sadhu (holy man) from India, began his own silent journey. He stated that he would refrain from speaking in order "to save mankind from the monumental forces of ignorance." He was born Merwan Irani of Persian parents, raised in India, and educated at an English school in Pune. It is said he had a normal life until the age of 19, when Hazrat Babajan, considered one of the five Perfect Masters of the time, befriended him. This encounter was to change Meher Baba's life forever.

Babajan kissed Meher Baba on the forehead, thus unveiling him to his spiritual perfection; and thus he fully realized himself as God. "This child of mine," declared Babajan, "will create a great sensation in the world and do immense good to humanity."

Meher Baba's last words before he stopped talking were to explain that his silence would be short. "When I break my silence," he said, "the whole of creation will hear and know who I am." Meher Baba said he would only end his silence "when the suffering on earth was at its height." He did, however, continue to communicate, at first by means of an alphabet board, and later by signs and gestures. He said, "You have had enough of words . . . it is now time to live God's words. It is not through words that I give what I have come to give." Meher Baba maintained silence for 44 years, until his death.

On many other occasions Meher Baba promised to break his silence with an audible word before he died, and he often stated a specific time and place where this would occur. His failure to fulfill these promises disappointed some of his followers, while others regarded these broken promises as a test of their faith. Some followers speculate that the Word would yet be spoken, or they say that Meher Baba did break his silence, but in a spiritual rather than a physical way.

Sometime during 1966, while I was living in Chicago, a friend passed me a card with a photograph of Maher Baba; he had a bulbous nose and a large, mustached, smiling face. His image warmed my heart. Under the photograph were these words: "Don't worry, be happy." On that very day he became one of my teachers, and I strove to follow his simple instructions: not to worry and to be happy. According to all contemporary accounts, on January 31, 1969, Meher Baba died without having uttered a word.

Four years later, on my 27th birthday, I stopped speaking.

I couldn't remember the last words that I had spoken the previous night, but when I awoke on February 23, 1973, I found myself waking on the Inverness mesa with no words to say. Having begun my own silence, like Meher Baba, I told myself it would be for a short time, just for the day.

I put my sleeping bag and plastic tarp in a large red rucksack that held my paints and journal along with some food and clothes, and I headed down one of the paths into First Valley. I crossed a wooden bridge to Inverness Way, turned right and walked three houses past the tennis court before I turned into the yard. I stopped for a long minute and looked at the low bamboo growing by the fence. Then I walked inside.

Jean was sitting in the bedroom. She was still wrapped in her robe, and the radio was tuned to the only San Francisco radio station we could get in the valley. Twisting her hair between her thumb and index finger, she looked up and smiled.

"Hey, happy birthday, honey. Did you have a nice sleep out? How about that rain? It's nice, huh?"

I nodded yes and gave her a big kiss and a smile.

Jean continued, "Well, you must have had a great time; you're in such a good mood. Maybe you should do more walking and camping out." Her lips formed a wry smile, and we lingered in another kiss.

Silence. Usually I would be chattering back at her a mile a minute about where I had been, what I had seen, and where I was going. Now I only stared back at her. Instead of speaking I took off my pack, reached inside, and retrieved my black bound journal. I showed her the pages of the last several days. All the paintings were of bamboo. Today's page was still blank.

"Yes . . . uh huh . . . I see," she said as she turned each page. "And you're not saying anything, so I guess you're going to be silent for your birthday. That is a great idea. I hadn't thought of that before. I would like to do something like that on my birthday, but keeping my mouth shut would kill me." She laughed.

The thought of Jean not talking for a day was hilarious, and I almost laughed out loud as well. On this first day of silence, I opted not even to allow myself to laugh.

"Maybe you would like to walk out to Limantour Beach and spend a few days of quiet camping," said Jean. "I would come with you, but I have stuff to do over the hill."

Between Jean and me there appeared to be some form of telepathy. We understood each other with few words and, now, with my few gestures. I got some fresh clothes, fruit, and trail mix and headed off into the dreamscape in search of a quiet place and solitude.

Limantour Beach was actually a spit of sand that stuck out into Drakes Bay, and between Drakes Beach and the spit, the waters of Drakes Estero flowed, providing the main drainage for the Point Reyes Peninsula watershed. It was one of our favorite beaches, not only because it was very isolated and had a locked gate, but also because it was accessed via a system of hidden dirt roads and trails that started across the road from our house.

Before I started the climb over Inverness Ridge and toward Limantour, I found myself walking down the rain-soaked path to the pitted asphalt road that leads into town. At the post office Helen

Giambastiani, the postal clerk, was just finishing sorting the first-class mail when I entered. From behind the counter she handed me a few letters retrieved from the general delivery slot.

"Good morning, John," she said with a smile as she turned back to the mail slots.

Inside I strained, wanting to reply in the usual manner by saying something like, "Good morning, Helen. How are you? Did you like that rain we had this morning? Thanks for my mail." But not a word escaped my lips. Instead, I was gripped by the reality of voluntarily not speaking. I asked myself how I was supposed to communicate, if not with the words that were now swirling around in my head as thoughts begging to be said. With Jean there was an intimacy that I didn't share with Helen.

A grin stretched across my face, and I made a feeble attempt at a salutation with my hand, but Helen was not looking at me, and I felt embarrassed. For a moment I was washed with a tide of relief, as I thought that she would not notice I was not speaking. Perhaps I would be able to get my mail and slip out before I had to explain something that I believed was so odd.

Helen turned from the mail slots and looked at me square in the face. "What's the matter, cat got your tongue?" she asked.

Smiling again, half out of embarrassment, I placed an index finger across sealed lips. I pointed to myself, and then lit and blew out the imaginary flames of an invisible birthday cake that I created in front of me with a few circular gestures.

"It's . . . uh . . . your birthday?" she asked in a halting voice.

I nodded yes and placed my index finger across my lips again as if I were going to let out a long "Shhhh."

"And you're not going to talk?"

I nodded. "Oh, that's interesting, John," she chuckled. "And how long is this going to last?"

I smiled and held up one finger.

She handed me another envelope and cautioned me to be careful. I was not sure why.

It took almost five hours to reach the beach. I was in no hurry as I followed the trails over the ridge and along the small creeks that make up the watershed. Up high, the bishop pines with gnarly branches dripped with strands of Spanish moss to haunt my imagination with forest ghosts. I reached the beach as darkness fell, in time to find a protected place among the sand dune grass.

I saw the white deer, a half dozen or more down close to the water. A local rancher had imported the deer from India as part of his stock development. Now they were wild, and they had become almost sacred in the local mythology. Seeing them was akin to seeing a white buffalo or an albino rhino or elephant. They possessed a kind of magic. The coastal fog closed around me.

From my pack I took out my paints and journal. I turned to the blank page that was today. I stared at its emptiness for a long moment, listened for the silence at the end of the wave, at the edge of the sea, and then with one deep breath I painted a circle. In this silence it was all that I could think to paint, to gather everything around me. Then the next wave advanced, and before it retreated there was again a silence, and inside this circle I painted a dot, and I peered into the dark, wet, diaphanous veil. It was all that I could see.

I lay down on the sand and fell asleep to the shushing of the sea rolling onto the shallow beach. The white deer danced across my dream with their magic. I knew I would have to follow.

In the morning, when the dark of night turned to silver gray, I woke up alone to the crashing sounds of the waves. I was still silent. There was no reason for me to speak, and at the edge of this sea each passing moment took me farther and farther away from the chattering shore had I left only the day before. I had never been here before. The experience of this newness begged me to stay and explore. The current dragged me into water profoundly deep. In this new place, I decided to spend another day.

I was anxious about my decision not to speak for another day. I feared that I might be lost, but the white deer, which were rarely seen, now grazed on the hillside that overlooked the beach.

When the next day came, it was hardly a decision for me to make. My reality had been altered, and I was intoxicated as if I had taken some powerful drug. Nevertheless, I asked myself when I was going to speak again. And the answer was that I did not know. The current had swirled tighter around me, like a small whirlpool, and I knew that this deep water had taken me.

Once I got back to town, the reaction of some of the townspeople and many of my friends to my silence was sometimes amusing, but often not. Some people in the community thought that both my walking and my silence were signs that the end of the world was close at hand; some thought it the mark of my sainthood; and others simply wrote off my actions as those of a certified nut and paid little attention except for their own amusement. Still others were righteously angry, the most prominent being a dear friend by the name of George Ludy.

George was terribly angry with me, and, as I sat in his real estate office, he was not afraid to let me know. He was a big man, over six feet tall, and he smoked a big cigar that fit the size of his hands and personality. On the wall behind him was an oil painting of the U.S. Coast Guard ship *Bear*. He had told me about the time when he had been an able-bodied seaman on the ship and had sailed to the Arctic on a rescue mission.

"It was a really hard life on that ship," George had said, and he wrung the cold from his hands as he remembered a long-ago pain.

We talked almost every day. George told me stories of his past and the history of Marin County—he had been a county supervisor during the building of the Golden Gate Bridge. I talked about my family and about my dream to build a boat and sail around the world.

But as I sat, silent, in his office, he was clearly not happy.

"We have had too many conversations for you to just shut up," said George.

He looked at me in disgust. I looked at him and smiled.

"Look at you. I know you're intelligent, but now I am beginning to think you are just an ass." He tapped the ash from his cigar and told me not to come around anymore.

It was upsetting to me that he felt this way, and I wondered what I could tell him to make a difference. But that was just the problem: I wasn't telling him anything.

Before I left, George said he didn't mean it about me not coming around; he just wanted me to talk to him again.

"But I still think you're an ass," he said.

As for me, I was pulled in many directions. Inside I was arguing with myself about whether I had lost my mind. I asked myself what I thought I was doing. I figured I would definitely speak the next day because my actions were clearly crazy. Weren't they?

But the next day came, and I convinced myself that I should remain silent another day, even at the risk of insanity.

One day while I was painting on the side of road, in front of the Inverness Grocery Store, a milk truck drove by. It was loaded with goods from one of the dairies out near the point. A cloud of dust rose into the air, and a light brown, gritty patina settled on the painting I was making. Instead of complaining, I followed my new practice: to do something to correct or solve the problem. My solution was to ask the store owner for a broom and to sweep the street. Soon I made it my job to sweep the street every morning as my community service.

Not everyone was happy with this. Some people felt that because I was a black American and a racial minority, it reflected poorly on the community to have me cleaning the streets. Inez Storer, a friend and teacher at a state college, was one of those who felt offended. She told me that my street sweeping and not talking made her "mad as hell."

I had nothing to say.

Later in the month, Inez's feelings changed. She surprised me with a book that explained, at least for her, what my silence was about: *The Creative Process,* edited by Brewster Ghiselin. It consisted of essays written by various people in the creative arts in an attempt to discover what was common in the experience of creating. Each artist had a unique approach that seemed to work for him or her. I was even more touched when Inez gave me a sable watercolor brush to replace the bristly brush I had been using.

"This will make a big difference," she said with a smile.

I wondered at Inez's transformation. I felt that perhaps it had occurred in part because of the transformation that was happening inside me. No longer did I hold malice toward anyone because of what they may have said or thought about me. I was still drunk with silence and with the miracle that sprang from the stillness, which demanded that I listen without judging. I was grateful to be helped along the road.

Still, as the days went by in my silence, there was at times a cacophony of thoughts, conversations, and arguments that persisted inside my mind and begged to become words. I argued with myself about not speaking. Along with the "What are you doing?" and "When are you going to stop?" questions remained a host of dangling conversations and arguments from before I stopped talking.

It seemed I could not turn off the voices and internal chatter. Something else was going on, however. I can only describe it as a shift in awareness. Physically I was feeling different. While fierce conversations raged inside me, I had not heard my physical voice in over a week, and that in itself began to alter my consciousness—not to mention what interrupting the physiology of speech was doing to my mind. I understood that I was experiencing an altered state.

So one day, after much thought about the merits of not talking, and to end my almost constant inner struggle, I decided to continue my silence, as an experiment, until my next birthday. By now I intuitively knew that I was on a path that had no clear direction or end, and so by calling this an experiment, it put the silence in a context that was familiar to my community and me. The experiment was my attempt to make a rational decision.

Still, my mind raced with a thousand and one ongoing conversations and unanswered questions. Any fantasies I may have had about some mystical inner peace or happiness that would automatically come with the closing of my mouth soon vanished in the dissonance of my thoughts.

Some months passed, and my friend Inez's feelings continued to change. One day she told me she was so impressed with the evolution of my art that she wanted me to be a silent guest lecturer in one of her classes at Sonoma State College. She felt that her students needed exposure to new ways of seeing the world.

It took me two days to walk the 30 or so miles to the campus. When I arrived, Inez met me in her office and took me to an auditorium, where the class was waiting. After hearing about my visit, about half the 20 students had chosen to be silent for the day.

I was a little nervous when I arrived. I had never stood silent in front of a group this large to act things out, and it became more like a performance. But the walk had been a good one, full of new vistas in the hills of Sonoma. It had refreshed me, and I felt present. I was also gratified that some students would actually be silent for the day in honor of my visit, as that meant we were already sharing some part of each other's journey.

I loaded the projector with transparent slides of my watercolors and enlisted the aid of a grinning, mute student to change the image at my nod. Inez made a brief introduction, and I launched into a little banjo riff while the house lights dimmed. The screen lit up— *The Road, Friends, and Places*—and then dissolved into a watercolor montage of landscapes and people accompanied by my music.

I was surprised at how much I enjoyed myself in front of the class. I freed myself of any inhibitions and stage fright until I felt as though I were flying. I was not sure what lessons I imparted during my performance, but I left feeling that the students had taught me how to listen and to receive gracefully unexpected teachings. Afterward, when students asked questions, I felt the connection with them even more powerfully. I knew that as artists and human beings searching for truth, we were speaking the same language.

"How did you get here?" someone asked. I put on my invisible backpack, walked my hands through the air and then acted out walking over the hills by walking around the stage. All the students took part in feeding back to me what they thought I was trying to say.

"Why be silent?" one student asked. To answer that, I cupped a hand around my ear and strained to listen. When they supplied my intended answer, I had my two hands arguing with each other.

But when the question "When will you speak again?" came up, all I could do was hunch my shoulder and draw a large question mark in the air.

Unlike Apollonius, I could not speak in silence to thousands of people or quell any riots or arguments. My way to deal with disagreements was to avoid them, and to avail myself to listen. And unlike Meher Baba, I did not have an alphabet or writing tablet to communicate. I had no message to speak of. I used my body to answer questions. I did not know when I would speak again—or if I would ever speak again—and that thought frightened me.

There was still so much for me to learn.

Lesson in Silence: Feeling Your Body and Environment
Objective: Discovering yourself in your body, as an extension in the environment where we live

First, if you are able, take a walk. If you cannot walk, at least go outside and feel the outdoor environment. Now take time to feel the weather. How does the temperature feel? Of course, with a thermometer you can measure the exact temperature, but what is important for this exercise is discovering how the weather makes you feel, which is a qualitative and not a quantitative measurement.

Is the rain warm or cold on your face? How hard is it falling, or is it a gentle mist? Is the sun shining? How does it feel on your skin? Maybe it is cloudy. The purpose of this exercise is to feel yourself in your body.

LIFE IN A JOURNAL

Eight months into the silence, I begin to write with paintings.

October 16, 1973

Point Reyes, California

   Near Drakes Summit the sun is rising behind the trees and the hills behind Point Reyes Station. The air is cold in the early morning. Later in the day, the sun warms everything and the sky is clear. The bees can be heard buzzing and humming in the trees. Butterflies and birds flutter nearby. Summer makes one final stand before the inevitability of winter. The wind comes out of the north, and the calmness of the bay is interrupted by the chop and the whitecaps. The moon is still high in the sky, and an incoming tide adds to the turbulence of the bay. In the evening the stars appear. The sky is clear.

The image I created is of sunrise and evergreen trees. The sun was a red and orange ball, dark blue in its center where it was difficult for me to look and obscured slightly by the trees and shrubs. A line represents a ridge in the distance. The words are not about silence, though that is where they are formed. They exist on its edge.

I liked the painting-and-writing journal because each day allowed me the time to practice these arts. Usually I did my paintings in the mornings, but sometimes I painted in the afternoon after I had walked somewhere different. I usually did the writing in the evening after I had experienced the day, so I could reflect on the day as a whole. Then I could sit quietly and meditate on my perceptions. There were also times when I needed to write in the moment of the experience.

I looked at painting as beginning a learning process, maybe because I hadn't really done it before—or when I did, I didn't do it very well. My first attempts at painting on the blank pages of my black bound journal were no more than colored splotches of paint that later progressed into very delicate representations of bamboo. Probably the one saving grace of painting in my journal was that I only made one painting a day, and after that I simply turned the page to another day to paint: a new day.

Also, painting came from a totally silent place and could exist in a silent space, like on a wall in a museum, where we are asked to experience a work that seldom offers any words and that, often as not, is untitled. While I have used words to describe the painting at the beginning of this chapter, it exists in and of itself without words and without explanation, and yet it can convey meaning.

Most linguists agree that spoken language predates written language, which is symbolic of the spoken word. However, there is little or no assurance that petroglyphs, incised in rock as far back as 10,000 years B.C., or pictographs, paintings found in caves, came before spoken or organized sound language (meaning anything more sophisticated than mere animal cries). But for the purposes of my recapitulation, I began with painting because for me it came from silence.

Writing seemed much more difficult, however, as there were already lots of grammar rules that I felt I needed to adhere to, and, as with painting, I felt I was not a good writer. There may have been good reason for this feeling, as during my first attempt at college, I failed freshman composition even though my teacher—who was 82 years old in 1964—had been a student of Mark Twain's. I do recognize that the skill of writing is not transferable with one's relationship with great writers; however, I believed in the interconnectedness of all of us, present and past.

When I began writing from silence, I started by describing the weather. I wrote on the page next to my painting for that day. There was a simple complexity about the weather, as it sometimes seemed to be a metaphor for how I felt. Because the writing and the paintings were so close to one another, I looked for clues in the painting to reveal what the weather might be like. For instance, if I looked at the way the trees looked against the sky as the crows raised up in a flock, I might notice the coming of rain or a changing season.

After a few months of writing only about the weather, I changed my focus and wrote about the physical surroundings, thus learning to describe my immediate environment. I began with descriptions of the outside environment (as in the example at the beginning of this chapter) and then moved indoors. My journals turned to animals and then people. I had a whole journal that was devoted to portraits of people.

My first portrait was a self-portrait, because I wanted to practice on myself before I asked other people if I could do theirs. I figured that if my self-portrait pleased me—and it did, sort of—it might please whomever I painted. I began painting faces as if I were painting the parts of a landscape, because we are all indeed just that: parts of the landscape.

This method fit in with my philosophy on how to approach the environment in our lives. We are all part of the environment. We have to learn to take care of each other in order to learn how to take care of all that surrounds us. It seemed natural that I would learn how to paint portraits in the same way that I approached the environment, because we are it.

I first approached my friends. I would show my portrait, point to my friend, and then point to a blank page. I can't think of anyone who said no, even though it was usually a time commitment of 15 to 30 minutes. While I painted, most often my subjects would talk about what was going on in their lives, and I would get to know them. Sometimes neither of us spoke and we would share the silence as we got to know each other.

A part of journaling was like notetaking in a class. I would write down something that I had learned and wanted to remember. Then I would reflect on it and integrate it into my life.

I first learned about keeping a journal from Dr. Benedict Kimmelman. He was my dentist as I grew up, and later he became my friend and mentor. In the beginning, and during each of my visits to his office, I noticed that he would sit quietly for a few moments between patients and write in a thin notebook about half the size of a standard piece of printer paper. I simply liked the way he looked—with his leg crossed and his head bent—and the sound of his pen as it scratched words onto the paper. I remember wondering what he was writing, because he looked so deep in thought, so dark and serious. It was as if the writing had transported him to some distant shore, and for the time that I watched him, I was magically transported with him—I just didn't know where.

One day Dr. Kimmelman explained that he wrote things that had happened and that he thought about, and maybe one day he would write a book. He had been keeping a journal for over ten years. He wrote first thing in the morning, throughout the day, and then in the evening before bed.

Dr. Kimmelman and I shared a special relationship that began when I was eight years old. One day I was in the basement, and I had found a book hidden away in a dusty box of paperbacks. The book had piqued my interest. On the cover was an illustration of a man tied to a post. He was slumped forward, and his hands were tied behind his back. A white hood with no eyes cut was drawn over his head. The title of the book was *The Execution of Private Slovik,* by William Bradford Huie. The book was about Private Eddie Slovik, who was executed during the closing days of World War II. Slovik had been the only American to be executed for desertion since the American Civil War.

Within a few days I had read the whole thing. It was the first book I had ever read, and it was my first real consideration of the realities of war. I did not know then how it would help to shape my life.

Considered by many as one of the best examples of investigative reporting ever written, *The Execution of Private Slovik* reconstructs the soldier's hapless life before and after he was drafted into the U.S. Army. Through hundreds of letters, interviews, and official records, Huie was able to paint a picture of Slovik as an unlikely pacifist who raised the ire of the military he had been asked to serve. As it turned out, Slovik was a soldier who realized he couldn't kill another human being.

I was six when I saw my first death: a robin crushed beneath an automobile's wheel on a Philadelphia city street in front of my home. It had fallen from the tall elm with new electric green leaves. It was too young to fly and had slipped out of its nest. The adult robins hovered anxiously above the concrete curb. I begged my mother to let me take it in, to care for the baby bird until it could fly. It seemed as if everyone on the block was out on their porches that Saturday morning. They swept sidewalks and washed their granite steps as they watched the drama unfold. The odors of bleach and pine oil cleansers wafted in the clean spring air. Finally my mother gave in. At that age it seemed as though I could always sweet-talk my mama.

But it was too late.

In excruciating slow motion, the car wheel turned and crushed the life from the feathered body. Only the dream of flight remained. Standing on my parents' porch, I began to cry. The neighbors sighed in concert. Alone, I wept as I swept the robin's flattened body, still warm, filled with bloodied worms, into a pile of trash and leaves beside the curb.

My parents tried to soothe the hurt with love and wise words about life and death, but in the darkness of my room my mind replayed the robin's death. Clutching a pillow, I cried each night for weeks.

A year later my mother's family began to die. Tuberculosis. The disease wracked the community, and within a year three of my mother's siblings were taken away. It took Audrey, my youngest aunt, first. At 18 she was beautiful, with golden brown skin and soft, thick lips. She sang opera, and they said she was going to be a star. I was flat out in love with her.

I didn't really understand the dying kind of death. I mean, I understood lying there with all the red life running out of you, the blood and guts of a squashed baby bird on a warm spring street, the irreversibility of shattered glass. I could kind of understand that, though there seemed no fairness to it.

What was still a mystery to me was the lay-yourself-down, get-sick-and-die-in-the-back-bedroom kind of death. Audrey did it that way. Grandmom, with her silver hair and almost toothless smile, said she knew the moment that Audrey died because Audrey started singing and then stopped.

So as I read about Slovik, I took on this specter of death.

And then I came across something that would change my life. In the process of writing the book, Huie had interviewed several of the surviving members of the military court marshal board. One survivor was Capt. Benedict Kimmelman, who, according to the author, had retired from the military to open a dental practice in Philadelphia.

"Hey, Mom," I said as I showed her the page with Captain Kimmelman's name. "Do you think this is our Dr. Kimmelman?"

My mother looked at the page as if she were studying the spelling. My parents had already questioned me about why I wanted to read such a book. It looked pretty gruesome to them, and they weren't sure how they even got it.

"No," she said. She paused and thought more deeply. Then, finally, she said, "No, we don't know anybody like that. Maybe it's someone related to him."

Okay, that was it. I didn't think much about it until my next visit to the dentist. Dr. Kimmelman always talked to me about what I was doing in school and asked questions when my mouth was filled with little cotton logs. I came back with muffled answers that would make him smile—that is, until this one day when the logjam broke.

I asked, "Say, Dr. Kimmelman"—he was smiling his usual logger smile—"do you know Eddie Slovik?" The logs fell and clattered silently onto the floor, and shock ran through his face before his usual calm returned.

"Who asked you to ask me that?" His voice had an accusatory tone, and I was surprised that anything I said could elicit such a response or be so interesting.

"No one. I was just reading this book that I found." I told him the title.

"Who gave you the book?" asked Dr. Kimmelman.

I could see by his expression that I had brought up a sore point from Dr. Kimmelman's past. It took some time for me to explain how I had gotten the book and why I had read it before he accepted that he was not the target of some cruel subterfuge, but that I was there as something else—that fate had brought us together. That's when the fact that he had been keeping a journal for several decades came up. Slovik's death had been the source of a lot of angst in Dr. Kimmelman's journals. It had had a great impact on the way he now viewed life. That I had read about Eddie Slovik on my own, and was now standing before him, was as if Slovik had reached out from beyond death to touch Dr. Kimmelman.

Dr. K, as I grew to call him, was a researcher as well as a family dentist. His studies demonstrated that fluoride in drinking water reduced cavities. While I was still in high school, I became Dr. K's research assistant at his Hahnemann Medical College laboratory, where he did work on tooth histology as related to tooth decay. He oversaw my study on the feasibility of dental implants.

An important part of the scientific process is being able to document your discovery or to repeat an experiment and reach the same results. During this time, Dr. K showed me how to keep a research journal. He taught me the importance of being accurate with words and numbers. A research journal is a record of what a scientist does during the process of making a discovery. It helps scientists figure out which factors affect their outcome. Later scientists share these journals with peers and other researchers to see if their findings can be repeated.

Dr. K's personal journals documented his journey and the inner work that he was doing as a result of the Slovik case. Dr. K had been captured at the Battle of the Bulge before Private Slovik had been executed. He didn't learn that the death sentence had been carried out until he had been released from prison camp.

During his experience as a prisoner of war, Dr. K came to an epiphany that basically forced him to reassess the death penalty and his part in it. Through his writings and his friendship I learned about the human cost of being responsible for taking another person's life, even when sanctioned by the state.

I vowed then that I would never take a human life.

While most court marshal boards found the defendants charged of desertion during World War II guilty, all the death sentences given by the board were eventually commuted as the decision made its way up the chain of command—all except one, that of Private Eddie Slovik, who was shot by a firing squad on January 31, 1945.

Throughout the years my painting-and-writing journal has helped me in many ways. My daily paintings, especially the landscapes, helped bring me to where I am now, but in a very different way from photography. When painting I am usually not so much concerned with the way the work looks, but with the way it makes me feel. I enjoy bringing something into my being, processing it, and then creating an artifact of the experience. I might use this artifact to tell a story or to help me better understand the inner development of my journey. The subjects all had some significance to me as the artist, as well as to others. More important, the paintings were silent artifacts created out of silence.

The writing journal, like the painting journal, was an artifact of an experience, except the symbols were different in that the words represented speech that had moved from the pictorial to the linguistic. Writing journals often reflect the quantitative analysis of experience as well as, through images of poetry and metaphor, the qualitative. With both types of journals we are able to step outside the linear representation of our experience and look at moments, processes, or developments more holistically. Nuances of our experience that can be lost in the passage of time can more easily be recalled and experienced in a different place. These nuances may yield a different truth or meaning, based on where we are now.

Gaining clarity and solving problems are but two benefits of keeping a journal. As a gateway to the unconscious and to inner life, it was uniquely useful for me. What Dr. Kimmelman gave me was inspiration to keep a journal during a significant time in my life. More important, he gave me a tool to know myself better.

In town I listened to all the compliments and criticism with no argument. Not speaking precluded argument. And the silence instructed me to listen. From this new place lessons—or perhaps realizations—came. The first was that for most of my adult life I had not been listening fully. I listened only long enough to determine whether the speaker's ideas matched my own. If they did not, I would stop listening fully and my mind would race ahead to compose an argument against what I believed the speaker's idea or position to be. Then I would interject at the first opportunity. Often I did not listen long enough to understand anything that the speaker had to convey. Giving myself permission not to speak, not to attack some idea or position, also gave me permission to listen fully. In an uncanny way, giving myself this permission gave the speaker permission to speak fully his idea or position without the threat of rebuttal.

This was both a sad and a joyful moment for me. I realized that because of my inability to listen fully, I had missed many opportunities to learn. The joy of this moment came from the realization that if I practiced listening fully now, perhaps there would still be opportunities for me to learn.

The days continued to pass without my lips uttering a sound. For the small amount of money I needed, I cut wood with some friends.

I spent the next few months walking alone, usually up on the ridge and out to the beach at Limantour. I slept there and listened to the pounding surf. Sometimes I visited a family in one of the several houses that had been built before the land was purchased for the national seashore. Other times I constructed a driftwood shelter and built a campfire in the sand. I'd stay for several days, watch the birds, and explore the ragged edge of sand and sea.

On the ocean side of the ridge, the tall, gnarly bishop pines ended and the old ranch trail made its way along a green canyon wall that bloomed in season with crimson paintbrush, purple lupine, and lilac shooting stars. It was a watershed, and alders grew around the little brook that started out as a spring higher up. The trees became denser and hid the panorama of the low green hills and the blue sea as the trail continued into the valley. This was where I went to be by myself.

Farther on was the pond where I fished. From here the rutted dirt road led back up to the ridge. It was only a mile or so and could be driven in a four-wheel-drive vehicle. I had driven it many times, but walking made it even more real, more remote.

The months passed slowly. The din of inner chatter faded into quiet echoes in my written journal. Now the daily watercolors in my black bound book took on new meaning. I looked forward to this time each day as a meditation, and I used the paintings to communicate with friends and people I met: stories in watercolor images without words. I continued to write the occasional letter to my mother, however. Once she wrote me that she had seen Dr. K, and he had asked her about me. When she told him what I was up to, he smiled and asked if I was keeping a journal.

I learned that there were all kinds of ways to do journals, different ways to use them, and all sorts of smaller practices that I could utilize within each style or practice. There was journaling as a practice to help you be more in the place where you are, or journaling as an artifact of your life and a snapshot of where you were. When I reread my journals, the snapshot was what was most apparent. Another part of journaling was being able to find the story that we all share, and then to retell it. Journaling was something that I could do in silence; it could become a time in the business of life to reconnect to the space of silence or at least to dwell consciously on its edge. It was Dr. Kimmelman who inspired me to keep a journal. And so, soon after I began walking, I painted my first page.

It was the silence that inspired me to continue.

Lesson in Silence: Meditation
Objective: Beginning to be still

The average human's walking speed is about 2.7 miles per hour, but during the rush of today's modern world, we may feel like we're hurtling along at hundreds of times this most natural pace. Even when we stop moving, our minds often continue to race along with all the cares and worries of today's worldly turmoil. Meditation is a technique to still the mind and to gain inner peace.

This first introduction to meditation is very simple.

Find somewhere to sit that is comfortable; a chair in a quiet room or a quiet corner of a park on a park bench is fine. There is no need to sit in any special position. However, I like sit up straight in a comfortable chair, feet on the floor. Close your eyes and be still. Breathe naturally and be conscious of your breathing.

It is usually good to set a special time of the day and to use a timer—or you can begin and end your meditation naturally. Five minutes is what I started with, and I increased the time as I felt comfortable.

FATHER'S VISIT, 1974

Silence, no matter how much we speak, is a necessary occurrence. Throughout the day, it dwells between our words and sentences. When we listen closely, the silence lays a fabric to clothe our thoughts, punctuated with words that linger on the tongue, until it finds its ragged edge. Silence, when held between us, is the most profound force in existence.

Still, I was afraid that while my parents thought my decision not to ride in motorized vehicles was merely eccentric, their reaction to my silence might be a little more severe. When I wrote to explain why I wouldn't be calling for at least a year, my mother explained that my father would be coming to California immediately. They figured that either I had been entrapped by some California religious cult they had read about in *Life* magazine or I'd been imprisoned for selling drugs.

I suppose there was reason to fear. Synanon, a drug rehab group, had moved to Tomales Bay with shaved heads and talk of establishing the promised land; instead, they harassed local residents and stockpiled assault weapons while threatening anyone who disagreed with their philosophy. In southern California, the Manson family had gone on a killing spree. And then there were a half dozen other groups who promised salvation in one form or another, if only you would sign over all your worldly possessions.

Jean picked up my father at the airport and drove him to Inverness in her old blue VW van. She and my dad had met a few years earlier when I had taken her to Philadelphia. She had gotten sick and stayed in my old bedroom for a few days while I went to New York City to try to get a record contract for the music group I represented. My parents liked Jean, who had compelling stories of being black, white, and Native American, though they were a little concerned about her being 20 years older than I.

Jean and Dad found me walking alone along the road that skirts Tomales Bay and the San Andreas Fault. I was trying to get home from Point Reyes Station before they got there. The van stopped, and my father looked at me through the open window. We were both surprised to see each other out of the context of Philadelphia. Fragrant laurel trees bent their heads in an arch and whispered in the wind above us.

I didn't know how to react. I didn't have words, naturally. And my father and I no longer had that easy bond we had enjoyed when I was growing up.

I remembered that, when I was a child, my dad spent most Sundays taking me somewhere interesting, like a golf driving range or a museum. One of our favorite places was the Franklin Institute, a science museum with interactive exhibits. I think Dad liked it so much because he learned just as much from the exhibits as I did, maybe more. He worked for the Philadelphia Electric Company, first as a lineman and then as a foreman, so the electricity exhibits and the story of Benjamin Franklin's discovery held both our interests.

Sometimes my father would borrow his younger brother's car and we would drive across the Benjamin Franklin Bridge into New Jersey and visit Uncle Walt. My dad told me Walt wasn't a real uncle; he was my mother's first boyfriend. Walt was Cherokee or Lenni Lenape, and he traveled in the black rodeo circuit. He could jump off and on two horses at a full gallop and then ride them with one foot on each. Spending time with him was like having my own private circus. If my father loved another man, I believed it was Uncle Walt. I loved him too.

My father and I had gone through some life-changing experiences together as well. As I grew older and became increasingly exposed to the racism that devoured young black men, my father let me be privy to his own pains and frustrations, and this helped me learn to deal with mine. In 1952, 12 years before desegregation became law, he took me on my first bus ride in the segregated South as much for my education as to visit relatives.

When the Greyhound bus pulled in front of the Howard Johnson restaurant, several hours' ride out of Philadelphia, I followed the line of hungry travelers right past the sign that clearly pointed the "White" passengers into the restaurant and the "Colored" passengers around the back. There, I saw the other line snaking around two rusted metal shacks—one an outhouse, the other a place to buy snacks. Hot dogs rolled around on a small Ferris wheel cooking under hot lights.

We stood in line to use the bathroom, and someone let us in front of him. I was upset at having to follow the "Colored" sign and at being barred from the restaurant, but what really made my tears fall was when we returned to our seats on the bus. We all had to sit in the backseats, behind a thickly painted white line on the floor.

This was the last straw for me. I was prone to car sickness if I couldn't sit next to a window, and now I was relegated to the very last seat. I began to cry, and nothing my dad said would console me. Then, to the right of me, a very wise woman offered me a cherry Life Saver, and for the moment its sticky sweet redness was all that mattered—that and the big, toothy smile the lady shared with me as my dad and I made our way south into Virginia. I snuggled tightly in his arms—and I didn't get sick.

But there was also physical punishment. It was part of the lifestyle. My father would dole out beatings with belts and straps so that I would learn to behave. This is now clearly seen as abuse, but back then it was merely a way of bringing up a child. If I made an error, my butt would pay the price.

I knew from my mother's letters that Dad thought my pledge of silence stemmed from what I had suffered at his hand. I assured her that this was not the case, but I don't think it mattered. It was what he had in his head, and it would take more than a few words sent in the mail to change his mind.

The last time I had seen my father was five years earlier in Philadelphia, on my birthday, when he had driven me to the airport to catch my plane for California. He had wanted me to see his cousin Shep, a musician who now lived in San Francisco, so he had given me Shep's address and phone number. We had parted on good terms.

All this and more was going through my mind as the blue van carrying Dad and Jean pulled up beside me.

"Hi, son." Dad's greeting was warm but tentative, as if he were afraid to hear my answer.

I smiled my biggest smile and reached to touch his hand.

"Do you want a ride to the hotel?" he asked.

I walked my fingers through the air, and in the silence of my answer I heard his breaking heart. I shared the confusion of his pain.

"Damn!" he said. His eyes fell. "What is this?"

For my dad, knowing intellectually that I didn't speak was one thing, but the reality of his silent first son, who he dreamed would become a doctor, was just too much. I knew this, but just the same his words shocked me. I felt upset that, after all this time and all the miles he had traveled to see me, I had caused him this disappointment and confusion. I wanted to pull him from the van, give him an hour-long embrace, and tell him how happy I was to see him, how he shouldn't worry about the past, and how there was only love between us. Then we would walk arm and arm to the motel, where we would stay and talk until dawn about our lives and the journey that we were both on.

I wanted to drink this moment in small sips and, once our bottle was nearly empty, throw back the last little bit and savor the memory of its rich flavor. But cars were passing close enough to keep me concerned about the traffic.

For a moment even my father was speechless, as clouds moved across the dry, dark landscape of his face. I was not sure what kept his tears from falling, or what kept me from opening the door and riding with him the final mile to the hotel, but the depth of our silence deepened, and for the first time since my childhood, I felt both the depth of his love and the gulf that pretended to separate us.

Later, at the hotel, we explored our relationship and our family in new ways. First Dad tried to understand my miming, which had become my way of communicating. I gave it time. By this time I knew that my decision not to speak put an imposition on people, and I had developed the patience and willingness required to explore it.

Change, I realized, is a part of life. Still, certain tacit agreements among people make everyday life easier. One is that we will stop at a red light and go at a green one. If, during the night, a couple of revolutionaries were to get together and change the rules, there would no doubt be a plethora of car accidents—not to mention pedestrians getting smacked in crosswalks. Another agreement is that we will talk to one another, even though the Fifth Amendment guarantees us the right to remain silent.

So imagine how disconcerting it would be if one of the people in your life decided not to speak. The world, if only for a time, would be a little harder to understand. One of the tacit rules would have changed. As such, I understood my father's difficulty in accepting this and being able to work with it once he had.

I decided to write notes on small scraps of paper. I explained to him that I seldom wrote notes for anyone, and that I was making an exception. But no matter what I wrote, it was not enough.

"Okay," he said, once Jean had gone. "No one is around; it's just us. You can talk now."

"This is for real," I wrote. "It's not a scam."

For a moment he looked disappointed. "It's not because I used the belt when you were growing up, is it?" he asked.

I shook my head no, but in truth I didn't know if my silence was in part a way of searching to heal the pain I had felt on much of my journey, a way to find forgiveness for my own transgressions and for the transgressions of others. I let him go on talking.

"You know that if I knew then what I know now, I would never have done that. It's just that that's what happened to me when I was a boy, and that was the way everyone thought it had to be done."

I nodded as he spoke about his childhood—how his father had beaten him and how he had left home to support the family. When he finished, I held on to the silence that was between us.

After a while, he looked at me, shook his head with a little smile, and said, "Man, you're something else."

He worried about me as an American black man walking around the countryside with a banjo; quite clearly, this image of a wandering minstrel held negative connotations. And as for the not talking, he said, I had already placed a stone around my neck by not riding in cars. Not talking was just another handicap piled onto the fact that I was black.

"How could anything good come of this, John?"

I didn't have an answer for him, only that I was here now, that he and I were together, and we were sharing another important moment in our lives. Thinking that he would approve, I wrote that I would like to go to the local community college, as a step in completing what I had started and what my parents had hoped for me when I finished high school. The College of Marin was a good 20 miles from Inverness, however, and I hadn't yet figured out the logistics.

He laughed at me. Displaying a further illustration of his chief concern, he wondered how I could even think of going to college when I didn't even talk. For me it was the first time I had told anyone of my dream, albeit in writing on a scrap of lined paper.

My father must have sensed my disappointment at his reaction. He said, "Look, don't think I don't want to see you go to school and finish; I do. It's not the walking so much, it's the silence that's hard for me to understand."

I searched the pile of scribbled notes until I found a clean scrap of paper and wrote, "It keeps me from telling lies."

In not speaking, I had come to realize that lying was a practice I had acquired as a kid. When I finally came to terms with it, I found no reason for lying other than that I had developed a bad habit. But as I explored the issue in my silence, I came to see that I had not been satisfied with who I was. I had felt more comfortable pretending to be someone else with knowledge, skills, and abilities that were not mine.

Growing up a Negro in America, I had never heard of anything such as low self-esteem, but I did live it. We were all trapped in it. It was pervasive in the popular media—the newspapers, the radio, and TV. I remembered not liking who I was even at a young age. I did not like being colored. I felt as though I was cursed and trapped, and I was embarrassed—not really embarrassed by myself, but rather embarrassed by how the dominant culture looked at and portrayed me. My defense was deception. I lied in order to pretend.

I deceived myself into believing that I was someone else, not black and not white, but a pretender, more chameleon than anything. It seemed simple enough. If you don't like who you are, you just invent someone else. It was not that I never liked myself. I started out with parents and a family who let me know pretty quickly that I was a unique and lovable individual with all the potential in the world. But back then I felt it was the world that did not live up to *my* expectations.

It had taken me years to understand that my propensity for deception was actually a reflection of my society, because society attempted to deceive me. In the short term the deception seemed to allow me acceptance of self, but the ultimate outcome was the loss of self. By pretending not to be myself, I had lost track of who I am.

The walking and silence saved me. They not only gave me the opportunity to slow down, to listen, and to watch others; they also afforded me the opportunity to listen to and watch myself. Silence, I discovered, was not something negative. It was not simply the absence of speech; it was a whole and independent phenomenon, existing in and of itself. In the silence, I rediscovered who I am.

And, perhaps more important, I was able to do something that had been impossible only a year earlier. I was able to listen to my father, and not only hear him, but also understand the validity of his feelings. And even though his feelings were different from my own, I could now accept them as truth; I could respect his words.

Later, I took my dad next door to meet my friend George Ludy. George was older than my dad by about 20 years, and I knew my dad would appreciate that George was also part Native American.

I sat on the floor and worked through my banjo repertoire.

"You never mind that stuff," George told my father as I strummed a few chords. "He's been playing that same tune for the last two months."

Soon enough, my dad took out a package of Pennsylvania Dutch scrapple, often described as a mush of pork scraps and trimmings combined with cornmeal and flour. He had brought ten pounds of it from Philadelphia. Dad began cooking up a mess of scrapple in the little office kitchen. Jean and some other friends dropped by, and I shared some of my journal and paintings with everyone. The little office filled with smoke as my dad passed out samples of scrapple.

Later, from the phone booth outside the motel, my father called my mother back in Philadelphia. "Yes," I heard him say, "I've seen him. He's standing right here." He paused, and I watched him listen. "No, he seems healthy enough. He doesn't smoke, and he doesn't drink. And the people here seem to like him."

At the door of the phone booth I began to play a nameless tune I had composed on the banjo. It was still raw and unsure. The notes toppled from my fingers, and my father spoke loudly over them.

"Yeah, he paints and plays the banjo." The music annoyed him. He shooed me away and closed the door. Now I could barely hear him, but I just caught his next words: "I think we should just leave him here and hope that he doesn't show up in Philadelphia. No, this wouldn't work in Philadelphia. Yeah . . . Yeah . . . Okay. I'll see you when I get back."

Since I was at least physically healthy, and I hadn't joined some strange California cult, it seemed deprogramming was not necessary; my parents, at least for now, felt they could leave me to my own devices, even if my part of California sat precariously on the

San Andreas Fault. In her quiet way, my mother prayed for me and planned to monitor any seismic activity through sporadic visits and weekly letters.

As my father stretched to understand my journey, I realized that maybe you can't change the world by your actions alone, but you can change yourself. And when you did, the world around you might also change in the very act of attempting to understand you, just as we all try to understand each other.

Several days later my father returned to Philadelphia.

Back at our home in First Valley, Jean was talking to me in the kitchen over breakfast. "So last night you were speaking," she said nonchalantly as she put butter to toast.

My ears pricked up. I wondered if I had been talking in my sleep. It had been only a few months since I had stopped talking, and I could count on one hand the instances when words had slipped from my lips during that time: once when I had excused myself after bumping into someone at the grocery store, and once when I had gasped, "Oh, my God" while watching Charlton Heston part the Red Sea.

On each of those occasions, lacking any evidence except my own awareness, I had wondered if I had actually said anything. Now Jean was telling me that I was talking in my sleep. This was too much. Crestfallen, I looked at her and waited for the details.

"That's not all," she continued. "You were riding in a car, too."

I knew that Jean would not lie to me about something like that, and I was relieved to find out that she was talking about her dreams. I drew a big question mark in the space in front of her face. She looked at me with a blank stare. I drew the question mark again, flapped my hand in front of my mouth as if I were talking, and hunched my shoulders.

"Oh. What did you say?"

I nodded yes.

"I don't know, I can't remember. All I know was that you were in the backseat of a car talking; it was night, and we were driving somewhere with some other people. I remember I didn't think it strange at all for a little while. Then it dawned on me, 'Hey, John is in the car, and he's talking.'" Jean looked at me and asked, "What do you think it means?"

I hunched my shoulders again. I didn't know.

A few days later Ken Fox, a neighbor, told me about his dream. He and I were sitting on the roof of a nearby house, and we were talking as well. "I don't know exactly what you were saying," he said, "but I got the feeling everything would be all right."

I soon learned that many of my friends and neighbors were having dreams about me talking to them. They were generally happy about this set of circumstances, but no one could remember what I had said.

I had had the same dream, I confessed to Jean. I had been in the VW van with her and Dad; we'd been driving to the motel, and we had been talking. A shock had fluttered through my heart when I had realized what was happening. I woke up drenched in sweat. I didn't remember a word I had said.

The silence grew deeper.

Lesson in Silence: Discovering the Landscape
Objective: Finding place

More and more, as we become consumers of industrialized transportation and other commodities such as food, shelter, and clothing, we become insulated and separated from our surroundings. As our society becomes more complex we focus on getting from A to B, passing through our environment without regard. Finding place is rediscovering our connection with our environment and ourselves. This connection is healing and essential to our well-being.

Along with the weather, we are greatly affected by the physical landscape we live in. Are there trees, a highway, a back road, or hills around you? Is there a park, a body of water, a pond, a stream, a lake?

Get a map and see where you live in relationship to other places you know, to where you were born, to where your family and friends live now. If they have moved away, see where you live in relationship to the names of some of the places you have heard about in stories, in the news, in school.

Make a point each day to walk or sit outside and to take in what is around you. Look for a quiet place where there are natural sounds such as birds, water, and the movements of trees.

If you live in an urban setting, look for a park or a vacant lot or community garden. In some urban settings a natural and quiet setting may be a cemetery. The point of this exercise is to find your physical place as well as to discover your physical body in the place where you are.

ENDING AND BEGINNING: THE NEW YEAR

It was Christmas Eve in 1973, and I was delivering some Christmas gifts I had been gathering for community children: little wooden toys and carvings that I'd collected during the year, paintings, socks, and cinnamon buns from my mother's recipe. I also included little jars of huckleberry jam. I had picked the berries, canned the jam, and made hand-painted labels of Black Mountain and Tomales Bay. George Ludy had given me the laundry bag that I slung over my back like the iceman on a hot summer day.

It felt good to be doing something for children again. Before I had stopped speaking, I had enjoyed visiting my friends and reading stories to their children. I think it was the only thing I truly missed. There had been Lucy Shoemaker and her seven children; the Richardson boys, whose dad had been restoring an old schooner; and many more.

I started out in the afternoon and visited a few dozen houses. I walked four miles from Inverness to Point Reyes Station and back, then eight miles over the ridge to the house on the beach where the Saccamano family lived behind a locked gate. Even if the children were asleep, their parents would wake them and explain that Santa Claus was here.

Sure, I was a different-looking Santa, skinny with a black beard and hair. I wore old, patched jeans, a blue-green plaid flannel shirt, an orange DayGlo reflector vest, and a floppy, red homemade hat that I had put together from an old red backpack. The sack especially was a dead give-away, as it had the word LAUNDRY spelled on it in faded black.

Nonetheless, I was Santa! I had the toys, and I'd walked all night.

I had not expected, however, that here at the end of this journey, it would be I who received possibly the greatest gift of my life.

It was late Christmas morning when I awoke just off Sir Francis Drake Boulevard in the redwoods of Samuel P. Taylor State Park. This wasn't a grove of 2,000-year-old giants—it was only a second-growth forest—but waking among living beings that were a few hundred years old was still inspiring. I took my time to linger in the quiet that pervaded the grove and then found myself back on the road to see one of my friends, Okanta.

She was a Lenni Lenape, a First Nations people who lived in the area of the Delaware River that includes New Jersey, eastern Pennsylvania, Delaware, and the Lehigh and Lower Hudson Valleys. She had moved from Pennsylvania to California, and now she lived in a tepee with her partner Van and son Little Bear on Barnaby Mountain.

Usually it was an all-day walk to Okanta's house from Inverness through Olema Valley, over Tocaloma Hill, a few miles through the redwoods to Lagunitus, and up the backside of the mountain. I would usually stay for a few days and help in the garden or explore the woods of virgin fir where I could sit in silence. Today I was over half-way there. I brought a jar of honey and a wooden toy for Little Bear.

Okanta liked to talk of Native American culture. She derived great pleasure from remembering stories and rituals. We used American Indian hand gestures and signs that people of different language groups had used to communicate for hundreds of years. For instance, to say "spirit," we twirled two fingers in the form of a V and slightly raised our hand at each larger circle, so that the motion resembled a small tornado or dust devil.

I was raised as an African American, though my great-grandmother insisted she was Indian. My mother said that my great-grandmother was not. But when I pushed her on the issue my mother would say Great-grandmother was part Navajo, which never made sense to me, because Navajos lived so far away. I did understand, however, that if we admitted to the authorities that we were Indians, we might indeed be sent away. Whether this was a real fear or something that adults told a little boy to make him stay in line, I never knew for sure. Later I found out that the policy of removal started with the Indian Resettlement Act of 1830, when the U.S. government forced the Five Civilized Tribes in the Southeast to reservations west of the Mississippi River. This had happened earlier to the Delaware, also known as the Lenni Lenape. These forced resettlements had allowed unscrupulous people to seize property and land from native and black Indians, much like the government took property from Japanese citizens and relocated them to prison camps during World War II. But as I walked up the mountain, reservations and prison camps were far from my mind.

Okanta spoke to me about *manitou,* an Algonquian word meaning "spirit." Everything possesses an invisible essence that makes it what it is, she said. Her stories of a vision quest had always intrigued me. In First Nations culture, vision quests, or laments, were a rite of passage from adolescence to adulthood. The quester would often gain insight from visions that came during four days and nights of fasting in the wilderness, away from the tribe or community. Silence and fasting were allies of the visions. Once the quester returned, she would relate her visions to the community, thus helping the people as a whole to live in peace. This ritual is very much like mystical escapism, in which a pilgrim would escape the norms of his community, journey to a sacred place, and find knowledge to bring back home so that he could improve the lives of his people.

My own journey seemed more organic and without conscious form; I found my way as I went along and, at different times, was claimed by pilgrimage, wandering, and all forms of the human journey. The various phases of my quest often overlapped, joined, and became indistinguishable. Slowly, on this day, as Okanta spoke of the rites of passage, the idea of my own vision quest began to take root.

Vision, as understood by Native Americans, stands for several things. Vision stands for wisdom, insight into the nature of things, balance and harmony with all creation, forging one's future, learning from one's own dreams, and, most important, opening one's eyes to see life free from pretense and distortion. Before I started on my journey, I was enamored by different makes of cars; they spoke to me of who I wanted to be and conveyed the worth of the people who drove them. I coveted certain brands of clothing, not because of their styles per se, but because by possessing them I felt I would be better than my brothers and sisters around me.

These preoccupations left me as I walked silently on my journey. But the most dramatic change was my letting go of the pretense of race. I began to understand the social construct, to see only that we were all different and all the same. I knew then that I had to allow this vision to rule my life.

Okanta said that one of the main purposes of a vision quest is to awaken the Great Spirit or God, and thereby to explore a deep state of consciousness and self-discovery. As I discovered, wisdom itself is rooted in silence. This was clearly the case in the vision quests of the North American tribe of Algonquian. Whenever adolescents sought the vision that would direct and give meaning to their lives, they left their people to fast in solitude and silence. During this state, the Spirit came and spoke to them.

Even before I gave up the use of motorized vehicles, I walked and fasted, and though I spoke a little when I was alone, I was close to silence. I just didn't abide in it. My longest fast lasted 30 days, though I drank water and some juices. I heard no voices as such, but I did take meaning from many things around me, such as the voice of an owl on a new moon night; I felt that perhaps some communication, maybe a letter, would be coming to me. If I saw a discarded tire on the road, I might think of the circle of time or the unity of all people. Or if I saw the white deer on the beach, I knew to find the sacredness in the moment.

As many people have found, the most important aspect of being silent is to be attentive and focused. The Native American people believe that in every act, in every thing, and in every instant, the

Great Spirit is present, and that one should be continually and intensely attentive to its divine presence. Black Elk, an Oglala Sioux elder who was revered as a holy man, believed that being attentive in silence is of utmost importance because nothing happens by accident. Since all created beings are sacred and important, everything that happens to them is significant, clothed with symbolic meaning. By paying attention, we gain a little more wisdom and understanding of our own lives.

Toward the end of his life Black Elk revealed a number of sacred Sioux rituals for publication, and his accounts have won wide interest and acclaim. He also claimed to have had several visions in which he met the spirit that guides the universe. He believed that the most important reason to ask for a vision is that "it helps us to realize our oneness with all things, to know that all things are our relatives, and then on behalf of all things we pray to Wakan-Tanka that he may give us knowledge of Him who is the source of all things."

Steven Foster and Meredith Little, who pioneered the modern-day vision quest experience and were vision quest leaders themselves, find that this type of journey is highly effective as a means of accepting and finding the meaning in life's changes. They believe that vision quests empower individuals to be vital forces in their communities; engender self-reliance, courage, endurance, and self-control; activate self-healing mechanisms; catalyze personal encounters with the collective, archetypal unconscious; and ignite insight, wisdom, and illumination.

During this remarkable silent retreat in nature, the quester usually gets in touch with the divine. The quester ultimately returns with something even more powerful and rewarding: what the ancients called vision.

John Muir, the great American naturalist, believed that when a man went out into nature in search of wisdom, he would find more than he expected. In this respect, I would be hard-pressed not to agree with the benefits of questing. But I am still reminded that for me, life's journey is an ongoing process, and that the most important part of a vision quest is in the experience and its ineffability, that in its beginning and in its end is a vision of the eternal.

In Native American traditions, as well as in both Western and Eastern ones, an individual must periodically withdraw from the material world in order to attain peace and inner knowledge through silence and solitude. In the Native American belief system, shamanism, the vision quest ritual, as well as the modern-day vision quest, is directly related to the experience of silence.

This tradition can be characterized as an earth tradition, in which the four worlds—mineral, plant, animal, and human—are seen as interconnected, in absolute harmony and balance with each other. It is a tradition based on a silent dialogue between an individual and nature, where nature is perceived to be one of the universe's most powerful teachers.

Nature is a mirror of the Great Spirit and, as such, is truth. For the Native American, the teachers are death, change, silence, and the sacred rocks; to know truth is to know the White Buffalo Woman of the plant realm and the sweet medicine of the animal realm. These are considered to be the realms of wisdom because it is uncontrived, a place where thought does not interfere. Here is where I did not speak; I did not write; I only walked and sat in the silent space between the words, the steps, the breaths, and the heartbeats. As I practiced weaving the experience of each tradition as warp in the tapestry of my journey, I found silence was the weft to the varied expressions of that which is divine.

In Native American cosmology, shamans are the keepers of a remarkable body of ancient techniques that are used to achieve and maintain well-being and ecological equilibrium both for shamans themselves and for members of their communities. Shamans are seen as the guardians of the psychic and ecological equilibrium of their group, as intermediaries between the seen and the unseen worlds, as masters of spirits who become the shaman's helpers in these worlds, as supernatural healers. They are able to transcend the different cosmological planes for healing and power-obtaining processes.

As in many traditions, there are often hierarchical structures that denote not only levels of attainment but also one's position in a community or organization. These roles include chief, roshi, medicine man, and holy man. Depending upon each person's journey and experience, these denotations take on different meanings.

While reading *The Autobiography of Malcolm X,* I was impressed with Malcolm's shift from promoting a vehemently antiwhite ideology to embracing one of global goodwill following his pilgrimage (hajj) to Mecca. He was the first American black Muslim to journey to Mecca. Malcolm X approved of the fact that all pilgrims to Mecca dress the same, thus leaving behind any signature of rank. He described the feeling as "communitas," in which all pilgrims were one. It was this feeling of unity, regardless of color or station, that led to Malcolm X's conversion to global goodwill. I experienced similar feelings of communitas as I passed deeper into silence and recognized that each person held the same place that I did.

The mind plays an important role in Native American tradition as well. Shamans believe that the only way to tame the mind is to make it an ally. One must find a way to dismiss the ordinary discursive mind, which is culturally conditioned. The shaman accomplishes this through extended periods of silence, isolation, and fasting in the vision pit, a cave in the mountains or the desert. These periods awaken the senses and break the perceptual and conceptual habits conditioned by culture.

Ethnographers studying pilgrimage have identified three parts of the journey; these stages are so distinct to me that I believe anyone can understand them. They are relevant to both walking or silence. The operative expression is that of journey, whether exterior, interior, or both. Thomas Merton, the Trappist monk whose silence led him to the ecumenical understanding of the divine, wrote many books about pilgrimage, contemplation, and silence. For example, in *Seeds of Contemplation* and *The Dark Path* he explores both the concept and the practice of silence and concludes that either journey has merit, but it is best to take part in both.

The first part of the pilgrimage marks the point where we separate from the familiar. For me, refusing to use motorized vehicles was stepping away from the familiar and actually making physical journeys. In the vision quest this happens when the quester leaves her community for the wilderness, which exemplifies the nature-based modality of the journey, as opposed to other traditions, when the journey begins by entering a monastery, convent, ashram, or other such place that is intentionally set up outside the ordinary community. We can also see this first phase in the world of ideas—on the spectrum of an inner journey—as letting go of a familiar or even comforting idea or concept, like being at war or forging an alliance.

The second, or liminal, stage marks a sort of ambiguous state during which the pilgrim is part of no fixed social structure. This stage is often said to be the most powerful. In a physical pilgrimage, you are traveling through a place or places where you have never traveled before. In this stage, however, you are in an antistructure, as you are not expected to live by all the mores of the town or culture that you are passing through. Because of this, the establishment may be cautious or fearful that you might impart to the community something that is new or upsetting to the status quo. It is these new thoughts or ideas that are the true gift of the pilgrim. If you are fortunate, your community recognizes that you are on a journey—even a sacred journey—because the mechanism of pilgrimage is available to all human societies.

The third stage is the reaggregation, which occurs when the pilgrimage is complete and the pilgrim returns to society. Now that the pilgrim has returned home, he is no longer outside the morals and standards of the community. It is at this point that the community begins to look to the pilgrim for some new insight in order to learn how to live better.

It was at this stage that Malcolm X returned from hajj and told us that we don't have to be hateful. It was at this stage that Black Elk spoke of the maker of all things. And it was at this stage that

Nelson Mandela showed us how to forgive transgressions and build a country. For each one of us, the reaggregation will be our own to give to the rest of mankind. The stages may not be as clearly marked as a map, however. There may be journeys within journeys, beginnings overlapping endings, weaving a fabric that is both smooth and ragged, of light and of dark, of sound and of silence.

Lesson in Silence: Keeping a Journal
Objective: Record your journey and its landmarks

Besides being a good snapshot of where you are in your life, keeping a journal provides an opportunity to discover something about yourself that thus far you may have been overlooking, if only because you did not take the time to articulate in words what you felt. Likewise, it is an opportunity for to express your inner journey outwardly. It is a good discipline. Besides, the more you write, the better writer you will become.

Begin your journal. It can start as a simple notebook, in which you write about the weather or the things you notice while out on a walk. You can write, draw, take digital photos, or collect items to make a scrapbook—whatever you want. What's important is that you do it every day. Choose one day a month as a free day; on that day reflect on what you have done over the previous month.

I usually write in the evening, but often I make an entry in the morning and sometimes in the afternoon. The idea is to get into the habit of writing, and as your journey progresses you will usually be present to capture what is going on. Don't be afraid to share your journal with others.

VISIONS

My personal vision quest was a gift that began on that Christmas Day in 1973. As I began writing and painting, I left what had become familiar to me to explore instead the wordless silence of the inner self. I composed words to express my inner journey, where once only paints flowed on paper and hands danced in the air. All this continued. My eyes sparkled or were dulled by what they saw, and my heart was moved by the music I played or the music that played around me—how it touched me on the inside.

It was ironic that such a gift came to me that day, after I had carried all my heart and love in a laundry sack up through the mountains over long nights and days. At each home my burden grew lighter until I had nothing left to give. Oddly enough, on my previous birthday it had been the same. Motivated to give the gift of one day of silence to my community, I received even more.

Walking in the forests and along the wild shores of Point Reyes, I began to gather inside me a space where ideas formed without words and begged to be expressed. Painting became an outlet for this expression, as was the music that I learned to play from listening to the songs of jays and the wind through the trees.

On this Christmas Day I walked along the road and began a poem. It was about manitou, the Great Spirit, and the words came to me as easily as each step. This poem and these paintings followed.

They are the artifacts, the footprints in the sand that point in the direction traveled.

Manitou
Upon the road, empty sack, full heart.
Clouds play amongst the mountains.
Tide rushes toward the sea, returning.
Wind whispers softly in the trees.
Feather dance, lying on the road,
One flight is done another just begun.
Manitou calls
December 25, 1973

I came down from the mountain and started back to Point Reyes. Okanta and her family's presence were still with me, as was my father's. I was still holding the silence that was between Dad and me when last we met. It moved with me through the first small village and into the redwoods. I was walking slowly, in no hurry, letting each foot feel the earth before it raised into the air and down again. Cars passed, their tires hummed, and I felt myself reaching for the banjo and touching the steel strings. I allowed the music to accompany my steps.

It was dark, and several miles were already behind me when I had the first waking dream. I was in a hotel room with my father; he was at peace with the silence that we held between us. There was nothing to say and everything to say, but it was said wordlessly. I was on a journey that we could not share, and he was going to leave soon. Already I was missing him, the presence that had traveled across a continent to be with me then, and now in this dream. He took me to the mirror, and we looked deeply until I knew that I was looking at myself and he would always be with me that way.

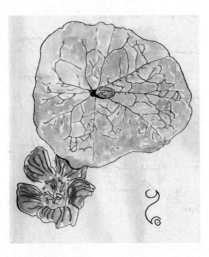

Manitou is the rain today, wetting road and making clay.
Manitou is a drop on leaf, enlarging worlds beyond belief.
Manitou is the screaming Jay, wanting rain to go away.
Manitou is the flower.
December 26, 1973

It was raining lightly when I finally crawled out of my sleeping bag. The bishop pines with crooked tops were all around. Their arms in grotesque shapes were nevertheless welcoming. I made a small fire and boiled some water for a strong black tea. I stared into the fire and felt the warmth in my hands and my chest. The flames settled down to coals, glowing brightly at the kiss of gentle breeze. The white deer appeared, and I watched them all morning as they appeared and disappeared in the mist.

My father and mother appeared to join me in watching the deer. My mother had come so that I would know that she was with me too. And I started to laugh but then did not. I let the dreams run their course and made sure the fire was out before I started down the trail to the beach.

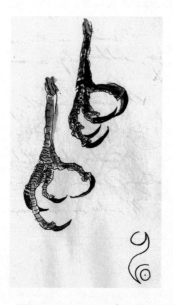

Manitou sits upon the trees.
Manitou's rain drips from the leaves.
Letting go of shape and form, Manitou is the endless sky.
Letting body, feather torn, fall to earth.
Manitou is the tear.
December 27, 1973

I came out of the trees and looked for my parents or the white deer, but all I found was the body of a hawk, desiccated and torn. I was taken back to a Philadelphia street, where a robin fell out of its nest. It was at this moment that the significance of both my silence and my walking settled upon me. Each was its own journey, along with painting, music, and now writing. I felt a little dizzy thinking about each beginning and each end. And then I let go of any thought and lost myself in the walking and the way the sky touched the sea.

When I arrived at a pond surrounded by a meadow, I decided to stop and sink into the grass. From here I could see the ocean, and in the sky two ospreys circled. In Native American mythology, the totem of the hawk is that of a messenger and observer, one whose job is to look over everything and to convey these sights to others.

In the night I had another fire and wrote words from the silence. There were so many words, I wondered how I would choose the right ones. I fell asleep and dreamed of riding in Jean's blue van with my father. We did not speak.

Manitou is the yellow gold of daffodils as they unfold
Manitou is all that unseen something rather like a dream.
Manitou is the fragrance.
December 28, 1973

When I arrived at the beach I was restless. All I wanted to do was leave. But walking between land's end and the edge of the sea, I felt myself being pulled by each. I had not eaten in three days; I had only consumed tea and water. The white deer grazed up on the hill and looked back the way I had come. Their meaning was that of family protection. I did not see my mother and father, but I knew that they were with me.

As I climbed back into the cover of the trees, the image of Dr. K came to me, and he talked about respecting life and going back to school. I listened closely to him as the trail through the bishop pines turned to a dirt road and the dirt road to asphalt. Night was coming by the time I reached my redwood friends. This was where I stopped to spend the night. I needed their strength, wisdom, and protection before I could climb the mountain. This time I slept without dreams.

Manitou is the rushing stream, moving swiftly through the trees.
Voice, the wind comes from the sea,
Calls the falcon flying free.
Manitou is on the Mountain two where tipi stands and sky is blue.
Inside, Manitou is the fire, glowing coals.
December 29, 1973

I spent the last day of my vision quest just like the first—walking up the mountain from the redwood grove. When I reached the summit, I found Okanta, Van, and Little Bear just as I had left them. Here time had stood still. In the tepee, Okanta was cooking bread in a large black Dutch oven over hot coals. That evening I shared my paintings and, for the first time, the writing that had come from silence, together with the vision quest that I had begun on Christmas Day. Okanta had kept the laundry bag so I could return it to George Ludy.

In the morning I broke my fast with the bread Okanta had cooked. As for my vision quest, I was filled with a deeper silence and a deeper understanding of myself. To me that was the journey I was on, and that is the journey we are all on: to discover who we are, to find our places in the world, and to understand that we are all one. Relatives. It was a place where I wished to linger. This was my vision as the year ended. And as the new year began, I found these words. It was a prayer that is often attributed to Chief Yellow Lark of the Lakota. I let myself rest in their meaning, and it became contemplation as I continued on.

Oh Great Spirit, whose voice in the winds I hear,
And whose breath gives life to all the world. Hear me.
Before you I come, one of your many children.
Small and weak am I.
You strength and wisdom I need.
Make me walk in beauty.
Make me respect all you have made,
My ears to hear your voice.
Make me wise that I may know all you have taught my people,
The lessons you have hidden in every rock.
I seek strength not to be superior to my brother,
Make me able to fight my greatest enemy, myself.
Make me ready to stand before you with clean and straight eyes.
When life fades, as the fading sunset,
May our spirits stand before you without shame.
January 1, 1974

On the following morning I headed back to Inverness and saw Jean. I walked over to see George Ludy to return the laundry bag. Inside the bag was my new journal. He smiled when he found it, and he read each page slowly and chuckled to himself. When he finished, he looked up to me. There was a tear in the corner of one eye, and in his crusty voice he said, "Well, at least you're writing now, you bastard. Merry Christmas."

I almost laughed out loud.

Lesson in Silence: Vision Quest

Objective: Make your own four-hour or four-day vision quest

A vision quest is really about the age-old search for meaning in our lives. This is even more difficult in the modern world with all its distractions, where a rite of passage usually means getting a driver's license.

While choosing four hours or four days is symbolic of the four directions, it is also a metaphor for the four stages or hills that are to be climbed: in infancy you are being nurtured by your parents and family in preparation for life's responsibility; in youth you learn how to master the requirements to take care of your physical self; in adulthood, if you persevere, you will receive the gift of your vision; this culminates with the realization of your vision in the final stage, your old age.

After reading the chapter on vision quests, plan your own vision quest by allowing for the time that you can afford. If you cannot take four days, try one day divided into six-hour parts, where you can practice fasting, walking, sitting, and dreaming.

Be open to your own vision. If you feel you need more help, you can find modern-day vision quest leaders in your area or online.

SIGNS, DREAMS, AND VISIONS

When I first stopped talking, inner peace and quiet were the immediate results I expected, but there were also the inner dialogues and arguments with myself. My inner turmoil wasn't so much about when I was going to end my silence, because my decision not to speak for a year had ended that discussion. Nor was it about what I should have said to someone after having a heated argument, because I just didn't have any arguments. Now the inner talk was about what I would have said if only I had been talking.

It was the residue of all those years of being a certain way that came and went with its own ragged edge. It was the laws of inertia, which specifically said that putting on the breaks of a speeding freight train required time, distance, friction, and gravity. The same applied to stepping out of the mainstream of culture by avoiding motorized vehicles and walking.

All the things that I wanted to do, all my dreams and aspirations, didn't dry up when I altered the way I transported myself. But some dreams I let go by the wayside every easily, such as wanting to be a fire chief or a famous band manager. And I had newly found dreams that came along with the vision quest.

Two dreams occupied my thinking and waking hours. The first was to build a sailboat and to sail around the world. I'd nurtured this one from when I was a small boy growing up in Nicetown in North

Philadelphia; the closest I had come to sailing, however, was being in a rented motorboat on the Chesapeake Bay with my dad and our neighbor, Mr. Tip.

I suppose the adventure I'd experienced with Mr. Tip should have turned me against the sea, but it had the exact opposite effect. When the shearing pin broke on the propeller shaft, we were dead in the water with the tide dragging us into the sea-lane, busy with freighters and oil tanker traffic. Our motor ran furiously, but the propeller did not turn, and we continued drifting into the channel. After a while my dad resorted to throwing the small anchor ahead of us and then pulling the boat toward the anchor. It was painstakingly hard work, and we didn't make much (if any) progress.

It all seemed fun to me as I sat with a half basket of crabs, until I could hear the panic in Mr. Tip's voice when he said we really had to do something. I have never forgotten the look on my dad's face; it held horror for him but more for me, as the sun began to set and darkness rose from the water. I remember him taking off his white T-shirt and waving it frantically at a passing cabin cruiser. It stopped and towed us back to the rental dock in a little inlet.

"You sure are lucky," the man who towed us in said. "I would have missed you if I hadn't seen your shirt in the dark."

My dad and Mr. Tip thanked the man profusely and offered him both our crabs and money for gasoline. But the man wouldn't take anything. Although I knew my dad might not want to tell my mother this story, there was no keeping a secret with me around. I was such a talker that I looked for things to talk about. Sometimes I made things up to have something to talk about and to gain approval.

Right up the street from where I grew up, a commercial boat-building shop turned out sleek wooden inboard boats. My mother let me look inside, but my father walked right in and talked to the workers, and we dreamed together. After our near-fatal boating incident, the size of our dream was the size of a cabin cruiser. Together we walked on unfinished decks and cabins. Later Dad found boat-builders who showed us how they used steam to bend the plywood into exotic shapes that glided across a glassy lake or eased through a choppy sea.

Growing up, I liked to look at picture books of motor yachts, which seemed more modern and therefore more desirable. I was drawn to one particular book, *The Boy Mechanic,* which promised that a boy my age could build anything from a soapbox racer to a plywood kayak and even a six-foot sailboat.

Down in the basement I could spend hours with a piece of wood on two sawhorses. This piece of wood grew from a keel to a large boat in my imagination. Eventually I moved to motor sailers. They were far too big to be built in the basement, even in my imagination, but all through my childhood to my adult years, I carried that dream with me.

My second dream was far too practical to be romantic, but it was just as real. I wanted to complete college. As early as I can remember, my parents stressed education as the key to success and happiness. Every occupation choice in front of me required an advanced degree. It didn't take me long to understand that they hoped I would become a doctor, which required the most education and training of all the professions. At every opportunity they held this up as *the* dream.

My father's youngest brother, Uncle Henry, had become a doctor, and it was apparent that the family wanted me to follow in his foot-steps. As for my part, I played the doctor card for all it was worth, and thus was able to garner approval for any of my wants as long as I showed how it kept me on the path of becoming a doctor. But while I loved the idea, living up to this dream was another story. School was not my favorite place, and academic study was not my favorite pastime.

My dreams changed as I emerged from my vision quest. I now knew that I had to devote myself to promoting peace, living in har-mony with the environment, and striving to the highest realization of myself and all my relations, while at the same time living in gratitude for the present moment. I wondered how, or if, I could do all that. It seemed a tall order. I wasn't even sure what it all meant. But visions are often like that: the meaning is to be figured out along the way, and usually in community. I would do what I could do. For starters, I would live in gratitude for the present moment. And for sure . . . in this present moment . . . there must be room for me to build a sailboat.

A week had passed since my vision quest, and I had been looking all around me in my sleep, my walks, and my waking dreams for some sign or some direction after such a powerful experience. It came on the evening of January 8, 1974, when I looked into the sky and saw a small wisp of white smoke, comet Kohoutek, between Jupiter and Venus. I had never seen a comet before, and for that reason it portended something great. I was going on a great journey, not metaphorically but literally—at least that's what I took from my sighting. Yes, I was to build a boat and sail around the world. I did not realize that sometimes signs are only what we want to them to be.

When I'd first arrived in California, I had found someone with the same dream, but we needed money to buy tools and materials. We raised some money, which we gave to a man who promised to invest it for us; but, not surprisingly, we never saw him or the money again. I suppose I could have accepted that as a sign to stop my pursuit, but I interpreted it as a sign that we must always overcome obstacles in order to achieve our dreams.

The sign of the comet sent me plunging full force into the project. First step: I would have to drive a wagon pulled by mules up to Port Orford in Oregon to saw a few Port Orford cedars into planks.

But it was the vision of my quest, unbeknownst to me, that moved with mystery along the road. As I sat in the shade on a narrow wooden bench shoved against the light blue aluminum siding of the Sir Francis Drake Garage in downtown Inverness, I watched the cars and pickup trucks pull in and fill up. I recognized most of them. Fulfilling my duty as the colorful local resident, I smiled and nodded in their direction as I dreamed of sailboats and wagons loaded with pungent, creamy yellow-white lumber pulled by mules down the curvy Highway 1.

My clothes were variegated with a splash of worn-out this and patched with a faded that. I wore dusty boots and my ever present banjo, topped off with a crocheted rainbow hat from Pearl, the wife of my San Francisco cousin Shep. Ted, the mechanic, was sitting beside me in greasy striped overalls. A shock of mussed blond hair set off his square face, which always seems bemused. We must have looked like a postcard scene sitting there, me with my legs crossed as I quietly plucked rusty steel strings, just enjoying the day.

Then a stranger at the pump slyly pulled out a camera from his black sedan and started to take our picture. Years ago, I probably wouldn't have thought twice about someone taking my picture, but since my vision quest I had become filled with a native sensibility, and I actually feared that cameras could capture your spirit.

Now, exactly where this belief came from I do not know, perhaps from some long-ago television show or a story in *National Geographic*, but there it was. I stopped playing instantly and, with every fiber in my being directed toward the would-be photographer, I projected, "NO!"

Feeling those vibrations and thinking better of it, the man began to put the camera away. Just then Ted came to life and shouted out, "Hey, go ahead and take our picture. We don't mind."

"What?" I thought. "Doesn't he know that a camera can steal your soul?" I turned and look at Ted, who was still bemused; he put his arm around my shoulders, quickly drew me to him, and smiled a big smile. I looked back toward the pump. The camera shutter clicked, the man ducked into his car, and without a word he drove away.

Feeling wounded, a hole straight through my middle, I sat there for a moment; but nothing leaked onto the ground.

"Aw, come on, John." Ted was standing now, wiping his hands on an oily rag. He sounded as if he had a mouth full of marbles. "It weren't all that bad, and it didn't hurt none, now, did it?"

I did not answer any of his questions. I was too busy writing down the license number and noting that it was a State of California official car. My mind raced with fantasies of dark activities. The picture was for a secret database, a file kept somewhere for some evil purpose. Or maybe it was going to be published in a "Come to California" ad. No matter. The next day I walked the four miles to Point Reyes Station to see John Maderes, a local attorney.

John's office was above the old Western Saloon and looked out onto Highway 1 where it passed through town. Cecil Roca's horse was tied to the hitching post outside. John's secretary ushered me into his office. He came out from behind his desk to meet me with an extended hand.

I explained everything that had happened in Inverness through a performance of mime that would have made Marcel Marceau proud.

Trying to deal with me logically, he explained, "There is really nothing you can do. You know you're a public figure, and unless people are going to use your image to make a profit, there is nothing you can do about them taking your picture."

John continued to explain the intricacies of privacy infringement as I pantomimed ripping my soul from inside my chest and throwing it on the floor. He watched me with amused and sympathetic eyes as I expressed my fear that this picture would be used to hurt me. If I could find out what agency took my picture and what they intended to do with it, I could tell them how harmful this was for me. An idea came to him, and he stopped me in the middle of a silent sentence.

"I do know someone at the comptroller's office," John said as he thumbed through the Rolodex on his desk. "I'm not sure what they'll be able to do for you, but they have public hearings at least once a month, and I can schedule you to, uh . . . 'speak.'" He thought for a moment. "I'm sure you will manage."

That was enough for me. I smiled and walked my fingers across the back of my other hand, up my arm toward my elbow, through the air, and onto his desk to Sacramento.

The irony of my crusade did not escape me, as I had begun painting my third book of watercolors; in place of the usual landscapes, I was painting the faces of people. It was a practice that I had devised to keep connected to the community. Each day I had to ask a different person if I could paint his or her portrait. That way I could share my silence with others. But was painting a portrait another way of stealing people's souls, even if I had their permission?

I felt a subtle warmth from the portrait pages when I looked at them. It was the warmth of a connection to my subjects. I decided that my paintings were more a reflection of each person's spirit passing through my soul, a mingling of our spirits that left us both with something more.

It took me five days to walk the hundred miles into Central Valley to Sacramento, the state capital, located at the confluence of the Sacramento and American Rivers. My first long walk passed through an unfamiliar landscape of faces and geography. The Central Valley is a great trough about 400 miles long and 50 miles wide, between the Sierra Nevada and the Coast Ranges. The Sacramento and San Joaquin Rivers drain most of the valley before converging in a huge delta that flows into San Francisco Bay.

After four days I arrived in Davis, about ten miles southwest of Sacramento. Davis's residents affectionately call their town the bicycle capital of the world. Lining both sides of the streets were bicycle racks with a multicolored assortment of mountain, hybrid, and racing bikes lined up side by side. Signs proclaimed that bicycles and pedestrians had the right of way.

I found a place to camp just outside of town and walked in to meet Debbie Nelson at Denny's. Debbie was a friend who lived on Tomales Bay. She had offered to help interpret my sign language to the comptroller board. My language now consisted of pantomime and some sign language gleaned from a book by Iron Eyes Cody on Indian Sign Language.

The son of a Cherokee Indian named Thomas Long Plume, Iron Eyes learned Indian Sign Language from Two Guns White Calf, a Blackfoot; Buffalo Man, a Cheyenne; and the Arapaho chief White Horse. Iron Eyes became an expert in the language and traveled throughout the United States and Canada. He was also a prize-winning dancer who was once asked to dance before the king and queen of England. However, he was best known in the United States for the public service announcement of the "crying Indian" that aired on the first Earth Day in 1971. In the spot, Iron Eyes paddles a canoe up a polluted stream past a smokestack belching black clouds into the air. Then he walks along the edge of a busy highway piled with trash. When the camera moves in for a close-up, a single tear rolls down his cheek, and the narrator says, "People start pollution. People can stop it."

A few weeks after I stopped speaking, I found Iron Eyes's book in the library. I was so touched by his television spot and so inspired by Native Americans' concern for the environment that I did something I had never done before: I wrote a fan letter. A short time later I received a letter, along with an autographed photo of Iron Eyes in an eagle headdress, from his wife. She wrote to say that Iron Eyes appreciated my letter and that he encouraged me to continue to work for a clean environment. I carried the book and the letter until the cover wore away.

Using Iron Eyes's sign language, I felt connected to him on this day, as I tried to reclaim my very soul.

In the early morning darkness I walked the last several miles to the capital city and to the hearing where I was to present my grievances. Inside the chambers, state officials gathered around the state comptroller as he called the meeting to order. All eyes turned to me as I entered. I was dressed in brightly patched denim jeans, a frayed denim shirt, a DayGlo orange safety vest, and my skullcap. My banjo was slung over my left shoulder on a knitted strap with the same variegated colors as my cap. There was silence, a deep weighty velvet that hung like a winter tapestry from every wall. At that moment I realized I was where I was meant to be. Something was working through me, and all of us were going to be playing a part in it.

The comptroller whispered something to a woman beside him, and she nodded as he cleared his throat. "We have with us this morning a visitor from Inverness," said the comptroller. He looked down and shuffled through some papers. "Ah . . . a Mr. . . . ah . . . John Francis." He looked up and smiled. "He walked all the way here from Point Reyes to address this committee." The committee was wide-eyed, and mouths began to open.

Debbie edged past me into the center of the room. "Because John Francis has taken a vow of silence, I will translate his sign language," she said.

I moved to her side but kept my eyes focused on the 15 or so people who ringed the small room. Moving my gaze from one to another, I grabbed at the empty space outside my chest and threw it violently to the ground.

"My heart feels bad," translated Debbie.

Eyes widened.

I touched my chest with the palm of my hand, made a V shape with two fingers, and twirled them in the air in an ever expanding circle like a tornado. With the same hand I snatched away the invisible storm.

"My spirit has been taken," Debbie said on my behalf.

A sigh escaped into the room.

I went on to pantomime cameras, cars, and tears rolling down my unhappy face; I displayed the walking that had taken five days—the rising and setting of the sun became a circle coming up and disappearing behind my hand. Showing fear, supplication, and my plea for help, my hands continued and trembled until there was no more to tell except to thank the people who sat there in total silence for one long moment.

Then the comptroller spoke. "Well, that was quite a story," he said to Debbie. "All of us here appreciate how Mr. Francis feels." He cleared his throat again. "What would Mr. Francis like us to do?" He looked at me. I held out my left hand, palm up, and touched it with the forefinger of my right hand.

"He wants the photograph back," said Debbie.

"Well, we don't have the photograph," he said, "but we can assure him that if we did, we would give it back. The best we can do is to make some inquiries, and if we find out who took his picture we will get it and give it back to him."

He nodded again to the woman on his right, who scribbled something in a notebook and showed it to him. He took a moment to read the page and then looked at me. "Your friend Mr. Maderes in Point Reyes Station mailed us the license number of the car, the time, and the date, so I think that's all the information we need."

I seemed to become deaf or invisible again as he looked at Debbie and said, "Please thank Mr. Francis for coming all this way to speak to us today. You can tell him that he can go back to Inverness and not to worry. We will take care of everything."

Moments later, we were back out on the street. Debbie asked me how I felt. I hunched my shoulders. I was not sure if I ever thought that I would actually get my photograph back; neither did I know what I would do with it if I did recover it. I was no expert in putting back a stolen spirit. I didn't remember if I had ever heard that part of the stolen spirit myth. Maybe I would burn the picture, smudge myself with the smoke, and scatter the ashes to the four winds; or perhaps I would keep the ashes in a little medicine pouch around my neck. Anyway, I imagined I could only have lost part of my spirit, as I still seemed to have some left in me.

What I did know was that this was the longest walk I had made so far, and that I had changed. Before the vision quest, I had taken steps and had changed my life; both the walking and the silence were amazing in and of themselves. What was lacking, however, was the totality of a vision, a goal worthy of getting up each morning, taking the next step, and embracing the journey—the mountains to be crossed. The vision quest had prepared me for something larger than myself, something that I could take back to the community and share, something that we all could learn from to make our lives better.

It all had changed me, the five days walking, the miles, the geography, and the people I had met along the way: the journey had changed me. I knew this because outside the comptroller's chambers I laughed, a big silent laugh, and I slapped my knee so hard that it hurt. It was the first silent laugh that had come out of me in over a week. Debbie looked at me and seemed a little worried at first, and then she laughed too.

Besides recognizing the absurdity of our Kafkaesque performance, something else became clear to me. Notoriety had become part of my persona, and as a public person I could do very little to prevent someone from taking a picture of me in a public place. If I allowed myself to become sad each time someone took out a camera, I would be a very unhappy person indeed.

Right then I decided to embrace my vision—to grab the tail of the tiger and use the notoriety to further the cause of environmental protection. In this moment, I was transformed from a man expecting to live a quiet and idyllic life on the shores of Tomales Bay into an activist with a vision. I decided to use my life for change—to devote myself to promoting peace, living in harmony with the environment, and striving for the highest realization of myself and all my relations, while at the same time living in gratitude for the present moment.

Finally, I had begun learning what that meant.

A warm, euphoric feeling settled into the space of my stolen spirit. It filled me with a vision of purpose, laughter, music, and poetry. It followed me home. In the spring, it would accompany me on my newfound search to understand this thing called "environment" that I now so passionately wished to defend. I would soon make my first walk along the coast, 500 miles north to Oregon, and begin my environmental education in earnest.

A new man.

Perhaps.

My old dreams dragged behind me.

They rattled like old cans tied to a honeymoon car.

Lesson in Silence: Music

Objective: To evoke a consciousness from a place before industrial noise

Lacking the natural quiet of a previous age, we can accept the benefits of meditation and silence as a way to counteract the anxiety and depression often generated through our association with a noise-polluted world. One bridge I have found most helpful to escape from this pollution is classical music, which can soothe the weary soul.

Aside from playing your own music, there is a growing body of research suggesting that classical music can play an important role in good health and in the treatment of pain as well as depression, without the side effects of drugs. Classical music that was written and performed before the industrial revolution has the unique distinction of coming from a quieter time when natural sounds were more prevalent; at least the sounds that were heard during this time were not electrically amplified. Classical works from this period then possess a certain quality in the play of stillness and silence as part of its composition.

Find a piece of music or a genre that you like, from before the 1800s. This is a time before machinery and the noise of industry, and so the music reflects this. Find a time and place to sit and listen, each day or on a special day.

Keep a log of the music you listen to, as well as associated experiences and feelings, in your journal.

WALKING NORTH

Thomas Merton was a Trappist monk who wrote eloquently on silence and contemplation; when discussing pilgrimage, he wrote about the inner and the outer journeys and how we could have both at the same time. In this deep silence I started walking north. As I became more and more familiar with not speaking, my goal for my inner life became to know and dwell in silence ever more deeply while the physical journey of my daily life continued. My physical goal was to discover wilderness. It was something that I had heard of as I had grown up in the city, along with stories of pioneers and the California gold rush.

The first story I remembered about wilderness and the frontier was that of Johnny Appleseed, whose real name was John Chapman, and how he walked across the country and planted apple orchards. Then, in elementary school, we studied the adventures of Lewis and Clark as they crossed North America with the help of Sacajawea. These adventures played out before a backdrop of the American settlers' movement. As I sat before my weekend TV shows and in front of the cinema screen, I took in the legends of Davy Crockett, Daniel Boone, and the Lone Ranger with his faithful companion Tonto. My childhood wilderness accompanied me to California; it was still a part of my own personal mythology, but it had become illusive and more complex, now mixed with getting back to the land, living on a farm, and growing your own food.

One day I was looking at a road map of the Pacific Northwest when I noticed a tiny patch of green in the southwestern corner of Oregon about 500 miles north of Point Reyes. Green on a road map usually meant trees—a forest or a park. This particular patch had small letters running through it: Kalmiopsis Wilderness. It was located inside the Rogue River-Siskiyou National Forest.

At the library I found the address of the ranger station in Brookings and sent a letter requesting information. A few weeks later I received a large, brown envelope from the U.S. Department of the Interior. Inside were brochures on all the designated wilderness areas in the United States, with pictures and descriptions enough to dissuade a tenderfoot like me from wanting to have a wilderness experience. "Brushy low-elevation canyons with poison oak, rattlesnakes, and hornets," said one brochure. Even though I regularly walked great distances and had some experience camping, the wilderness seemed a little beyond my skill level. I thought I should wait for the following year.

I also wanted to learn about the Port Orford cedar trees that Bob Darr, a boatbuilding friend, had told me about. Boatbuilders the world over prize these particular trees because their wood is durable and resistant to rot and insect and marine infestations.

Feeding my dream of building a boat and sailing around the world, Bob gave me the name of a sawmill near Port Orford, Oregon. I imagined myself using a whipsaw to fell and mill the trees into the lumber I needed. Using mules and wagons, I would accomplish this with only hand tools. I would build a seaworthy vessel for my journey.

As I made my way north, I left behind all that was familiar, and I became a little afraid of what I thought I might encounter, what I did not know. Over the miles, a mantra became part of every step.

A mantra is a word, a group of words, or a sound that is believed to be spiritually transformative when repeated continually. The most common sacred word or mantra that Indian disciples use in their meditation practices is this word "ohm." In the Eastern Orthodox Christian tradition, in the icons depicting the image of Christ, an inscription around his halo reads, "I AM THAT I AM," which, when voiced, has a similar sound as that of ohm. The written depictions of these two similar sounds are also quite alike in their calligraphic shapes.

Sri Ramana Maharshi, a famous Indian master, received the ancient contemplation of "Who am I?" which both Westerners and Easterners practice today. It leads the aspirant to a state of self-realization.

There are several ways to receive a mantra or contemplation. It can come from a recognized teacher, from the glance of a master, or from a dream or other state of consciousness. People used "Who am I?" as a form of self-inquiry well before Sri Ramana Maharshi popularized it. He called the self "Silence." Real silence is a still mind, which, once controlled, becomes natural.

About that same time I received the Upanishads contemplation of "Thy Divine Self" from an Indian teacher visiting San Francisco. At the time, it was little more than a curiosity, a mantra to practice during my meditation; however, it turned out to be a powerful way to focus on my deepest and most true identity, that which we all share at the core of our humanity.

Now, as I walked north, another mantra—yet part of the same truth, the same contemplation—helped take me out of the fearful place I was in, to a place more mindful of the remarkable journey I was on. This contemplation of "Thy Divine Providence" put me into the present.

"Thy divine providence . . . " It was more like a prayer of protection.

"Thy divine providence . . . " until it came at each breath.

"Thy divine providence . . . " and then it became breathing.

The theological terms "providence" and "divine providence" generally refer to the activity of the divine to provide for its creation through its activities in the world. For me providence was expressed in the symbol of the tree. Trees get all that they need just by being present, by being where they are and waiting for the rain, the sun, the soil's nutriments—for everything.

I was rooted to the ground in a different way; I walked. There was no escaping from where I was unless I walked away, and at that speed, I was always there where I was. It was the same way with speaking, because I didn't do it. There was no calling on the phone or shouting for help, except in the way I might write a letter, but even then I had to be in the place where I was writing the letter, and at the speed of writing, and by the time I could get a letter in the mail, I might just as well be present.

When I left Point Reyes, I had a little bag of dried fruit and nuts and a little money, not more than ten dollars. After a week of moving up Highway 1 I had even less money and no food. I looked for the inner journey to be reflected in the physical journey. If my physical journey was a reflection of my inner journey, however, I was nearly broke and on the verge of spiritual starvation.

As I walked, the mantra grew inside, and I realized my journey was really not a matter of food or money; these were just the manifestations of something other than what it seemed. Only for a moment did I see it, all at once, like a lightning flash that illuminated the path beside the jagged form of a winter oak, branches bare, scratching at diaphanous clouds racing in a midnight sky. For that instant it was all very clear, so that when the darkness came again I could walk along the path based on that sudden glimpse,

The mantra was not a prayer asking for protection, safe passage through an unknown wood; it was only for the brief encounter with myself, the letting go of all I carried, that weighed me down so as not to walk. But that is what I did; I walked. And as I did, I found both money and food along the road.

With me I had my banjo, which more times than not rested in my arms and hands simply to play a tune. People stopped me on the way. They would turn around in their cars and come back to see the person 'they had passed so quickly. Sometimes they parked beside the road and sat with me. They would ask questions and listen to the banjo play. Often they offered me food to eat and then gave me more to take along with me. In the small towns I found cafés and restaurants where I could play music for food. I would pass my weathered hat to collect change.

Fear vanished with the sound of music. And not just for me, but for those around me.

At night I often found a beach where I could camp. I would build a fire into which I stared until the flames had turned to coals and the dark had enveloped me. In the stillness I saw the lightning flash and could see the winter oak.

I walked for a month to reach Port Orford, a town on the Oregon coast about 60 miles north of the California border. Once there, I was told I needed to see R. D. Tucker if I wanted to learn anything about Port Orford cedar. He lived in Langlois, just north of town. I walked there and met this gruff, barrel-chested lumberman, who took an instant liking to me because I had walked all that way to learn about his trees— and because he liked the way I played the banjo. What surprised him most, however, was the knowledge that even though I did not speak, we understood one another. He invited me to his house and showed me old pictures from when the cedars had lined both sides of the highway.

"But they're dying out," R. D. explained. Something was attacking the trees' roots, and no one knew what it was. He theorized that it was a virus transmitted in the water and talked about a recent flood that may have had something to do with it.

As a friend had once told me, "Find a mentor, not a hero. In fact, find many. Because we walk in the shadow of others and must begin by acknowledging and honoring those who have taught us. To be effective one must continually search for mentorship regardless of our age or years of experience. We must be humble and learn from those who teach us."

That was good advice for me, because I knew nothing about felling and milling trees. R. D. was going to teach me about the Port Orford cedar and show me how to mill it into lumber with a handsaw. I knew that if I was going to fulfill my dream of building a boat by hand and then sailing her around the world, this was something I would need to know.

For a week I camped at R. D.'s mill and ate with his family, while he schooled me in what it would take to accomplish the first stage of fulfilling my boat dream. He told me that people in this country had stopped using whipsaws to saw logs into planks a long time ago. He smiled at me and shook his head in a fatherly way, as if I were his son and he had something important to tell me.

"Well, the only place where I know you can find a whipsaw is in an antique shop," said R. D. He shook his head again. "I suppose we could make one out of one of our mill saw blades. And then we could find a couple of cedars and move them with the front loaders over a pit, or we can rig something so you can do the sawing."

As R. D. spoke I started to realize the amount of work involved in the undertaking of my dream, and for a brief moment I let the dream go and felt a certain lightness of being. But more important, I questioned how this dream fit in to furthering the outcome of my vision quest—that of promoting peace, living in harmony with the environment, and striving for the highest realization of myself and all my relations. Inertia carried the dream forward.

Then, in mid-sentence, R. D. stopped talking and scratched his head. He remembered that at an old, abandoned homestead in the mountains, he and his son had seen a whipsaw rusting in an orchard. He drew me a map.

Mantra, mentor, and maps: my life was filled with them, leading me to places where others had been before, in search of something uniquely mine that I could share with us all. Now what I was searching for was a saw.

In September I started walking south, back to Point Reyes, but this time I followed the Rogue River from the ocean at Gold Beach into the Siskiyou Mountains, the national forest, a green patch on the map. As I made my way back through the deep forest of southwest Oregon's Siskiyou Mountains, I felt the inner journey and the outer journey become one, and I let that be reflected in my writing and painting.

I concentrated on letting the experience of each moment impress itself upon me without making any precondition as to what that might be, until there was no need to concentrate at all.

Meditation is at the heart of Buddhism; consequently, silence has a central role in the spiritual unfolding of the aspirant. Meditation is a practice of gently freeing oneself from concerns of the world in order to experience only the moment. It is an exact yet simple method of becoming aware of who one really is.

Among the founders of religion, the Buddha (sixth century B.C.) was the only teacher who did not proclaim himself to be God, to be God's incarnation, or to be inspired by God. He taught that existence is impermanent, full of suffering, and unsubstantial. The way to enlightenment, according to Buddha, was to see through the illusion of separateness among people, as well as the insubstantiality of the ego.

Walking, painting, playing music, and writing were the forms my meditation took within the invisibility of silence. The vision quest, the mantras, all the forms of my meditation folded into one because they, like all of us, were related. In the meditation of painting, more important than the material result of the practice was the process of letting go of the desire for certain results. So in painting, I let the act of painting be part of what I painted. I entered a space that was more about the connection and less about me being a painter, and I let the ink and paint be whatever they might in order to reflect the inner landscape and meaning that hitherto had remained invisible. Like parenting, it's more about the connection between parent and child and less about the intellectual perception of being a parent.

In writing, I let the words come out as well. As I painted and as I wrote, I more easily entered that altered state, because after a year of living with silence, I found that I dwelled on its edge. It was a ragged edge as I moved from the quiet path in that deep forest to finding peace and wilderness beside the busy road. Nature, our mentor and teacher through our peak experience, embraces us and can be embraced by us.

As you move through your daily life, see if there is some correlation between your inner journey and the outer landscape. In the simplest of terms, this means taking time to smell the roses. It is being still amid the rush in order to see the blade of grass breaking through a crack in concrete, to witness an act of kindness to another, or to be the act of kindness. In one moment you can lose yourself and then be found, to understand that the miracle is not the turning of water into wine, but the water itself.

For me this practice was at times so joyful that tears would well in my eyes and spill over my face. This could happen not only while I sat beside a busy road in a patch of dandelions and buttercups, but also while I walked, while I played music on the banjo, or while I sat by an evening or morning fire. For you, it is any activity in which you can lose yourself, like playing with your children, cooking, or cleaning for your family. As with the mantras I spoke of earlier, these moments can be transformative.

On the fourth day after I'd left R. D., I noticed crows circling in the sky ahead of me. Next, an old single-bottom plow beside the trail told me I was near the old homestead R. D. had drawn on the map. When I came to where the crows were flying, I found an abandoned apple orchard loaded with the apples that the crows were feasting on.

Farther on I saw the building that must have been the barn, where the whipsaw was suppose to be. Next to the barn, however, I saw a small dog, which meant that the homestead was not really deserted. I thought I might lose my opportunity of gaining this whipsaw, or at least be forced into doing more work in order to gain it. As I drew closer, however, I found that the dog was really a coyote, a trickster in Native American cosmology.

I searched unsuccessfully for the saw and found my way back to the trail. I was disappointed, especially after R. D. had seemed so sure.

The meditation I contemplated today dealt with disappointment. It began in a faraway country, where a young man sought the meaning of life. His teacher explained that all his questions could be answered by a very wise hermit who lived high in a mountain wilderness. The young man made up his mind to go there, even though it was a long and dangerous journey that would take him from his family and his village, and even though he might never return. Several months passed before he reached the foot of the mountain. Without stopping to rest, he climbed into the wilderness. Four days later, when he reached the hermit's home, he found that the man was gone.

The young man stayed for a long while, but when the season changed he decided to return home. When he got home, his family looked at him in amazement because he was no longer the same young man who had left. He was older, and his ways were very wise. He hadn't realized how long he had been away. He saw his old teacher, who asked if he had found the hermit. "No," he said. "But I did find the wilderness. It did not disappoint me."

Likewise, I was not disappointed. I had learned my way through this forest, and I had learned the juxtaposition between the inner and the outer journeys. Perhaps next time I would even attain a saw. And I knew there would be a next time.

I loaded up with a backpack of apples before I headed off down the trail and refocused on my meditation.

Walking meditation was now so much a part of my life that I was a little surprised when, as I made my way through a section of pathless forest back toward the highway, I became lost. At this point, however, "lost" was a relative term. Following only a general direction, I had expected to find the asphalt highway as I emerged from the trees. Instead, I came to an old dirt logging road on the side of the mountain.

As night began to fall, I became anxious. Even if I did know the general direction, this was my first time in a forest so large I could not walk through it in less than a week. Since I was alone, I knew also that I had to take great care that I did not fall or hurt myself; it could be a long time before someone happened by. I was also anxious because when you are lost in the woods, the common wisdom is to stop before dark to prepare your campsite for spending the night. This usually means finding shelter, firewood, and water.

My largest concern was whether I should go up to the right or down to the left. With little more than a pack of apples remaining, I worried that if I went the wrong way it might be days before I realized my mistake. But the roads and trails were circuitous. They started out in one direction and then turned with the contours of geography to go in another. Otherwise, the mountain was nearly empty of cover. There were no food sources to speak of, and while broken trees and limbs littered the ground, they were not suitable building material to be taken to the sawmill.

Both choices, left and right, were strewn with cut and broken logs that would have made walking difficult. I lost control and silently cursed myself. This was when I saw the chipmunk. It was scurrying about its business, carrying nuts, seeds and such here and there. Then it stopped, sat still on a log, and stared at me. I stared back. For a while, we just stood watching each other. It went back to scurrying about, but after a few moments it stopped to stare again.

It crossed my mind that if this little chipmunk wasn't concerned, why should I be? I had stopped early enough to get firewood. I had enough water for the night and part of the morning, and there was no place I had to be. I had, however, fallen prey to backpacker's syndrome: after eating sparse amounts of dried pack food, I fantasized about a diner with my name on an order of French Fries and a milkshake. Then again, maybe I was still scared of the bear I'd seen a few days earlier. Since then, in the darkness I jumped at every snapped twig, rustling leaf, and bouncing pebble.

After I set about cooking my last bit of beans and rice, I couldn't help smiling at myself as I asked internally, "Why am I in such a hurry?" Yes, perhaps it was ursaphobia, the fear of bears, but it felt more like being on the ragged edge, where silence and awareness come and go, where one gets lost and then is found. It was not simply black and white; it was more like peace, real peace: alive and dynamic, a state where one can discover and explore one's true self.

After I ate, I washed my dishes and set some water on the hot coals to boil water for tea. Then I played some music, "Night Rain," its repetitive notes becoming themselves a mantra that took me to a familiar place, where I was falling asleep, protected only by the fraction of a millimeter of fabric stretched above my head that was my tent. There were no words, just the metal strings vibrating low in G, the thunder of a distant storm; flashing D, the lightning ripped the velvet sky, then fingering the thrill of C until the rain so far away fell a light staccato on my tent.

The rain fell, lightning flashed, and thunder rolled across the sky, yet I was at peace. The sound of the music had faded, yet it was still with me. The fire crackled. I sipped hot tea in the golden firelight surrounded by velvet darkness.

Silence.

Lesson in Silence: Grounding in a Quiet Place
Objective: Bringing the outer journey inside through place

We all on occasion may feel out of sorts, scattered, nervous, or even overwhelmed by the stressful demands of our modern society. Even when I had given up using motorized vehicles, I sometimes felt this stress when I interacted with the modern world, such as when I attended graduate school or dealt with the daily business of life. I discovered that visiting a favorite quiet place in the park by my apartment or at the lake across the street and sitting quietly and meditating was enough to restore my calm so that I could go on.

Once you find a natural, quiet, or tranquil place, practice the meditation that you have been working on. Focus on the physical place that you are in, and think about its physical characteristics. As you are walking throughout the day, try to recall this image and your feeling into your world.

Carrying with me this physical place, as well as the peace that I discovered there, was a way to bring a grounded feeling wherever I went. By the lake I would touch the water, and in the park I could touch a part of the tree as a way to reconnect to that part of the earth and to recognize my own part in it.

GUNS AND SPIRITS

In the morning, when I left my camp, I turned neither left nor right on the dirt logging road, but rather started climbing where I had seen the chipmunk the day before: straight up the mountain over broken trees, sawn tree trunks, and rutted earth until I reached the summit and felt the cool sea breeze. The ocean was covered with soft cotton clouds, and in the distance I heard the sound of the road. No longer lost, I fell to the ground in relief. Slipping out of my pack, after the last steep climb, I stared into the morning blue sky in mute celebration.

The sun was warm as I descended slowly. Once on the black asphalt road, I turned south and followed its broken yellow line past fields and farmhouses. My banjo was out, and I touched the steel strings in celebration of life. My body was smiling. Two cars, filled with laughing people, passed in opposite directions. According to my map I was on the old Oregon Coast Highway, about two day's walk north of Brookings.

I contemplated divine providence, complex enough to keep me and, indeed, many theologians busy for eternity. My interpretation of divine providence is that we are all provided with what we need to be who we are and to do what we need to do.

Many people would have problems with my interpretation. For example, some Christian churches see divine providence as providing only for the support and success of the Christian church. Then there is the thorny issue of predestination. If there is divine providence, which assures us how things will turn out, then it doesn't matter what we do; it is all predestined; all is fated; it's a done deal. Now, when we couple this with the idea of free will, which means we are all able to choose—and thus to influence—our destiny, it gets even more complicated.

If we do indeed have free will, and we can accept that free will is a precondition for making choices—and therefore is also necessary to accept responsibility for one's actions—then providence and fate seem to contradict each other. I let myself breathe this in and out at each step. These days it had become a mantra, which ultimately led to the place where I could let go of all of my ideologies and isms.

Silence.

In Hindu, Buddhist, and other major religious traditions, breath and breathing are integral parts of meditation practice. Beginners in Buddhist meditation are often instructed to count their breaths to the number ten, and then simply to be aware of breathing and to let go of other thoughts entirely. If some great idea comes to you during your meditation, write it down for later and return to your meditation. This is a form of mental concentration.

When I was walking, especially when I was exerting myself by climbing a hill, breathing became a more pronounced force that was easier to concentrate on than my moderate breathing. Each breath was almost vocal; it almost touched the invisible. As I walked, eventually I became my breathing, and things like worrying, wallowing in anger, and feeling ill will toward others simply fell away. It was such that, when I breathed in the contemplation of divine providence, free will, and fate, which had begun to exist on the ragged edge of doubt and certainty, they became one. It was through this fusion that I was able to let go of the distractions.

Lost in my reverie, I was playing the banjo and passing a tattered farmhouse when a young boy came running down the driveway. He was dressed in gray striped overalls and a faded, red plaid shirt. His shirtsleeves were unbuttoned, and a shock of dirty blond hair obscured part of his face. He wore heavy work boots that looked a few sizes too big for him.

"Hey mister, where you going?" he called to me from the driveway.

I stopped playing the banjo and pointed down the road. I could see that he was about 11 or 12. He had a baseball and a glove in his hand, as if he were in the middle of a game.

He grinned at me. "You walkin'?"

I nodded yes, and since I hadn't seen anyone for several days, I felt inclined to stop and visit with him.

"You really play that banjo nice. I never heard one played like that. Where are you comin' from?"

I pointed back over the mountain, and his eyes grew.

"You walked over the mountain?" asked the boy.

I nodded yes.

"Don't you talk?"

This time I smiled a little smile and shook my head.

"You wait here, " he said. Then he turned around and ran back the way he'd come.

I waited a few minutes and then decided that it would be best if I kept moving, so I resumed walking down the road. I had walked for about an eighth of a mile when I noticed that the kid was running after me with something in his hands. When he caught up to me he was breathing hard, and I could see he was carrying a large jar of canned peaches.

"My mom told me to give this to you." He handed me the jar and a spoon. "And she said that you can keep the spoon." He turned and walked away.

I was filled with such warmth that when I later sat down beside the road and imagined the sweetness inside the glass jar, tears came to my eyes. I put the peaches in my pack and thought how wonderful it would be to stop for the night and sit by the fire while I filled myself up with this wonderful sweet fruit.

There wasn't much traffic on the Old Coast Highway, as most cars stuck to Highway 101 at a lower elevation along the coast. The old road meandered higher along the easy contours of the mountain until it joined with the 101 about ten miles farther on. As I walked, I let myself think about the kindness of the people I had met on my journey and the peaches that I carried inside my pack. When I passed a green pickup truck parked in a driveway on my right, I noticed there was a man sitting in the driver's seat. He flashed his brake lights and called me over.

"Hey, where you headin'?" He looked at me through the truck's side mirror.

I had already passed him, so I had to walk back. My eyes were smiling. Our eyes met, and I pulled out a map and pointed to California. A little while later I was in his living room with his girlfriend. On a wall were about 30 guns; they mostly looked old. They were mixed in with several sets of antlers of various sizes, as well as photos of him holding the heads of assorted deer, elk, and big fish strung from a line.

He smiled. "Have you ever seen so many guns?" He took down a particularly lethal looking rifle. "I like to hunt," he said.

I had never seen so many guns in someone's home. I knew my dad kept an automatic pistol in a drawer in his and my mother's bedroom. It wasn't loaded, but I had found the shells above the bedroom door. At Uncle Walt's he kept a 22-caliber, single-shot rifle that we used for target practice at the dump. We shot cans, and I thought it was great fun.

My new friend asked me if I would stay for dinner, and something in his eyes encouraged me to accept his invitation. As I sat in the living room with Delmer Cosgrove and his girlfriend Dottie, he turned to me and said, "My friends call me Stubbs."

My life in Philadelphia did little to prepare me for this encounter, and as much as I was a mystery to them, they were a mystery to me. It was in that moment I realized the great opportunity I'd been given: to listen to what these new people had to tell me, to try to understand them, and to hear something I had not heard before. So that is what I did. I listened.

In order to listen actively, one must suspend judgment. It allows you to listen fully without prejudice, and it encourages the speaker to feel free to tell his whole story without fear of being challenged, even if ultimately I would disagree. To sharpen this skill, I used a little exercise. While I listened to someone, I put all my judgments into a cup of tea, and then I put that cup somewhere just within reach. Too often people barely listen. They hold the cup of tea at their lips and wait for their mate to pause so that they can sip deeply on their own thoughts and reactions. We're often so eager to share what's in our own cup that we can't listen to what's inside of others'. I knew I could reach for this cup at any time, but preferably after I had listened fully. At any moment I could pick up the cup and drink the tea, play a familiar tune, or read, write, or paint something in my journal.

What often came of this was that I learned something. At least I learned how someone else perceived life on the planet, a new point of view. After I'd taken this in, more often than not, my tea tasted a little different—I could play a new tune, or I was able to work out a different melody, or perhaps I could read a passage and understand it with renewed perception.

Stubbs had lived on this land all his life. It was a family homestead that went back generations; he hunted and trapped in these mountains, and he raised sheep and cattle on his land between here and the sea. As a young man Stubbs was a guide for the Western writer Zane Grey, and he had once climbed a tree to corner a cougar. He said that Grey had written about that wild episode but had used a different name. Stubbs made me promise that if I wrote about him I would use his true name.

I smiled at the idea of my writing a book.

"Oh, you'll write a book," Stubbs said. He took a sip of the tea Dottie had poured for us. "You know, I don't usually invite fellas I don't know, walkin' down the road, to come have dinner with me." He settled back into a stuffed leather armchair. "But you're different. First, you didn't look hungry." He stopped talking for a moment and looked me dead in the eyes. "You know what I mean by hungry? I don't mean hungry like you could eat a good meal, I mean hungry like you could do something mean to someone because you want what they got. You don't got that look. What's more, you don't talk. That's another thing that's interestin'."

I crossed my heart and held up one hand.

"Yeah, I know; it's a promise you made. Now that's real different too. I haven't met anybody like you before." He paused a long time.

"'Cept maybe an Injun, they don't talk much either. But they don't carry no banjo neither. You play that thing? We've been waiting to hear if you can play."

As I began playing, smiles grew on both their faces. Shortly thereafter, good old Stubbs picked up the phone to make a call. He was inviting his daughter over for dinner to meet me. Problem was, she was just sitting down with her own family and had to be satisfied with hearing the music over the phone. Then they decided that I could take a shortcut through the ranch, and she could come meet me in the morning.

What followed was a dinner of macaroni and cheese, prepared in honor of the fact that I was a vegetarian. After that I had a good night's sleep in the camping trailer they had parked beside their ranch house.

In the morning Stubbs's daughter showed up briefly, more to see her dad than anything else, but I was happy to meet her. She seemed like a piece of her dad, straight and honest. I was slightly disappointed that she didn't have very much time for small talk, as her chores were waiting and her kids had to get on to school, but I relished the opportunity to meet her at all.

Stubbs drew me a map of how to get to the New Coast Highway through his ranch. He cut off five miles from my own plotted journey. Dottie packed me some fresh fruit and a cheese sandwich for lunch.

"Now we might get to see you on the highway tomorrow," Stubbs said. His last words were to watch out for the "coyote-getters": shotgun shells buried in the ground and baited so that when a coyote pulled at the top, it would explode and send a lethal dose of cyanide into the coyote's mouth.

I had almost made it to the coast road when I decided to stop for the night. Sleeping in the tranquillity of the ranch was more appealing to me than camping beside a busy highway; I felt safer sleeping in a natural area. I settled down and finished the food that Dottie had packed for me, as well as the peaches that I had been saving. They were just as I had imagined: syrupy sweet perfection. There was a full moon to enjoy, so I had not built a fire. I was already in my sleeping bag and asleep as the moon was making its long arc into the sea.

I was awakened by a scratching sound, which I immediately assigned to a bear. I turned my head slowly so as not to cause any startle and peered into the brushy moonlight. I waited a long moment before I heard the scratching again. It took me awhile before I was able to discern a deer about 30 feet away. It took cautious step after cautious step. Mesmerized by the sight, I did not move for fear that I would frighten the young doe. Then I realized that 30 feet had closed to 10 feet . . . 5 feet . . . and then it was only inches away from my head. I remained still for fear that if I startled the deer it would kick me in the head as it tried to get away. I closed my eyes, breathed gently, and waited.

What happened next I attributed to the supernatural. In the moonlight, the deer kissed me on the face. Then, as slowly as it had come, it left. When it was gone, I lay motionless for a long time. I touched my face and felt the wetness of the kiss. The closest that I had come to a deer in the wild was the time when I was running on Inverness Ridge and came across one coming the opposite direction as we turned a blind turn. We were both startled at our accident. But tonight's meeting was something other, something deliberate, on both our parts. My mind raced as it tried to settle on the significance. Sleep was hard to recapture; instead I remained awake until the moon dipped into the sea.

The sun was peeking over the trees and I was walking down the dirt road when I heard a four-wheel-drive truck grumbling down the mountain behind me. It was Stubbs and Dottie on their way to town. I could hardly contain myself. I acted out the deer stalking through the brush in the moonlight and ended the performance by kissing into the air and pointing to the spot on my cheek.

"Licked your face, did she? Must 'a' been after your salt," Stubbs said as he scratched the side of his face and smiled. "They'll do n'ar anything for a little salt."

I realized that was probably true: I had sweated profusely during the day, and a slight white rime had caked on my eyebrows. No matter. As far as I was concerned, a deer had kissed me on the face. We made our final good-byes, and as I walked on to the highway I felt I was blessed.

Lesson in Silence: Mantras
Objective: To introduce a mantra to your meditation practice

Repeating a mantra is another technique for achieving concentration and inner peace, which is a particularly important goal when considering all the distractions of daily life. We can view meditation as similar to prayer; however, unlike prayer, it is best when done without intention and not as a way to ask for something.

In Tibetan Buddhism, one mantra is "Om Ma Ni Pad Me Hum." While it is very difficult to translate, it is one of the most widely used of the Buddhist mantras. Gen Rinpoche, a Tibetan master, says the mantra is the essence of all teaching. "Om" helps you achieve perfection in the practice of generosity; "Ma" helps perfect the practice of pure ethics; "Ni" helps achieve perfection in the practice of tolerance and patience; "Pad" helps to achieve perfection of perseverance; "Me" helps achieve perfection in the practice of concentration; and the final, sixth syllable "Hum" helps achieve perfection in the practice of wisdom.

Simply say this to yourself as you sit in meditation. Tibetan Buddhists believe that saying this mantra to oneself invokes the powerful benevolent attention and blessings of Chenrezig, the embodiment of compassion.

In my own practice I use a personal mantra that I discover for myself: a word or idea that comes in the course of my meditation, such as "peace" or "divine grace." You may use your own personal mantra, or prayer, until even these words fade into the silence of the page.

SHAKING THE TREES

A few days later, I crossed into California. It was nighttime when I arrived in Smith River. There were no streetlights, and I was tired from walking all day. Then I heard music and followed the sound of it in the darkness. As I got closer it sounded more like a party, accompanied by the loud bass of a rock band. In the darkness I could make out a small, white building that looked like a town hall. It was hard to imagine a party in this little town so late on Sunday evening. I walked up the steps, took off my pack, and leaned it against the wall of the covered porch. The beat rocked the building. I knocked but decided that no one could have heard me over the noise. So I just opened the door and walked in.

I found myself in a room illuminated by what seemed like a hundred candles. I guessed that the town hall was actually a church. Most of the candles were on the altar at the front, but additional candles lining the wall gave the church an ethereal light. A white cross was on the altar, and there were smaller crosses around the room with the candles. Native people, mostly middle-aged and with bells on their ankles, danced and stomped in a circle that went around the perimeter of the room. The women were all clothed conservatively in print dresses, beaded bracelets, and porcupine quill earrings; some had their hair up tightly in a bun with wood barrettes, beaded with native symbols.

It was the stomping that provided the bass I had heard. They were chanting and waving their arms as they moved together. The dancers passed around handbells with fist-long wooden handles that fit nicely in the hand—the kind teachers had used to ring us in from recess at my elementary school.

There were chairs placed against the walls around the room, and a few older people were sitting. I had expected to see a live band with a big sound system, party food, and some young people having a good time. But faced with what was before me, I thought of turning around and leaving. I didn't leave, however, because I felt committed to stay. After all, everyone was looking at me. It felt rude to just turn and leave. Instead, I sat down in one of the chairs as inconspicuously as I could.

It was clearly a religious ceremony, and it had a clear leader. The biggest person in the room, he wore dark pants and a white long-sleeved shirt without a collar. Most of the other men wore the same type of clothing, but over his shirt the leader wore a vest with bead-work designs. His energy reached out over the group, who followed him with their spirit and their eyes.

The chant changed: "Come to the Lord; He will save you." The procession continued around the room as the group began clasping each other's hands and making the sign of the cross. Older people who were sitting beside me—I hadn't recognized I was the youngest person sitting—were brought forward, and the healing began.

The minister went to each person and asked if they needed to be healed. If they said yes, he would touch them and offer a prayer. When he came to me, he showed no surprise at my presence. He merely welcomed me and asked where I was from.

I pointed back to the door.

"Don't you speak?" he asked. Concern was written on his face.

I shook my head, and he smiled. He put his hand on my throat. "In the name of Jesus, heal this man, Lord, and . . . " The minister's words were full of power and resonance. I felt them stir my soul. When he had finished, he looked at me expectantly. I thought to myself that maybe I did need healing, and that maybe this was the time to start speaking. I thought of something I could say: "Hallelujah! Praise is to God!"

I was so close. It would have been so dramatic.

But I kept the thought to myself.

Tonight would not be the night I would break my word fast.

Looking a little disappointed, the minister told me it might take a few prayers. I nodded. I thought he was probably right. When the ceremony was over, I learned that I had stumbled upon the Smith River Indian Shaker Church.

I was introduced to some of the church members, who welcomed me warmly. I had the spirit of walking many miles. They recognized this. There really was no need for explanation. We held each other's hands for long moments and felt strong emotions stirring within us.

Afterward, I slept beneath a cypress near the church.

In the morning I went to visit the Shaker minister from the night before, Charlie Big Head. When he learned about my silence, he laughed a big laugh and told me that if I had chosen to speak last night, his reputation as having "big medicine" would have been assured. He laughed more, and we sat and had breakfast together.

Charlie Big Head talked a little about the Shaker church and its shamanic roots. It was not related to the Shakers that I had heard of, those who were commonly referred to as the shaking Quakers. Mother Ann Lee founded the shaking Quakers in America; celibacy was an integral part of their doctrine. These Indian shakers, on the other hand, were more related to the Ghost Dance movement, with elements of Catholicism and Native American traditional shamanic healing mixed in.

As the story goes, in 1881, John Slocum (Squ-sacht-um), a native logger in Washington, died. His wife and friend were holding a wake and waiting for his coffin to arrive by canoe. Just before the canoe arrived, John was resurrected. He told the astonished gathering that he had indeed died and had gone to heaven. An angel had explained to him that he was really meant to go to hell, but that if he returned as a witness to other sinners he would be saved. Thus started the Indian Shaker Church, which borrowed heavily from Catholicism. Not surprisingly, Slocum was reported to have had some Catholic instruction.

A few months later Slocum fell deathly ill again. As his wife, Mary, approached his sickbed and prayed, she began to shake uncontrollably, and miraculously, he was cured. Mary attributed John's second miraculous cure to her convulsive prayer, and thus was born the name Shakers.

The Indian Shaker Church spread through many different tribes primarily because it relied on the individual to make his determination on any matter of religion, in the sense that there were no strict rules to follow; it was up to the head of each church and its members. As such, the church preserved many Indian ways, even though there was a fusion of Christianity and Catholicism in particular.

The Ghost Dance movement arose in 1889, when Jack Wilson (Wovoka), the son of a Paiute mystic, had a vision during a solar eclipse. In Wilson's vision, Christ returned to Earth to bury the wicked, native and non-native people alike. Proclaiming that he was Christ returned, Wilson preached that any Indian who participated in the Ghost Dance ceremony would be saved. The movement, which spread across the country, called for the Indians to purify themselves through meditation, chanting, fasting, and, most important, the ceremony of the Ghost Dance.

The Ghost Dance was an adaptation of the circle dance, which native peoples had used in various forms for thousands of years. Different tribes and reservations adopted different elements. The movement's leaders preached that Indians would be saved only if they gave up the wicked ways of the white man. They would have to stop drinking alcohol and turn to farming and sending their children to school; generally, they would be expected to lead a clean and respectful life.

But as with all other Indian ceremonies, the Bureau of Indian Affairs forbade native peoples to dance the Ghost Dance because it was seen as a force that united the Indians against the U.S. government. In fact, the government cited the Ghost Dance as one of the causes of the armed resistance of the Lakota Sioux. This resistance resulted in the Wounded Knee Massacre, in which at least 150 Lakota Sioux died.

Native peoples believed that those who did the Ghost Dance would one day be lifted up in to the sky while a new soil was laid down to bury the wicked. Those who danced would then be returned to reunite with their lost ancestors. Women in bands that had lost their men in the Indian Wars were particularly fervent dancers. They danced until they were exhausted in the hope of insuring the return of a loved one.

The shamanic state of consciousness involves a deep respect for all forms of life, with a humble awareness of even the inorganic matter of our planet. The shaman knows that humans are related to all forms of life. He approaches all forms of life with familial respect and understanding. Sun Bear, a Chippewa shaman, said that everything has energy within, and the first thing that a person has to do in life is to learn how to sit in silence and feel the energy that abides in the earth, the trees, the rocks, the waters, and so on.

Both the Ghost Dance movement and the Indian Shaker Church allowed Native American cosmology to endure in a cross-cultural environment. While fewer tribes dance the Ghost Dance today than in times past, the Indian Shaker Church has survived and continues to evolve.

Charlie Big Head was very interested in my vision quest, my walking, and my silence. He found my silence especially interesting because the shaman contacts the spirit world in a state of silence. As shamanic philosophy dictates, when you approach the spirit world in this altered state of consciousness, in which you utilize love, respect, and inner stillness, nature will in return reveal itself in ways that are unimaginable and unapproachable in an ordinary state of consciousness.

Charlie Big Head asked me about the animals I saw. I told him of the chipmunk that had told me to be patient and to take my time, to be where I am; the coyote that I had thought was a dog; and the bear. He wanted to hear that story in detail, so I did my best to convey it in silence.

I mimed climbing up and down on a narrow trail, where I ducked beneath low branches. When the trail led down the narrow canyon, I stopped at the creek to drink from between the rocks. I was grateful for this stream of cold, clear water, and so I sat down to listen to its voice. It welcomed me and made me feel good.

As I sat, I looked across the stream. That's when I saw a large black bear ambling down the trail. I was motionless, not afraid but still filled with gratitude that I could share this stream and this moment with Brother Bear.

Problem was, I was still on the trail, and Brother Bear was moving right toward me. He ambled across the rocks until he stood not a foot from me. He look right at me and sniffed at my face, and in that moment I realized that there was nothing between us—no bars, no glass, no great distance, just a few inches—and in my mind I saw the universe filled with shooting stars and comets while an unimaginable array of colors, lights, and cartoon figures passed before me. After a short while, Brother Bear gave one final snort and ambled back up the trail the way I had come. In mime, I used large, bold bear strokes to paint him walking crouched over and sniffing with his eyes half closed (bears are notorious for having bad eyesight), and then I patted my hand over my heart and, my eyes wide open, made little dust devil signs near my head.

Charlie Big Head thought for a moment. "Well, John," he said, "a bear can mean power, courage, and introspection."

Yes, I could see that the bear was a powerful creature, one that deserved my respect. It brought very strong feelings to me and made me think of my father, who to me symbolized strength and deserved respect, yet I feared his disapproval. I thought this was a message for me. Perhaps my father was telling me that even though he sometimes disapproved of some of the things I did, he was always near, always ready to help, always by my side no matter what I might be going through or what choices I might make.

Then I told Charlie Big Head about the deer. He looked at me for a long time, until the silence had settled between us, and then he took my hand in his and spoke.

"Good things are for you," he said. "After you are finished, maybe you will come and see me, but your journey may be very long."

I left Charlie Big Head standing in his yard. No more could be said. But as I walked I began to understand that everything—all my encounters with both animals and people, together with what they said and what they did and what they represented—was a very important part of the journey. Even more, I realized how much more important it was to listen, even to the unassuming chipmunk.

The next afternoon, when I arrived in Crescent City, 13 miles south of Smith River, I went to Denny's. I had enough money from the cans I had been collecting from the roadside to buy lunch. As I ate, one of the waiters came over to speak to me about what I was doing. When he learned that I had walked from Point Reyes to Oregon, the place became abuzz with talk, and a young couple offered their home as a place for me to shower and to rest. They said there was a radio show broadcast from the restaurant in the morning, and they asked me to come back to be interviewed. It sounded like a great idea, even if I didn't speak. They gave me directions to their home. When I got up to pay the bill and leave, the restaurant manager said it was taken care of.

On the way to their place, I heard a pickup truck approaching me from behind. It was late, and there was little traffic. As the truck approached, I felt something was wrong; a numbness came over me, and a sudden hum in my head made me look up.

That's when I noticed my shadow appearing in the center of the headlights' beams. I squeezed to my right as far as I could without falling into a deep ditch. The truck sped up, and I felt the brush of the passenger side mirror against my left shoulder. As it passed, the driver turned off the lights. The truck turned at the corner and disappeared into the darkness.

When I made it to my new friends' house, I tried to tell them about the truck. I had a difficult time conveying this, however, so I ended up just thanking them for their hospitality.

I returned to the restaurant the next morning. Already the radio personality was on the air and telling everyone who could hear "to come on down to Denny's," where they were offering some great breakfast special.

The DJ, who had wavy blond hair and was dressed in a white shirt and striped tie, sat in a little area right by the front door. He did not seem to mind the clatter of dishes or the competing conversations that swirled around. Someone walked over, tapped him on the shoulder, and pointed to me. He nodded and waved me over.

"Hey, so you're the guy who walks and don't talk," said the DJ. "How are we going to do this?"

I hunched my shoulders and pointed to my banjo.

"You play that thing?"

I nodded yes.

"That's great." He was already back on the air and telling people that they had to "come on down to Denny's today, not only for their great breakfast specials, but to meet John Francis, who walked into town today but he doesn't talk. So you're not going to hear him saying anything, but he does play the banjo, he says, so I'm sure he'll give our listening audience a few notes."

I let loose a tune. He smiled and, telling me in radio sign language to keep it up, he rolled a horizontal index finger around and around.

When I was finished, he seemed truly excited. "Hey, isn't that great, folks?" he said to his listeners. "And he is right down here at Denny's. After the break we are going to talk to him . . . without him speaking, that is. This'll be a first for me." The DJ put a cassette tape into a player and flipped a switch. We heard a jingle about buying a new car from a local dealer. Meanwhile, he leaned my way and asked if I had ever been on the radio before.

I smiled and shook my head.

"You have a great story," he said. "Do you have anything to sell, like music tapes, paintings, or something like that?"

I shook my head again.

"That's not good, John. You gotta go commercial. Sell stuff. You hear what I'm telling ya?"

I nodded that I did.

The commercial over, he identified the station and, after introducing himself again, said, "Our guest this half hour is John Francis from Point Reyes, California. John doesn't talk, but we are going to talk to John and find out all about him. John, tell us what you are doing and why."

As I mimed he described, "Okay, folks, he is crashing his hands together, and . . . you saw an oil spill . . . while you were driving . . . and you threw your car away . . . and started walking."

There was a pause as I finished the mime and he finished describing it. The DJ continued: "But tell us, John. Why did you stop talking?"

I began to mime.

"Oh, oh, he has both his hands up in front of him, and they are talking to one another; no, they are fighting . . . no, having an argument." He searched for the right words. "To stop fight—having arguments."

I brought out my journals. The DJ stopped himself after reading a few entries on the air. "Hey, wait a minute, folks. How do you know that John is here, if all you hear is me talking? I could be making this whole thing up. John, how about playing a little banjo for us, and then we will open it up to the phones?"

I played the banjo for a while, and then the phones lit up like a Christmas tree. I began to take questions.

"How many shoes have you worn out?" asked one caller.

I hunched my shoulders.

"He doesn't know, caller."

"What do you think about nuclear war?" asked the next.

I pinched my nose.

"He thinks it stinks," said the DJ.

It went on like that until the show was over. I walked back out into the street and headed south.

I moved along the coast and through the redwoods—the ancient spirits of my dreams—until I climbed a high road above the sea. Charlie Big Head had told me my journey was going to be long, but at this point I wondered if it would ever end.

———

A week later, I was walking the Sea View Road that parallels Highway 1 at a distance of about a half mile and an elevation of about 1,500 feet. It was quiet, isolated, and lined on either side by Douglas fir. There was little traffic, and my spirit was full and at peace. I felt the meaning of every step and breath as I breathed myself into and out of existence.

As I walked I softly played "Life's Celebration" on the banjo.

Lesson in Silence: Find Another Teacher
Objective: Open yourself to other possibilities

There are many teachers from whom you can learn different techniques of meditation, and different religions and beliefs have various techniques for finding silence. You would be wise to at least investigate them in pursuit of your own understanding. The exercise that I have offered here is one of listening. Even when you have settled on a practice or a teacher, remember that even students can teach, and that we all learn from and teach each other. This comes from my own experience, which I am sure has been influenced by many students.

Reading is a special form of listening, and what you will gain is a greater understanding of self and the journey you are on.

MR. DEATH

The blue pickup truck passed me heading north and then returned, driving by slowly, before coming to a full stop just ahead of me on the side of the road. As I walked by, the two men in the truck turned their heads as if to keep me from seeing their faces. The air was charged, and my body tingled.

Suddenly the quiet was shattered, and my music stopped. I let out a long breath.

"Hey, boy, just a minute." It was the driver's voice, gruff and irritated.

Looking over my shoulder, I stared back at the truck and then at the two men. There was something familiar about the long, gray expressions on their faces. I thought maybe they were people I had met before. I turned and walked over to the open window on the driver's side.

It was a small, imported truck, and it was easy enough for me to place my left arm casually on the roof and peer inside into two wary eyes. Both men were blond, the driver with a short military crew cut and his passenger with medium-length hair that dropped down like that of a shaggy dog. The passenger seemed nervous, and he was hiding something beside his legs.

"Boy, are you lost or something?" The driver was almost friendly. I was thinking that he just wanted to offer me directions or maybe a shortcut, except for the way he had said "boy." If he had addressed me as "sir," "mister," or "buddy," that could have been friendly, but "boy" made the hairs on my neck rise.

I shook my head and walked the fingers of my right hand over imaginary hills. I ended by pointing down the road the way I was walking, south.

"Are you heading south?" asked the driver.

I nodded yes and repeated the motion of walking my fingers over the hills, only this time a grin had formed at the corners of my mouth. I was not sure why, except that I was thinking that maybe these guys were lost, and the thought was amusing.

But I knew they were not lost. We were all where we were meant to be. I knew this from the very core of my being as the driver's right hand came from beneath his seat and revealed the dark gunmetal of a .44 revolver, the barrel of which he placed against my head.

In that moment of crystal clarity, I recognized the face of death. He was like an old friend I had forgotten, but he had always been there, always walking with me in the forests, over mountains, over hills, and into valleys, through the fullness of my journey to when the tears flowed from my eyes as unquestioned rivers.

I breathed in.

"We don't like niggers around here." Death said these words, but the words seemed not to matter. They were like a code that I had heard before but never understood. All that mattered now was that we were here together.

I breathed out.

He pulled the trigger, and the hammer fell.

Click.

I heard no explosion. My body did not slump to the asphalt road. I was looking past the gun into his frightened eyes. It happened so fast that I hardly realized the flash of light that came through. A rush of thoughts passed through me, but one got stuck:

"Damn, I did not make a painting for today." I almost said the words out loud. But now I was pulling back with a large smile, pointing at myself, and walking my fingers across the invisible hills again, as if it was all I knew. I gave the sign that everything was okay.

A puzzled look passed between Death and his companion. They looked at each other and then back at me. Time was standing still.

"Now get going," the driver said.

I signed "okay" again and moved slowly away from the truck, turned, and started walking down the road. A minute later I looked back, and the blue truck was gone. A little farther on I found a break in the trees and sat down beside the road. From here I saw in the blue distance the Point Reyes Peninsula—home. It was only a few days away. An ocean of brilliant white clouds hugged the coast. Only the highest hills, ridges, and mountaintops were visible. In this afternoon light I had to paint.

The painting was a meditation. It kept my mind from spinning in continued replay and kept my hand from shaking. We are the mountains. We are the trees . . . but my reverie was short-lived. A big white truck pulled up in front of me and blocked my view. The two men inside were both wearing white cowboy hats, and I did not recognize either of them. They must be the good guys, I thought; and, just to drive home that point, one produced a deputy sheriff's badge and held up a gold star so that I could see it. I felt a wave of relief.

"Hey, boy, are you lost?" one of the men asked.

I shook my head no and showed him the unfinished painting of the road flanked by steep shoulders of summer grass, barbed-wire fences, and fir trees that headed down to the coast, crowded with fog, brown hills, and Point Reyes in the distance.

"Never mind that," he said, as he dismissed my journal with a wave of his hand. "The ranchers are all hot about you being up here."

I walked my hand in the air and pointed down the road.

"What's 'a' matter with you? You deaf or something?"

I shook my head, crossed my heart as if I were making a promise, and placed my forefinger in front of my closed lips. He leaned out the truck window across the lap of his passenger and took a good look at me. He shook his head and rolled his eyes.

"Well, it don't matter what you are. You do understand me, and you better not be sittin' here when I come back or there'll be some real trouble."

They waited until I packed my things and started walking down the hill. Once I did, the truck rumbled on up the road and disappeared in the trees. I waved as they drove by again. Once they were out of sight I took a few steps more. Still barely in the sun, I stopped again to finish my painting.

On my way down to Highway 1 I passed through the fog. After the warmth of the sun it sent a chill up my spine. I was both angry and afraid—angry that life could still take on such an ugly and familiar form, and afraid that death would catch me before I got home. I began to shiver uncontrollably.

When I reached the highway about an hour later, some friends from Point Reyes were driving by. They stopped, and we embraced. They told me that reports of my progress coming down the coast had been reaching home. I was so happy to see them that I began to cry big, silent tears through a silly smile. They looked worried and asked if I was all right.

I hesitated, then nodded yes; but for a moment I thought of getting into the car, where I could be safe. I might have done just that, only there was so much I needed to express while standing there at the side of the highway that I didn't even know where to begin. I could only wave to them as they drove on up the coast.

In the evening I camped beside the Russian River, just a few miles farther. Home was just a couple days away. I made a small fire and listened to the faraway surf and the barking sea lions. They sounded so much like dogs, but they never annoyed me. Closer still were the lagoon and the mournful call of a common loon.

In the stillness, I thought of a dead friend, Jerry, a Marin County deputy, lost somewhere in the vastness of the sea. I was still afraid of death catching me, but I was warmed by the fire, and I was breathing. With each breath I recommitted myself to the journey, to the work that needed to be done.

Sitting there, I was filled with silence that left me, filled me, and then left me again. I sat there breathing, in and out, in and out, until the silence and darkness of the night overwhelmed me.

A month later I was at home in Point Reyes and wandering around on the Inverness mesa. A sheriff's car was parked on the road. In the driver's seat was a deputy. He waved me over. As I got closer I realized it was my friend Tony Veranda. Besides being a Marin County deputy sheriff, he owned a jewelry shop in Point Reyes Station. I often stopped by to share some music, me on the banjo and Tony on the jaw harp. When I got to the side of the car, he greeted me.

"Walking-No-Talking John, how are you doing?"

Taking the hand that he had extended through the window, I smiled and nodded.

"I haven't seen you for a while," Tony said. "Where you been?"

I was already taking out my painting journal. I handed it to him. He carefully turned the pages and made sounds of approval.

"I see you been out to the lighthouse." He handed the book to his partner, who I recognized immediately as Death himself. For an instant I thought this was my time to die, but the feeling was wrong for that. There was no tension, no crystal clarity, just my friend Tony with a big smile on his face, even though he was sitting next to Death.

After flipping through my journal briefly, Death gave the book back to Tony, who returned it to me before excusing himself to leave for some emergency call that I hadn't heard come through. I imagined that Death was very busy in the course of the day.

The next day at Tony's shop, before we played our music, he told me a story about his new partner.

"We were just sitting there, and when we saw you, I said, 'There goes Walking-No-Talking John.' Then he tells me that you talked a lot when he put his gun to your head. After he was through talking, I bet him a case of beer that you didn't. He hated like hell to pay up."

Then Tony and I played "Night Rain." Even in the afternoon, that rain fell, lightning flashed, and thunder rolled across the sky; yet I was at peace: Even with Death so close, I smiled and climbed the ridge until I could see the ocean, brilliant blue in the distance.

Years afterward, Tony came to me and apologized for not being able to act when he heard the story from his partner. Neither of them was in a good place, he said. A few months later, Tony died.

I came to walking and then silence because of an environmental event that inspired me to act, and in that action I discovered other realities, such as the connectedness of all life. Through my vision quest I received a vision to hold: that in the course of my journey, I must devote myself to promoting peace, living in harmony with the environment, and striving for the highest realization of myself and all my relations, while at the same time living in gratitude for the present moment. I wondered how or if I could do all that. I wasn't sure of what it all meant. But visions are often like that. The meaning must be figured out along the way, beyond each mistake, alone and in community. And that was why, while the ugly world of race and racism and all the other isms that oppress and exploit swirled around me, I was grateful for the music with a friend and the opportunity to witness true healing, first within myself.

Lesson in Silence: Contemplation of Life and Death
Objective: Further explore the meaning of the ragged edge of silence

After we decide on a course of action or understand something to be true, it is a good thing to revisit that decision or truth from time to time, as our understanding may have changed during the passage of time or in the course of our further education. This was the case with my decision to be silent, which I revisited each birthday.

Revisit the first exercise of listening to see if your understanding of it has changed. If we can understand the ragged edge of silence, we can better look at other phenomena, such as life and death, love and hate. In your meditation practice, contemplate the edge of sound and silence, the ocean and the shore; let your mind wander and be open to the inspection of life and death as words of the introduction are grounded on the blank pages.

Use your journal to review and capture details. If your perception has changed, you may better redefine the meaning of sound and silence, life and death, and the journey that we are all on.

THREE EDUCATIONS

John Muir was one of the first people to look at the wilderness as a place where people, shaped by civilization, could go to be re-created and refreshed, not as a resource to be exploited for its minerals, timber, and wildlife. The words of Roderick Nash, a professor of history and environmental studies at the University of California, expressed a view shared by many contemporary wilderness proponents: "Wilderness . . . is a profound educational resource schooling overcivilized humans in what we once knew but unfortunately forgot."

This was the education I had sought since I began walking north from Point Reyes. Each spring, over the next three years, I journeyed north to visit the Kalmiopsis Wilderness, a gloriously green patch on the map that I had discovered in 1974, before my first walk north.

By the time of my first visit to the Kalmiopsis, I was much more comfortable with the idea and practice of camping in the mountains. My time on the road and exploring the Point Reyes National Seashore had provided ample opportunity to hone my camping skills without being too far away from home. My friend Jean had moved to an apartment closer to San Francisco, and I now lived in a small cabin without running water, up from First Valley and closer to Inverness Ridge. Next to a large fir tree, my home consisted of one room built of reclaimed redwood planks, a wood-burning stove, and a sleeping platform beneath a large skylight. I had windows on three sides, which gave me the feeling of sleeping in the trees.

The property belonged to Sim Van der Ryn, my mentor and a professor at the School for Environmental Architecture and Design at the University of California, Berkeley. He was also a founder of Farallones Institute Rural Center in Occidental. Located on 80 acres of rolling meadows and forestland 10 miles from the Pacific coast and 70 miles north of San Francisco, the institute was founded in 1974 to promote participatory education and appropriate technology—technology that is efficient, low cost, locally controlled, and adapted to local needs. Several of Van der Ryn's students had constructed my cabin and several other outbuildings as a class project.

When I arrived at the bottom of the Quail Prairie Fire Lookout (elevation 3,033 feet) on the western Kalmiopsis border, I saw the evening fog moving in from the coast, spilling over the mountains. Large thunderheads rose in the sky. Slowly, step by step, I carefully maneuvered with a 75-pound pack as I made my way up the stairway. As I moved higher, I became increasingly aware of the fresh breeze moving the tops of trees just below me.

Once inside, I silently introduced myself to the lookout on duty. He was busy observing an incoming storm and reporting it to the ranger headquarters in Brookings. His was a small room furnished with a little wood-burning stove for heat, a gas stove for cooking, a table, a few chairs, and a small cot with some storage space below. In the center of the room was a fire finder, which enables a lookout to report the location of forest fires.

Not much was known about the fire history of the Kalmiopsis prior to the establishment of the forest in 1907–1908, but charred stumps and blackened tree trunks gave silent evidence that, at one time, most of the area was burned over. People speculate that fur trappers, traders, prospectors, and early settlers caused some of the fires; others say the damage was done by lightning. And, as usual, both were probably right, at least in part.

The sun disappeared behind dark clouds. Night had come during midday. The temperature fell, and I shivered. A few moments later the storm reached us. Rain dropped in great silver-gray sheets onto the metal roof with a deafening roar, and the sky turned blue-white with lightning, adding to the confusion of the elements. I was grateful to be inside, but the lookout's face spoke our vulnerability without words.

Small fires ignited where lightning touched the trees, and plumes of white smoke rose into the stormy sky. At their camp near the Illinois River, the smoke jumpers were put on standby. In a matter of seconds, our visibility was cut to zero by the fog. The wind howled around us with gale force. More flashes of lightning were followed by rolls of thunder and driving rain. The tower trembled, and so did I.

"It's good to see natural powers and processes greater than our own," writes Nash. "The lessons of such experiences are precisely what are needed if the human-environment relations are to be harmonious and stable in the long run."

In a little while the fog was gone, and we had a clear view of the storm. The rain continued to fall for some time. It extinguished the fires, and the smoke jumpers were taken off standby. In the west there were no clouds, only the sun. Two rainbows arched across the sky and came down near Vulcan Lake. I watched the sun, crimson-orange, sink silently into the sea. This was my welcome to the Kalmiopsis Wilderness.

On this current journey, I passed through an area of *Kalmiopsis leachiana,* for which the wilderness is named. This is a small, unassuming shrub that resembles the rhododendron and is known to botanists as one of the rarest shrubs in the world. The plant's small, red flowers bloom from mid-May through June and may be collected by special permits given only for scientific purposes.

Three days later I reached Slide Creek and made my camp among some abandoned mining equipment and a few fallen shacks. In the eastern and southwestern portions of the Kalmiopsis, there were still a few roads constructed by miners to access their valid claims.

Most were built during and immediately after World War II for the excavation and stockpiling of chrome ore, for which there was great demand. However, Slide Creek and a few other places were known especially for their rich gold deposits.

When I first arrived at Slide Creek, I was put off by what I felt was the refuse of civilization, but even after just a day, nature's reclamation of me was too fierce not to be overwhelmed by her. I tried to justify my feelings in the poem I penned on the creek's banks.

Sometime the changes come from within
Seeing with no eyes
Hearing with no ears
We begin
September 23, 1975
Slide Creek, Kalmiopsis Wilderness

I somehow managed not to mind the silent clutter of abandoned mining equipment that lay rusting about—twisted cable, red- and yellow-painted motors with rods and pistons exposed—machines chipped to the bone. I became absorbed in watching the canyon wall and looking for the way I had come just days before. The trail was now lost in earthy colors among the trees and rocks. The trees were clinging, holding on with roots knotted to stone, others slipping, falling to the stream below. A few of them I got to know.

The wilderness I had come to experience is how they danced, the trees with long, green needles. How they stood in the wind, bending and swaying. And how they came to the water and drank there among the rocks like three sisters.

I saw movement. Mixed among the variegated hues of green . . . ferns and grasses, bushes and small trees loaded with blue huckleberries and red chokecherries . . . a flash of gray, and an invisible path was traced by a fat squirrel bounding with its tail high. It went down steeply along switchbacks through the trees down to the river . . . not the way I had imagined. But I did not really know the trail until I looked back—until I caught sight of the gray squirrel on it. I relaxed into a simple experiential knowledge that unfolded within me.

I felt as if I were finally learning to see.

I watched the blue jays, 50 or more, that came down each day. With utmost ease they swooped from limb to limb with raucous laughter and their feet curled under their bodies. And in the quiet I heard the voice of the river passing among the rocks and over stones, everywhere at once, making its way through steep green canyons to the sea. I tried to catch the words mingling with the shushing of the trees. Perhaps this was where our speech began. Maybe long ago, before there were words, there was only the river, and the people listened to the water . . . and the quiet whispering.

I could only hear the laughter. I was still learning to listen. The music that I played was the voice that I heard, the laughing.

Down by the water, I watched a nameless little bird standing on the rocks near the rapids and singing, its dark body bobbing to some silent music, before diving into the stream. I ran down to the rocks to find it. Surely it had drowned. But before I reached the stream there was another. Standing on the rocks, singing. Its dark body bobbed to silent music too.

Could it be the same bird?

It took most of the day watching, but I learned that this marvelous bird did indeed jump in the water, and then, just moments later, it would return to the same rock. It was something I had never seen before. I was filled with wonder for life's ability to surprise us.

In the night, the canyon rose black beneath a starry sky, and on this soft velvet I painted pictures in my mind of what is hidden there, until the moon lifted above the rim and silver shadows danced down to the river and splashed across the rocks. At Slide Creek I slowed down to a stop, and all the hurried miles, the noise and smoky choke of the speeding roads and highways, finally slid away.

I stayed for five days.

Then, one morning—when the fish-scale sky hinted rain—I left Slide Creek. I stepped on five stones across the Chetco River and continued south through the dense growth of poison oak. The trail greatly needed repairs, but I had grown to expect and accept it as part of the wilderness, as much as I accepted the large, striped hornets, dark and menacing, that suddenly appeared and grabbed moths from midair flight, and as much as I accepted the threatening sound of a rattlesnake's tail shaking in the knee-high grass.

Two days later I arrived at the mining claim operated for the last 17 years by two prospectors, Ruth and Perry Davis. I did not intend to stop, but I found myself walking up the trail toward Emily Cabin. Perry was sitting in a rusted folding chair, shaded from the midday sun beneath a clump of maple trees. He was so intent on unlocking some mystery of the rock sample at the other end of a magnifying lens that he did not notice me. I stood almost beside him and continued to make the little whistling sounds I had begun when I first started toward him. No one likes to be startled from a reverie, especially in the quiet of the woods.

Alongside the stone-and-cedar log cabin, spring water issued from a large, rusty pipe supported by stones and stuck into the earth. The water splashed over moss-covered rocks and made its way past Perry to the Little Chetco River a ways below. A fly buzzed around Perry's ear. He waved it away and looked up. Our eyes met for the first time. A sort of recognition passed through the lines of his face. Behind the push-broom mustache and grizzled, sour face, he smiled.

"Well, what do ya say," he exclaimed in a crackly voice that matched his appearance. "It's been a long time."

I was told that Ruth and Perry always welcomed wilderness travelers, and I would be no exception, even in my silence. But this greeting was unexpected.

I smiled and took his extended hand, knotted by years of hard work and river panning. For a moment we looked at each other a little harder than before and arrived at the same conclusion. This was our first meeting, but no doubt, we saw something familiar in each other, though we could not tell what. We both laughed.

"No matter," Perry said. He pulled at a shock of snow-white hair that hung from under his worn felt hat.

He offered me the hospitality of the chair beside him. "It's just that I thought you were someone I knew," he said.

Perry explained that his wife, Ruth, had gone to town for a few days in order to see the dentist. I handed him a recent newspaper clipping that explained my walking and silence. He read it slowly. When he was finished, he told me about a couple who had come the previous year.

"Didn't say a word the whole time they were here," he said. "They were on some kind of word fast or something—just smiled and nodded—stayed pretty much to themselves, down there, at the Copper Creek campsite."

I felt a certain kinship with those on the silent path before me, and I also felt a little relieved that Perry's recent life experience had prepared him for my visit.

"By the way," said Perry, "that's a good place for you to set up camp—water and a fire pit. You know how to handle fire, don't ya?" He gave me the once-over.

I nodded a reassuring yes that seemed to satisfy him. Just the same, he went on about how the cabin and the whole valley could go up in smoke in a matter of minutes. He snapped his fingers to illustrate the point. Then his eyes smiled from behind horn-rimmed glasses held together by wire and glue.

"What do ya say? Why don't ya come on up later this evening after you set up your camp and have something hot to drink." Perry liked to talk. He was not at all the unwelcoming, standoffish man I had expected. I'd anticipated someone who would be protective or secretive about his gold.

At night I sat in the prospectors' log cabin at Perry's invitation. Warmed by the old wood-burning stove and the soft yellow glow of the oil lamps, I let the music pour from my banjo—music inspired by my time at Slide Creek. It was staccato in G, filled with trills and rolls. Perry, dressed in his faded and worn pants and jacket, was inspired to dance. To my delight, he strutted about and kicked his heels. I continued playing as he puffed thoughtfully on his pipe, sending blue-gray curls of sweet smoke beyond the reaches of the lamp's glow.

"That music," he said, "reminds me of a mountain stream, a fast-flowing mountain stream."

He paused, puffed again, and stared into the shadows.

"It brings to mind," he continued, "a peculiar little bird that lives near the rapids of such a stream."

The banjo fell almost silent as the words passed from his lips.

"A water ouzel," he said with a smile. "Have you ever seen one?"

I nodded my head and laughed, not quite silently, at the communication of the music, and I danced around like the bird I had seen several days before, bobbing up and down and then diving into the invisible water. When I finished, for the first time I felt as if I had flashed back thousands of years to a time when humans communicated through dance.

In Native American lore, Raven and Water Ouzel visit each other's homes in stories about salmon, the river, and regeneration. The Ainu, indigenous people of Japan and Russia, believed that if someone were fortunate enough to eat the heart of a water ouzel, he would not only become an eloquent speaker, but also prosper in wealth far beyond his neighbors. Because John Muir heard the ouzels' song during the droughts of summer and winter, however, he felt that "the inner harmony of the water-ouzel serves as a simple but poignant lesson for man who endures different kinds of droughts abstract and real."

I camped near the cabin for three days. I visited with Perry, drew, and painted while listening to stories about his life and the wilderness. He told me about the grizzly he and Ruth had seen a few winters back.

"Must've been the last one in these parts," he said. "It was in pretty bad shape. No one believed us, but we knew what we saw."

"All that glitters is not gold," Perry said, and he smiled as if he knew some great secret and was about to let me in on it.

"You know that's been said before, but it's true," he assured me. The crackling fire took the edge off the evening chill. Perry paused again as if he were trying to remember something, an absentminded professor. "There's gold here, ya know, plenty of it, but it's not just the kind ya find at the bottom of your pan. Oh, there's enough of that too. But the gold I'm talking about is the gold of just being here. If you look around you'll notice that we keep our mining to a minimum. We take only what we need, and disturb as little as possible."

I had to admit that when I first arrived at the Davises' claim I expected to find monstrous machines, gouged and denuded earth, muddied streams, and signs that read "Keep Out." What I found was just the opposite; the place bordered on the serenity of a garden. I was interested in what Perry had to say. In spite of being a "retired" physical education professor, he liked to talk, and the way he talked about things could easily be called lecturing.

It must have been my own not talking, along with the word fast of the couple he had met earlier, that piqued his interest in the subject of being silent. It was obvious in the way he questioned me with his eyes that he had been giving the subject a great deal of thought. And then, one night . . .

"Recapitulation."

That is what he said to me in the darkness of the cabin.

"That's what I think you are doing with your walking and not talking: recapitulation. Do ya know what that is?"

I shook my head.

"Well, it's like going back to the beginning of things and then working your way through all the successive stages of human development to where we are now. You must be going back to learn something. Recapitulation is a good teacher. Why, we all do it some way or another, especially before we're born."

He went on and explained that the human fetus started out as one cell that multiplied into something with gills. Then it developed a tail that disappeared before it emerged into the world in the form that we're all familiar with.

"We're just goin' through all our ancestral stages on the way here," said Perry. "Somehow, whether you know it or not, you're doin' the same thing. I suspect one of these days you'll be riding in cars and jabberin' away again, but you'll be different. No doubt the world will be different too."

Ruth returned the day before I planned to leave. At 70, she was thin and wiry with an outspokenness one expects of a pioneering woman. She thanked me for keeping Perry company while she was away, as if we had planned it in advance.

"Dear, did you talk this child's ear off?" she asked Perry in mock reproach.

Perry only smiled and puffed thoughtfully on his pipe. They had been together nearly 50 years, and it seemed I had too little time to get to know her.

The following year, I returned to spend more time with Perry and Ruth, and the next winter, I took my friend Cherry snowshoeing into Emily Cabin.

Cherry was nineteen, athletic, and blonde. She liked to think of herself as a tomboy. I had promised her that she could walk to Oregon with me when she graduated high school. After her graduation ceremony we left from Point Reyes, walked along the California coast, and entered the Kalmiopsis.

Perry and Ruth had a question for us. "Would you two consider moving into Copper Creek Cabin next fall?" they asked. "We're getting too old to do it alone much longer."

It did not take long for Cherry and me to agree. Leaving the next day for the 500-mile walk back to Marin County, we exited the Kalmiopsis by the west gate and headed across the mountains through the Applegate Valley to Ashland. Filled with excitement, we headed south through the Central Valley and cut east around San Francisco Bay. It was spring by the time we returned to Point Reyes.

We arrived back at Emily Cabin the following fall and moved into the little redwood cabin next to Copper Creek. Before the first snow arrived, Perry, Ruth, and Cherry took the old Jeep out onto the mining road to Cave Junction to bring in the last of the supplies. When the snow came, the only way out would be by snowshoe or ski.

Around us grew the trees of my dreams: Port Orford cedars, standing tall and straight with deeply grooved bark, green, scalelike fronds in place of leaves, and tiny white X's on their backs. They mingled with the Douglas firs, pines, maples, and spruce.

I talked with Perry about sailing and building wooden ships, and he talked to me about the mountains, their gold, and the world around him. Then he sent me off to read *Walden*.

"It's what I've tried to model my life after," he said. "A feller could do worse."

Perry hadn't always been so environmentally enlightened, however. In fact, he told me about the time when he was about to flatten off a mountain to make a wilderness landing strip for a plane he wanted to buy. "It's best I read *Walden* early," he said.

"Here," he said as he handed me the box. "We want you to have this."

Inside the brass-hinged case was the U.S. Navy sextant that he had salvaged from his own sailboat years ago. It was the instrument that had helped them find their way on the open seas of the Pacific.

"You'll need it on your journey," Perry said.

Water welled up in the corners of his eyes. It caught what little light there was and glistened. I was touched. I had seen the sextant only once, while listening to a spirited and emotional episode about sailing. It was all Perry and Ruth had left of their time here besides the memories, and now Perry was even losing those.

"Ruth never liked sailing," he said after I thanked him. "That's part of the reason why, after the wreck, we moved onto dry land. Oh, it's been a good life, all right, but the one thing you should do, John, is to continue following your dreams." Perry spoke in the most fatherly voice that I can remember him ever using. I suppose he was right. The real gold was following your own dreams.

In the middle of winter Cherry and I snowshoed out of the Kalmiopsis to Kerby, a small town on the eastern edge of the wilderness a day's walk over and down the mountains; we had to cross Josephine Creek by a cable that was stretched from one tree to another. We

141

had come out to get the mail and a few fresh food provisions. We also wanted to visit our friends Joan Peterson and Chris Bratt in the Applegate Valley, another day's walk over the mountains.

We knew Chris and Joan from Point Reyes, where they had been teachers at the local high school. They had retired to Oregon to find a new life on a 160-acre farm. I would often stop to see them on my way to or from the Kalmiopsis. Now they were environmental activists working to protect the watershed and develop sustainable forestry practices on the land. In the middle of all that, they were fierce musicians. We played and they sang most nights after dinner.

It was after a few nights of music, just before we headed back to the Kalmiopsis, that Chris stopped me as I was telling him about the downed cedar trees I could use for building my boat. I was just about to mime driving the mule team down the coast highway when he spoke.

"Now let me get this straight. You want to drag some trees 500 miles down the coast highway to Point Reyes to build a boat and sail around the world?" His face was wrinkled so that the corner of one side of his mouth showed the half grin of impatient irritation.

I nodded yes, but slowly and tentatively, as I waited for what I thought I knew would follow.

"Do you know how much work that is?" he asked with a groan. One of his hands had reached up and was massaging his forehead. "You'll be working the rest of your life just moving the wood around and sawing everything with a whipsaw." He paused. "John, I really don't think you have thought about this. You don't even know how to build a boat."

I started flipping pages of an invisible book as if I were studying.

"Yeah, I know you can learn. But I have been thinking about your project ever since you told me about it years ago. What's the thing, really, about your building a boat like this?"

I couldn't do anything but hunch my shoulders and look into his eyes as he spoke, because I was sure that what he was saying was what I needed to hear.

"If you really want to travel around the world to learn, why don't you just walk? You can get a sailboat when you need one to take you where you have to go. I like what you are doing. Walking, listening, and learning is great, John, but I don't want to see you weigh yourself down with the other stuff."

Cherry and I walked back to the Kalmiopsis. We were happy about our visit with friends, but I was now in deep thought. This was the second time someone had questioned me about my plans. The first had come after a newspaper piece about me ran in all the major worldwide wire services. Soon I received a letter from a man who wished I would reconsider using mules or any other animals to transport the lumber. He wrote that because we had been so cruel to animals before the invention of mechanized vehicles, he would hate to see animal transport come into fashion again, even if I were a gentle man, which he felt I was.

Then there was the time when, a few years ago, as I walked a trail along the Rogue River just west of Agness, I encountered Mr. Smithers, a 90-year-old, grizzled prospector who had lived on his homestead perched above the river for over 60 years. In his tool shop I saw my first real whipsaw, hanging on the rough plank wall. I offered to buy it from him. He thought about it for a moment and then decided to make me a gift of the saw. He said he was tickled that I knew what it was, and he didn't think he would be needing it anymore. I carried the saw balanced on my shoulder for three days, all the way to the coast.

On my way south along the coast highway, I met a deputy sheriff who offered to send my saw via freight to me in Point Reyes.

I never saw it again.

Back in the wilderness, Cherry and I shared each other's silence.

Lesson in Silence: Painting From Memory
Objective: Further develop your inner landscape

In the business of modern daily life, we seldom take the time to sit and contemplate anything, let alone the landscape that we are living in, even when we are walking. When we do stop, we often think instead about some place else we have to, or would like to, be.

Unless you write in the moment as you are living an event, your written journal will be written from memory, which requires you to relive the event at a later time. At the same time, taking copious notes while someone is talking to you can also be considered a barrier to effective communication.

An interesting exercise that will help you gain the ability to stop and be present is to sit in front of a landscape or scene for ten minutes or longer as you take in the details and feelings that you experience. When the time is up, turn from the scene and make your drawing without looking back at the scene for reference. You can revisit the scene and compare your work to what you now see in front of you.

The idea here is to help you to be present in the moment of your observation, not in recording in any medium except your memory; this also helps us to better recall that moment throughout the day.

This will also aid in the exercise on pages 60–61, Discovering the Landscape. You can attempt through meditation to bring the inner peace you have discovered to another place. For me it is like bringing the Kalmiopsis Wilderness with me on my travels, or internalizing the bamboo that I painted that led to my silence to begin with.

SCHOOL OF REFLECTION: GATHERING THE TOOLS

Cherry and I lived in a redwood plank cabin, a quarter of a mile down the Little Chetco River from Ruth and Perry's cabin. Redwoods did not grow in the Kalmiopsis, so the planks had to have been packed in, maybe by mule. When we were alone, we did not speak; we were silent. When someone came into our circle or when we visited the Davises, Cherry would speak and translate my signs, turn my dancing into words. She was my voice as I had been Charles's eyes, and he my ears. But when we were alone, the silence would grow into shared gratitude and fullness that spilled over our ragged edge until we dragged ourselves to bed.

In the silence we never argued. As if we were a coyote and a raven, we watched one another during the day and the night until each knew how the other moved—until we knew each other so well that we could stay out of each other's way and anticipate each other's needs. Then, looking into each other's eyes, we switched. I would be the coyote, and she, the raven, until we knew each other's thoughts . . . no words, only feelings. We spent the winter this way, sharing each other's silence, each other's love. It was our winter crossing that we put into our music: Cherry on mandolin, I on banjo, and a poem.

Winter Crossing
In the Siskiyous,
Three days on the mountain.
Above our camp in blue sky
Hawks glide silently over frozen tracks,
Smoke from the morning fire
Rises into a bower of live oak,
The warmth melts snow
In a circle around us
Drips from green leaves splashed with light.

We pass through the morning ritual
Without words or smiles
Still on the edge of last night's dreams,
Alone with ourselves
Watching the fire die
Until the cold creeping in makes us move
Across a bare ridge
To canyon views
Filled with quiet emptiness.
Hearing only the soft swishing of webbed feet
The whisper of cold wind and
The sigh of our own breath
We came down from the snow.

Spring came, and when we left the Kalmiopsis, each went a different way. Cherry returned by bike to her family in Marin County, and I walked to Ashland, Oregon, across another set of mountains. I wanted to visit friends and to check out a small college in the town, so Cherry and I made plans to meet later, though we knew that life might end up taking us on different paths, just as the coyote and raven might part.

This particular college had been calling to me for three years now, ever since the day I had come upon it after a 14,000-foot climb up Mount Shasta in northern California. I remember coming down from the highway and discovering the lands surrounding Southern

Oregon State College (now Southern Oregon University). A tree-lined boulevard led into the center of town. Along the street, multicolored banners displayed images of lions flying from the lampposts; these heralded the town's world-renowned Oregon Shakespeare Festival. The town had a holiday mood. I stayed for a few weeks, made friends, and played music at the restaurants and in the plaza. I liked the town, and the town liked me.

I had finally found the college I wanted to attend.

Nevertheless, I was unsure about enrolling in a degree program while maintaining a vow of silence; this insecurity had kept me from attending school before. But as I sat in the registrar's office with Mr. Davidson, the registrar, my feelings began to change. He read some of the clippings and notes that I had offered him by way of explanation. To my surprise, he was receptive to the idea of my studying at the college.

"This is very interesting. *You* are very interesting," he said. "And you mean you haven't spoken in how many years?"

I looked up into the sky and counted the numbers off in my head. Then I held up six fingers.

"Six years, yes. Well, you seem to be able to do all right even without talking." He stopped, stood up, and retrieved some papers from his desk. "You may have to get permission from individual instructors to be in their classes without talking. You understand there may be some question about your motives or sincerity when it comes to your silence, but I'm sure you'll have no problem. You'll find we have some innovative programs here for the nontraditional student. The one that I think will interest you is the prior learning experience, or PLE, program. It gives up to two years of college credit for demonstrating knowledge gained from life experiences outside the traditional college setting."

Mr. Davidson went on to explain that to qualify for the program, a three-credit course in writing and documenting a PLE portfolio was required. The idea excited me. It ended up becoming the first class I signed up for. Here, finally, was the opportunity to realize one of the dreams from my vision quest.

Ann Deering, our PLE instructor, was a small, heavy-set woman with short, ear-length blond hair. She loved horses and dogs, subjects she was happy to talk about for hours after class. During class she talked about discovering who we were through looking at where we had been and trying to see where we were going. There were about a dozen students in our class, from 25 to 50 years old. Most had jobs and families and were returning to school for various reasons. Some hoped to make job adjustments and career changes. I knew why I was there. I had made it a life goal to get my college degree.

"What I want you to do," said Ann, as she drew a horizontal line with yellow chalk across a green chalkboard, "is to imagine this line as your life. This is the beginning, and here is where it ends."

The students groaned, and then there was an uncomfortable silence punctuated by sideways glances.

"How long do you expect to live?" she asked the class.

No one answered.

"How about 65, 70, 100 years?"

A pall dropped over the classroom. A woman of about 35 years raised her hand.

"What does this have to do with our prior learning?" she asked. "I have a family, and I don't like to think about dying."

It was clear that she was upset and that she spoke for the rest of us.

"I know you might think this is a morbid way to begin a prior learning class, but the important thing here is to realize that our lives are finite; they have a beginning and an end. When making our short- and long-range goals, we have to keep this in mind."

What she was saying was an obvious truth, yet no one had much to say about it except her.

"Look," said Ann, "suppose you were born in 1935; that would make you 44 now."

She scribbled the numbers beside the yellow line on the board.

"And let's say you would live to be 74; that would mean you would have 30 years to realize your long-range goal. It's nothing we have to dwell on, but it's something to keep in mind. If we can see our opportunity for accomplishment as finite, we can start to make steps to reach our goal."

An older man in the class made an uneasy comment about how he didn't want to know when he was going to die.

"It's impossible for me to know anyway," he said nervously.

Undaunted by the response, Ann asked us to make our own charts at home as an exercise. Not many of us did it, but I did, and after I had finished I knew that I was not going to haul Port Orford cedars down the coast to Point Reyes. If I were going to live my vision— to devote myself to promoting peace, living in harmony and gratitude with the environment, and striving for the highest realization of myself—then I was going to have to modify my dream.

So maybe I would not build a great ocean schooner completely with hand tools from trees that I felled and milled with a whipsaw. A great weight lifted from my shoulders. I knew that boatbuilding and boats were still going to be a part of my life, but not to the extent that I first had envisioned.

Ann asked us to do other, less threatening projects, like writing short autobiographies and chronological resumes and identifying life experiences that were similar to courses offered in college. But none were as powerful as the first, and no one could forget seeing his or her life as a dull yellow line scratched across a green chalkboard. I know I could not, and for a while all I did, and all I wanted to do, seemed to lose importance.

Once again I was forced to face death, and it made me feel very small and fragile. My head filled with images of oil-soaked seabirds, bodies rotting on a California shore, a friend lost in Tomales Bay, and the crushed body of a small robin on a Philadelphia street. Recalling these images made me feel a dull pain that I had buried deep inside but now made me feel life's immediacy. In facing death we experience the whole of life, and in that experience we find meaning and are obligated to act, often under great difficulty.

Attending classes without talking was difficult, though I had been preparing for it over the years. A few professors questioned my sincerity at first, but as long as I was able to do the work, they were satisfied. I communicated as I always did, via pantomime, acting, or, when all else failed, writing notes. Communicating in each class was easier than I thought. Since everyone was in the same mind-set, it usually required little effort to ask a question or to get a point across. But most of all I listened from within the silence that had grown to be so much a part of my life.

Some classes presented unique challenges because I did not speak, and some professors were still skeptical; I was not exempt from classroom participation or oral presentations just because I had chosen not to speak. I sat in the front of each class to be close to the teacher and to be ready to act out, mime a question or an answer, hand in a note or scrap of paper, or scribble something on the green board.

Classroom presentations were more problematic. One assignment in my natural history class involved making a presentation about mapmaking. Putting together the slides and overheads was easy. For the audio, I visited the county planning office with a tape recorder and a list of questions. Once the manager understood my problem, his face brightened.

"So, you want to learn about making maps," he said. "Well, you've come to the right place. We use all kinds of maps in the planning work that we do here. Let's go speak with the cartographer."

I played the edited tape in class while I showed slides of mountains and other landscape features. Working at my invisible drawing table, I produced an example of an unfinished and then a completed base map. At the end I stood there in the silence of Lincoln after Gettysburg. Not knowing what else to do, I bowed, and the classroom erupted into applause.

I enjoyed the discipline of attending classes and studying, and I savored the interaction of community. Not thinking that I wanted to be educated in anything but who I was, I took the classes that interested me—creative writing, anatomy, natural history. Then, one summer, my world changed. I took a course called living in the environment. In many ways, this is a class I continue to take every day as I walk on this planet.

I was amazed that the environment was something you could study. When I had started walking, the environment still had been something on the fringe, the ragged edge. Only Rachel Carson, a biologist who wrote *Silent Spring*—arguably the book that launched the environmental movement—knew how deeply we needed to delve into environment and into ourselves if we were to survive. And now I was reading Lynton Caldwell, who had been instrumental in the founding of the School of Public and Environmental Affairs at Indiana University, Bloomington. Caldwell spoke of how the environmental crisis was not one of pollution and reckless waste, but one of mind and spirit.

Wow.

I knew immediately that this was what I had to study.

Ann smiled as I handed her the black three-ring binder. It had taken me two years to write and gather all the necessary supporting documents to complete my PLE portfolio. She turned to the first page and read my short- and long-range goals aloud:

"My personal and immediate goals are to finish school and receive a general studies degree in science/mathematics with a concentration in biology and a minor in creative writing from Southern Oregon State College, continuing my self-directed study and involvement in the areas of environmental and related sciences.

"My lifetime goal is to sail and walk around the planet as part of my education with the spirit of hope that in some way I might help others and benefit the world."

They were pretty lofty goals, but after my vision quest, I was prepared to write them down. I had no idea how my lifetime goals would really be implemented, nor what they would mean to me or indeed the world in the long run, but I knew that I would find out along the way.

In June, when I was set to graduate, my father arrived with his cousins Shep and Pearl, his older sister Lucy, her daughter Maud, and Maud's 12-year-old daughter Maria. It was the first time I had seen most of them since I had stopped talking.

Aunt Lucy was a large, chocolate woman with full, soft lips and a large, toothy smile. After moving away from Philadelphia she had married a farmer in Stony Creek, Virginia, and had become a teacher and principal at a small elementary school during the era of segregation.

Now Aunt Lucy sat squeezed inside the breakfast nook of the 16-foot trailer that had been my home in Ashland for the past two years. She was talking in long, slow, rambling sentences about how proud she was about my graduation. Her voice carried the lilting sound of the West Indies. Nine years older than my father, she knew the value of a college education, and he was obliged to listen when she spoke.

"Johnny, it sure is something to me that you are graduating college. You know that is important to me, because if it weren't I wouldn't have come all this way. I mean *really*."

I nodded and tried to catch the eye of my father, who had somehow squeezed his large frame into the other side of the tiny nook. Strangely silent, he was looking out the window and gazing at the vegetable garden that my friend John Seligman had planted in his backyard, where my trailer was parked.

Lucy prodded him. "Doc, what do you say?"

My father came back from wherever his mind had wandered and gave his big sister a smile. He let go by quoting one of his famous sayings: "Well you know, 'You gotta learn to take the bitter with the sweet.'"

Aunt Lucy responded, "There isn't anything bitter about Johnny getting his college degree, especially with him not talking. I think this is really an accomplishment."

"Oh, I agree with you, and don't get me wrong," said my father. "I am really proud of him finishing school and all, but now what is he going to do? What can he do if he doesn't talk and ride in a car? I don't know how he managed to get through school without talking, but however he did it, that won't work out in the real world."

He turned and looked at me. "Things are difficult enough for black folks without you tying a stone around your neck. What do you think you're doing? Man, just stop this foolishness and start driving and saying something, because right now you ain't saying anything."

I just shook my head, as I had nothing to say.

Even though I was pleased with my accomplishment, I thought my father might be right. If I wanted to do more in the academic world, I would probably have to ride in a car and, sooner rather than later, start speaking. It was just too crazy to think I could find higher academia otherwise.

Graduation was over and it was Sunday when my family piled back into Shep's powder-blue Ford station wagon and headed back to San Francisco. I waved good-bye as they drove down the main street and disappeared in the traffic.

A half hour passed and I was in the grocery store when a friend ran up to me.

"Did your father find you yet? He's driving around looking for you."

I was sitting on a bench on the main street when Shep's Ford glided to a stop in front of me. There was excitement in the car as my family called me over. The San Francisco newspaper was in my father's hand, and his eyes were wide.

"You're on the front page, you're on the front page!" Dad exclaimed.

He held up the paper, and I read the large bold print above a picture of me in cap and gown: "Bay Area Man Graduates in Silence."

"Man, look at that, you're on the front page!" said my dad.

I gave Dad an embarrassed grin. I did not feel comfortable with my image in my father's hand, not because of a stolen spirit, but because the image was so important to him, as well as the opinions of others. I wondered if the criteria of success for my dad would ever be different. Lucy chided my father among all the congratulations that poured out the car window.

"You see, Doc," she said, "there is nothing bitter here. Now what do you think of Johnny?"

"Oh, I still think he's crazy," said my father. "For sure that's why they put him in the newspaper. They are always looking for strange things to put in the paper. I just wish he would start talking now and give this craziness up."

We shook hands, and they said good-bye again and drove away. I was left sitting on a bus stop bench saying last good-byes to friends and classmates. Some of them were going on to graduate school, but not me. I was going to walk and sail around the world, and that made me feel good . . . very good.

Lesson in Silence: Meditation
Objective: Lengthen your meditation

Because of the fast food and instant gratification that are so prevalent in much of modern-day society, keeping our beginning meditation practice at around five minutes is best as a way to head off boredom. There may also be the expectation that as soon as we begin our practice there will be an immediate result. I like to think of meditation as a long walk across the continent. If we take a few steps each day, eventually we will reach the other side, but during the walk we begin to realize that what is important is the journey and not the destination.

As we become more patient with our practice and ourselves, however, we may lengthen the time of our meditation.

Take a moment out of each hour of the day. Stop thinking about any turmoil, and spend the moment in contemplation of silence and the ragged edge, the physical place where you have found peace and natural sounds. You can sit down if you are not already sitting, but that is not necessary. You can keep doing the physical work that is required of you, but inside be contemplative. If someone talks to you or you are in a situation where you feel you want to speak, just speak and return to your contemplation when you can.

This exercise will bring silence and the sacred closer to all that we do.

DREAMING BOATS

The year before I graduated I had written to Bob Darr, a master boat-builder on Tomales Bay. I had told him of my goal to walk and sail around the world and had asked him if I could be his apprentice. If I were going to sail, I wanted to learn how to build boats. Bob had written back and said that he was starting a boatbuilding school in Sausalito, a little town across from San Francisco on the other side of the Golden Gate Bridge. He had said there would be a place for me at his school when I graduated college. I could hardly wait to begin.

I decided to ride a bike back to the Bay Area to the boatbuilding shop, and once again the cedar of my dreams surrounded me. At the shop, some of the planks were neatly stacked and stickered next to the walls; the rest formed glistening skins of sleek marine bodies in various stages of birth. It was lunchtime, and the shop was quiet.

Bob saw me standing in the doorway and came over to greet me. "John, you made it. I saw your picture in the Sunday paper and knew you were on your way, but I didn't expect you so soon."

I pointed to my bike, loaded down with four panniers and my banjo strapped lengthwise along the bike's frame.

Bob smiled. "Okay, John, you can start in right away. Your first project is to build a box for your tools."

For the next year, I learned the fundamentals of boatbuilding and design. In lofting we learned to draw the boat out full-size on the working floor. We shaped wood with sharp-bladed hand tools. I learned to hear the satisfying sound of sharpened steel against Port Orford cedar sent down by truck from R. D. Tucker's mill. Fragrant curls issued from the smoothing plane's throat and fell on the floor as I prepared the planking of a new sailboat order for the shop.

It was a place of few words and many quiet actions. Bob spoke very little himself; he preferred to communicate through the joining of one piece of wood to another. Still, the work was hard. We had to lift and move heavy trees. Bob liked to use local wood from trees that had been downed by storms but now could be saved and used in another life. Even when we used the power tools that made the work go easier, there was a quiet that pervaded the shop once the grinding and whining of the motors turned off.

I was glad to be learning the nature of the trees and the spirit of their inside growth. I was happy to have brought my dream to this place. It was something that I could take with me on my journey. It would not drag me down.

I thought of Chris Bratt in the Applegate Valley. He had wanted me to learn what it meant to build a boat before setting off with grandiose boatbuilding plans. I also thought of the South Carolina man who had written to me about the use of mules. I knew they would both be smiling, as I was now, with my hand stained with yellow chalk.

The shop was in reality a school, and the workers were the students learning on the jobs that came in. I was fortunate to be able to work from start to finish on the *Renegade,* a 28-foot cutter designed by Lyle Hess of southern California.

My skills were improving. I had received my first order for a rowing dory, an indication that at least someone trusted me to build a small craft. One afternoon, Bob came from his office in the corner of the shop to find me working on the *Renegade's* black locust rudder.

"John, I just received a phone call from your cousin Shep, in San Francisco." Bob spoke in a soft and ominous voice. At the sound of it, a hand wrapped itself around my heart and I waited for the bad news. "I'm really sorry to tell you this, but your mother called and it seems your dad is in the hospital and near death."

I stood there, letting the shock move outward from my heart to my motionless hands and feet. I tried to think of something I could do, but I could not.

"Your cousin wanted you to come over to his home in the city as soon as you can."

I nodded my head slowly and looked at my watch. It was only four o'clock in the afternoon. By the time I got off work the bridge might be closed to foot traffic, a new regulation following a recent spate of suicides. Bob saw me thinking.

"I think you should just go, John; don't worry about cleaning up." We always put our tools away and cleaned up after our workday. This was one of the disciplines that Bob had attempted to instill in us.

But today I listened to his words, and a few minutes later I was on my way up to the bridge walkway. Although the winter sun had set nearly an hour before I reached the gate, it was still open. As I crossed the bridge, I could see the situation developing. I would be asked to give up walking. What would I do?

My cousin lived in the Silver Terrace neighborhood of San Francisco, close to Candlestick Park. Inside, the mood was somber. Shep's wife Pearl met me at the door. Shep was behind her. We all embraced.

"Yeah, man," he said in a resonant voice, "your mother called yesterday to say your dad went in the hospital with a fever and chills. She called again today to say that his fever is up to 105 degrees. The doctors have no idea what's causing his fever. He comes in and out of consciousness, but he's delirious, and he's been asking for you. Your mother wants you to come home as soon as you can. So what you gonna do, man?"

Without hesitation, I flew my hand through the air as if it were a jetliner.

"Well, look, let's call your mother now and see how your dad is doing. You don't have to talk; you can just listen."

Shep dialed. "Hi, La Java, how is John?" He listened in silence. "Okay, Johnny is here; you tell him. Here he is." Shep gave me the phone, and I put my ear to the receiver.

"Johnny, are you there?" Mom asked. Her voice was tired. "Listen, your father is very sick and has been calling your name all night, saying that he has to see you. I promised myself long ago that I would never ask you this, because I know that you are doing something very special. But I'm asking for your father. Please come home and see him. You know that he would do it for you."

I had to exert myself strenuously to keep from talking and telling my mother that I'd be on the next plane. I allowed myself only a little humming sound in the affirmative and gave the phone back to Shep.

"La Java, he's going to fly out of here tomorrow. We'll call you in the morning to let you know what flight he gets on. Let Big John know." They talked a few minutes more and then hung up.

We spent the rest of the night in preparation.

I insisted on riding my bike to the airport. My idea was just to use the plane to get to Philadelphia, and once there I would use the bike. My mother had sent Dad's credit card by overnight delivery for me to use on the ticket. Before I fell asleep I thought of how different things would be when I awoke: a new adventure.

In the morning I had a quick breakfast with Shep and Pearl. My bike was packed and I was walking out the door when the phone rang. Shep called me back. It was my mother. I listened to the receiver.

"Last night your father's fever broke, and it's back to normal. You don't have to come. I only told him that you were at Shep's and that you were worried about him, but here, he wants to talk to you." She put him on the phone.

"Hi, son?" My father's voice sounded weak, and he did not wait for me to answer. "Mother tells me that you've been really worried about me, and I just wanted to let you know that I'm all right. So don't worry, hear?" He could barely talk, but I knew that he would be okay.

As the days passed I thought more deeply about my decision to jump on a plane. It was not a decision I had made lightly. I knew that even though I hadn't had to follow through with it, the decision had indeed been the correct one. If I were going to live my vision—to devote myself to promoting peace, living in harmony and gratitude with the environment, and striving for the highest realization of myself—then I would have to modify my dreams as events played themselves out.

As my apprenticeship at the Center for the Wood Arts progressed, I revisited my lifetime goals as articulated in my PLE portfolio: "To sail and walk around the planet as part of my education with the spirit of hope that in some way I might help others and benefit the world."

As I read the words, I realized that I had no idea of their true significance; I only knew that I looked forward to learning what they meant in the walking. Keeping this in mind, I joined a group of friends in Point Reyes to found and incorporate Planetwalk, a nonprofit education organization dedicated to raising environmental consciousness and to promoting earth stewardship and world peace through pilgrimage.

My friends Cindy Ohama, a small-business consultant; Tegen Greene, a clothing designer; and Sim Van der Ryn, an architect and professor at the University of California's College of Environmental Design in Berkeley, were Planetwalk's founding members and attended the first meeting.

Through my charades and the group's chatter, we came up with articles of incorporation and explored visions of what "planetwalking" could be. In the end, we decided that the initial goals of Planetwalk would serve only as a framework. At its core, Planetwalk was a journey of discovery. We were filled with excitement and hope.

I set a date to begin my journey and continued to prepare myself and gather resources. To create community on the road we began to publish *Planetwalker,* a newsletter that would accompany me as I walked. I planned to travel across the country on highways, roads, and trails, through cities, small towns, villages, forests, and deserts. I would seek wilderness. Stopping, I would learn to listen.

It was ten years to the day since I had stopped talking. Every year on my birthday, I gave myself permission to speak and asked myself if it was right for me to continue or to end the silence. It was no different this year when I walked into George Ludy's new Driftwood real estate office, smiled hello, and shook his hand.

"Did you bring this rain with you? And when are you going to start talking, you good-for-nothing son of a bitch?" George always teased me that way, so when I indicated that I wanted to use the phone he gladly gave it to me. He knew this was all part of the gag. I would pretend to call someone, he would laugh and take the phone back, and we would continue our visit.

This time I actually dialed a number, and while the other line rang I watched the grin disappear from George's face.

In the physiology of talking, airflow from the lungs is regulated through the nose, throat, and mouth. It is altered in various ways. For example, a whisper is produced when the vocal cords or vocal folds that are attached to the larynx are only partially closed. When the vocal cords are tensed, the sound is said to be "voiced;" when they are relaxed, the sound is "voiceless." Via the lips, teeth, hard palate, tongue, oral cavity, and a few other parts in the head—all of which make up the supraglottic system—words and speech are possible.

"Hello, Mother?" My voice came from ten years of silence, rushing from me like the south wind on Tomales Bay, and two big tears welled up in each of George's eyes as he began to cry.

"Yes, Dwayne, what do you want?" she asked. She thought it was my brother.

"No, this isn't Dwayne; it's me, Johnny."

"Okay, Dwayne, stop playing and tell me what you want."

"No, mother, this really is me." I guessed that my brother had played this joke before. "Ask me something only I would know."

"Well, if this is Johnny. . . . " She thought for a moment and then continued, "Tell me what I told you in the elevator in San Francisco."

I sat silent for a moment. At his desk, George had wiped away his tears and was now intently listening to one side of an unfolding drama being played out in his office and over his phone.

I replied, "You told me that if I was serious about what I was doing, I would not ride in elevators."

"Oh, lord, Johnny, it *is* you! Let me get your daddy." Suddenly her voice was filled with excitement. "John, John, pick up the phone. Johnny is talking!" In an instant my father was on the other line, and we exchanged our first words in ten years.

"I wanted to talk to you," I said, "to let you know that you will be hearing some things about me soon. I am going to begin a walk around the world. I just want you to know that I am all right and that I love you."

"We love you, too," they answered in unison. In my family, to give voice to expressions of love was, at best, unusual. The fact that I could say the words, and they could acknowledge them and answer in kind together, was this side of a miracle.

We talked a bit more about my plans for the planetwalk, and they asked if I would continue talking. I told them that I already had started walking and that they should not expect me to continue speaking. In part, breaking my silence after ten years was my attempt to keep the decision a living one, and to avoid simply not talking out of habit; I wanted it to be a living choice.

But more than that, I was speaking from silence.

In the dreams in which I spoke to dreamers, like those of my old girlfriend Jean and my neighbor Ken Fox, they could never recall the actual words that I spoke. They were of no matter and carried no meaning; it was the very fact that I was speaking that was important. The words I spoke to my family that day were as much for me as for them.

For me the force of my words was palpable, requiring a conscious letting go and then a push and pull of mind, body, and spirit all at once. Even though the voice was just a whisper issuing from my throat like breath, the words felt alive and had a certain power that stunned me, like explosions from the ragged edge.

In academic and religious circles, creationists and evolutionists have squared off over the "design flaws" of the recurrent laryngeal nerve, which make a circuitous route from the brain into the chest cavity, around the heart, and back up to the larynx, where, along with the superior laryngeal nerve, it controls the vocal muscles. The evolutionist argument is that the nerve should simply traverse a few inches from the brain to the larynx, which would provide a more efficient design; the circuitous route, which evolutionists see as unnecessary, proves the theory of evolution because it shows that nature cannot go back and correct a "design flaw," and thus the design is unintelligent.

Creationists, on the other hand, claim that the reason for the seemingly inefficient design is that in the development of the human embryo, many systems have to be functioning before development is complete. These systems are the necessary outcome of developmental dynamics and are, therefore, proof of intelligent design.

As for me, it was all a miracle, as synapses fired and a message from my brain moved through my laryngeal nerve around my heart and put words into my mouth; and so I knew that, creation or evolution aside, the words that I spoke had come directly from my heart: I love you.

After hanging up I spoke with George, who was starting to cry again.

He said, "I am so glad that you talked to your folks, and you did it while I am here. I won't tell anyone you spoke if you don't want."

"George, you can tell anyone anything you want," I said to him. Often people asked me if I talked when I was alone, as if my silence were something directed at them or something I did only when they were around.

This was not a secret. This was a moment that I wanted to share, especially with George and my mother and father across the country. George was over 80, and he was not about to stop smoking his cigarettes and cigars. He did not care if smoking shortened his life. I did not think he would be around when I got back, and I wanted to speak with him before he died.

"Well, I hope you'll be okay," said George. We talked a few minutes more. Then he said, "You don't know how happy you've made me by letting me hear you talk to your parents. Jeez, John, I remember all the talks we used to have. You're not a dumb man, but the 18 years you'll be walking is a long time to be gone. I won't be around much longer, so I won't be here when you get back."

I waffled my hand and hunched my shoulders in a gesture meaning "no one knows." He took my hand in his as we said good-bye.

By the time I reached Point Reyes Station I was again deep in silence, as if I had never left.

Lesson in Silence: Thinking of Our Relations
Objective: Step outside of your self and be of service to others

Social isolation is not a new concept in modern society. Even as we find ourselves more connected by technology—through the Internet, texting, cell phones, and social media—we seem to be losing the ability to connect meaningfully with one another.

During your walks, look for opportunities of service. These can be as simple as helping someone with directions, but they can also take the form of organized community service, such as working in a soup kitchen, mentoring students, or visiting and assisting the elderly. Speak to your friends about opportunities, and look online for community service websites where you can be connected with other people and community service opportunities.

Community service is a way to take yourself out of your normal workday and deliver yourself into another space with beneficial results for all. During your walks, leave cell phones at home or at least turn them off.

When walking across the country while not speaking, I was forced to reach out to people in a very physical way, and this helped me experience our interconnectedness.

STUDIES AND REFLECTIONS

From the beginning, when I had stopped speaking, I had felt intuitively that silence was something I needed not only to practice but also to explore. I felt the high of being in a place that was new to me but at once was very old. It was like seeing the Grand Canyon or the oldest redwood, like standing next to 2,000 years of living for the first time. During that moment on the road when a gun was put to my head, death and life reached their ultimate personification in one crystal flash; I had been transported to the edge of darkness and light. In that moment I was everything and nothing. My heart stopped; I died and was reborn. I soon discovered that hidden at the edge of silence was healing, not only for an angry mind but also for the spirit.

So it may stand to reason that for the most part, practitioners of silence are found in monastic settings; this is why so many of the writings and experiences of silence involve religion—involve places where one mates the self and the divine.

My first exposure to the concept of silence was my teenage interest in the vocation of a Trappist monk. The Trappist order, founded in about 1664, is a more austere offshoot of the Cistercians; its official name is the Order of Cistercians of the Strict Observance. Following the monastic rule of St. Benedict, they remove meat from their diet while practicing monastic enclosure and silence. They express a spirit of apartness from all worldliness and a dedication to prayer and penance.

My interest lay in my opinion that the robes were really cool, but when I learned that Trappist brothers maintained a vow of silence, I changed my mind. A very vocal person who was unable to keep his mouth shut for even a few minutes, except perhaps when sleeping, I questioned if I actually had a religious vocation at all. I decided that I did not.

Instead I wanted to travel the world and seek fortune and fame. What kind of fame I did not know, but I did like fast cars; sports cars were my passion. Ironically, ten years later I found myself living the life of an ascetic, walking through the countryside while maintaining a vow of silence. As I walked, I took the silence with me into community after community, and I was accepted in some manner, perhaps as an oddity or eccentric.

I was thinking of my youth as I wrote my first letter of introduction, as well as subsequent letters, to ask if I could visit the Abbey of New Clairvaux, a Trappist monastery near Vina, California, for a retreat. I was looking for a spiritual retreat, much like that of my vision quest, but within a community of silence. I did not mind that the community was a religious one because, like their most famous member, Thomas Merton, I had come to believe that all religions, though their paths may be different, lead to God; it is up to each of us to find his or her own way. Much of Merton's work involved exploring similarities and differences of Eastern and Western religious thought.

Someone once asked the Dalai Lama if he believed in God. He thought for a moment and answered, "It all depends. If by 'God' you mean the 'God' of Thomas Merton, then yes, I do." This was a testament to the ecumenical nature of Thomas Merton's beliefs.

I left for Vina before I received an answer.

While I was interested in Merton's take on religion and silence, I was equally enamored by his life journey and how he arrived at his understanding of contemplation through the mystery of his own life.

Born in France in 1915, he seemed to be an average, educated but disenchanted teenager who traveled in Europe and the United States.

Merton chronicles his journey in his autobiography, *The Seven Storey Mountain,* which reportedly sent scores of students, World War II veterans, and teenagers flocking to monasteries across the United States. After searching to find himself through a circuitous route, he finally answered his vocation and became a Trappist.

It was about 250 miles to the abbey from Point Reyes, through Sacramento, the state capital, and up the Central Valley. When I reached Chico, about 20 miles from the monastery, I had been walking for over two weeks. The thunderclouds that had been gathering above the mountains during the last few days of my walk finally burst and rolled into the valley with high winds, lightning, and heavy rains.

I stayed at the house of an old friend, Tom Peterson, who was attending Chico State University. Waiting for me amid a joyful reunion was a letter from Brother John Paul, the guest master at the Abbey of New Clairvaux. I had been writing to him since the previous August in an attempt to schedule this retreat. Up to now my indefinite travel plans had made that difficult, but Brother John Paul's most recent letter explained that due to a cancellation, a room would be available for a two-day retreat. I left for the abbey two days later.

The buildings gradually thinned out as I left Chico behind. In front of me the road ran straight through fields of wavy grass, golden brown and green with hints of mauve, on into the beautiful day. Clouds played in an azure sky fading into milky blue on the horizon. To the east the foothills rose gently and hovered in the hazy distance, where I could make out the snow-covered Mount Lassen.

The monastery gate was open when I arrived. Brother John Paul, dressed in blue denim overalls beneath a brown-and-white habit, looked unlike any monk I might have imagined. He greeted me in a booming voice from a vintage Schwinn two-wheeler: "Welcome, John Francis, to New Clairvaux. I didn't know if you were coming since I just sent the letter last week and was not sure it would find you." He got off his bike, and we shook hands. His enormous hands forced me to wonder if he had been a boxer in another life.

I nodded in answer to his question, reached into a cargo pocket, and took out the letter to show him as he walked his bike along beside me. A little in the distance I was surprised to see two monks working on a roof to the strains of the Rolling Stones, Mick Jagger unable to get any satisfaction in the midst of the sound of banging nails. When I heard snatches of conversation and laughter above the music, I gave a sideways look at Brother John Paul.

"Oh, they haven't taken their final vows," he said. "You know, over the years the strict code of silence here has been somewhat relaxed, and the monks are permitted to speak to one another during the course of the day, but long conversations are still frowned upon."

In my mind I saw Jagger wagging his finger at the two novices as he pranced across the roof ridge.

Brother John Paul spoke again. "I'm very curious about your silence, though, John. Have you ever thought of becoming a monk?"

I offered a silent laugh and nodded my head. I held my hand at about the level of my shoulder.

"Oh, when you were younger. I must say, your letter was very interesting. It was hard to believe you were going to be walking here from where you live. We wanted very much to accommodate you if at all possible. How long have you been silent?"

I showed him all of my fingers and smiled.

"Oh my, ten years. I didn't realize that it had been so long."

I hardly believed it myself as we walked along the shaded path and quiet shadows of the monastery.

Sitting in the guesthouse, Brother John Paul spoke in a whisper: "When you're finished walking around the world, you should come back and join us here. You should become one of us. There is a lot a community like this can offer you."

In the days that followed, I spent my time in quite reflection. Rising in the morning before the sun, I sat with the monks while they sang quiet prayers. For them silence had become not the absence of sound but a state that allowed them to leave behind the business of the mind. In this state comes the consciousness of all things, of unity, of the One. As the quiet of the morning darkness gathered close around us, the prayers became intertwined in quietude and silence. This allowed us to become empty vessels waiting to be filled with the mysterious— waiting to receive all that was necessary to be who we were meant to be and to do what we were meant to do, here in this moment.

Following in the footsteps of Thomas Merton, Brother David Steindl-Rast, a Benedictine monk, and was one of the pioneers in the dialogue that was taking place between the East and the West. This conversation was meant to bring two worlds closer together; Merton had been a part of this important process until his death.

Steindl-Rast talked about silence as being an "attitude of listening," a gift that each person is invited to give all others. This is a special kind of listening; it is a listening with one's heart, one's whole being. By listening in that way, we may find meaning in our own existence.

Steindl-Rast's words rang true to me, because I began to understand that my silence was a gift to my community and others; each day that I did not speak, I realized that the importance in listening was not only being able to receive the heart of another through my attention, but also having an opportunity to learn something that I might not otherwise learn. Being attentive to fellow human beings is being in communion, which is a sacred act. When we engage in attentive listening with silence and understanding, we can be open for the meaning of life to enter into our being.

Gratitude does this at each moment. In all religions, gratitude is part of the practice.

For me, when gratitude is on the edge of silence, it is prayer. It asks for nothing in and of itself; instead, it patiently waits for that which is beyond words, beyond the experiential. As a spiritual practice, gratitude affects our immediate world because it brings joy into our lives right away no matter what is going on. If we are grateful, there is always something to be grateful for. We can have all that we need, but without gratitude we will never have enough and will always want more.

St. Thomas Aquinas's direct experience of God expresses a mystic's own experience. When asked to communicate what he had seen, the only thing he could say about this profound experience was, "All that I have written seems to be nothing but straw . . . compared to what I have seen and what has been revealed to me." This was a poignant response on the subject of describing God and the ineffable, which can be neither qualified nor quantified.

As my experience with silence continued, I found myself in the same place, and I understood why I was unable to describe my experience accurately. More and more I was only able to point a feeble finger in the direction of the light at the edge of the darkness, because the words coming from the silence only briefly illuminated the path before falling back upon themselves.

Still, I felt a great sense of relief, of being at home, in the monastery, where silence is still a large part of the monastic life and is believed to be perhaps the greatest single contributor to spiritual growth. I felt my experience of silence deepen as the choices I had made were accepted without question. Traditions endured: rising for vigils in the quiet before dawn, then morning, afternoon, and evening prayers interspersed with the labors of the day. In my brief stay I found new meaning in the words "silent contemplation."

When I first arrived at the gates of the Abbey of New Clairvaux, it was in contemplation. I understood the concepts of gratefulness and prayer, but being in contemplation in the community of monks also left me with a profound sense of humility. This humility was neither self-effacement nor self-deprecation. It was acceptance of my relationship with the divine or ineffable, and it was acceptance of my relationship with all people.

Even as I claimed some new understanding, however, I knew that this new understanding was yet another human construct, a signpost on the path that must be left at the edge of silence; this was a place where the light and darkness meet, a place where our selves are all destroyed so that we may abide in the deepest silence, far from its ragged edge.

As I made my way up the Sacramento Valley, I found myself laughing inside. It was the humor of Brother John Paul that had me in stitches as I walked in the heat with sweat dripping from my forehead. This silent laugh brought a smile across my face, big enough that Patch Adams would approve. (Adams believed that the alternative treatments of laughter and good humor could cure illness.) Brother John Paul's gentle spirit, accompanied by the voice of Mick Jagger, grew inside me. I had to stop, take a deep breath, and slowly let it out before I could walk on.

"Silent contemplation" became my mantra, an idea, or the word or two I liked to have inside me as a way to approach the ragged edge of silence. For a brief moment I stood again on Inverness Ridge with Charles as I had so long ago; we were both blind and standing in the stillness that was the forest, listening for the other side of where we were, through the ragged edge.

Then, just as quickly, I was once more alone, with a new destination and goal in mind. Walking 500 miles through the Central Valley into the foothills of the Siskiyou Mountains, I stopped briefly to visit friends and forests along the coast, past the Port Orford trees, and into the Willamette Valley to Our Lady of Guadalupe Trappist Abbey. I had written ahead to visit before I had left the Abbey of New Clairvaux.

It was September, almost four months after I began walking from New Clairvaux, when I arrived at the gate of Our Lady of Guadalupe. It sat backed up against some green hills, burned and tilled fields up front, amid a field of clover and alders, with a bright garden of sunflowers before it. I found Brother Matthew far more serious than John Paul, but just as welcoming. He met me at the gate and showed me to my room.

There were five guest rooms looking out over two ponds. They were carpeted, with modern furniture and fixtures, and a simple cot to sleep on. Later, Brother Luke, the guest master, came to give me and another guest the official tour.

Over the next few days I fell into the routine of the Trappist. Vigils started at 3:30 in the morning and were their first community prayer of the day. They met for worship five more times before they turned in at 8 p.m. I actually made it to the chapel my first morning. But on mornings after that I only listened to the footsteps of the brothers from my bed.

All the monks gathered for their simple vegetarian meals. There were no words except a short blessing and a reading from scripture. In the evening I read *Thomas Merton's Dark Path: The Inner Experience of a Contemplative,* by William H. Shannon, published in 1981. The book illuminates the two approaches to knowing God: the *kataphatic,* or "contemplation," where one arrives at understanding God through affirmation; and the *apophatic,* an approach that uses darkness and negation in contemplation, and concepts and ideas are no longer helpful.

When news of my visit reached some of the monks who were involved in exploring the path of Merton's journey east into Buddhism, they invited me to visit. The abbot had given these brothers permission to sit and meditate in Buddhist fashion. Their meditation room was just a little space on the side of the kitchen where they baked fruitcake. They spoke, and I listened.

The abbey consisted of 26 monks and 11 priests, of which 6 monks were allowed to meditate as long as they did not cause any controversy. They came together to sit and meditate twice a day, at 3 and 6 p.m. The community used to make furniture until the business got too competitive; now their main industry was bookbinding.

They were very inquisitive about me, and more than one of the younger brothers found my life attractive. They wondered how I could live in silence in the outside world and, more to the point, whether they could. They were not the happy bunch of the monastery in California. The Rolling Stones were not singing on the rooftops, there was no laughter among the houses, and the brothers questioned their faith. Clearly the life of contemplation did not guarantee that you would find the happiness you sought. Perhaps the choice of Buddhism was difficult for some of the monks to live with. In the end they told me I had a better life than they, and said I should not come join them after my walk was over.

For my part, I looked again at the Trappist order as one for which I might have had a vocation, but I knew from my very core that I did not care to join it; I briefly felt sad for the young monks whom I seemed to have upset. I say "briefly" because I understood that questioning is one of the driving forces of our lives. Each year on my birthday, I continued a ritualized form of questioning whether or not to continue my silence. There is no stability in my liturgy; there is only the road, sometimes a narrow path, and sometimes no path at all. However, it is this road that I have decided to spend my life walking upon.

Lesson in Silence: Daily Practice

Objective: This exercise is meant to bring practice into your daily life, not like the practice of sitting in meditation, but living what is normal life in the moment and being open to opportunities of contemplation and reflection.

While we can practice our meditation and listening unbeknownst to the people around us, it's important to note that we can also share our practice. When we do so, our community becomes a part of our silence. For me this happened in the extreme when I stopped speaking; sure, it affected me when I was alone, but when I was out in the community, I had to recognize that the experience was not only my own, but also to some degree a part of all with whom I interacted.

For this exercise, I ask that you notice your morning routine when you wake up. Do you prepare and eat breakfast, read the paper, and interact with your family or friends? During some of this time, notice if you are usually silent—for example, while you make breakfast.

Carve out a ten-minute space of time during your usual routine where you can keep doing what you usually do, but now, each morning, try not to speak during that time. If you eat breakfast, be silent during breakfast; if you read, be silent then.

If the time includes time when you usually don't speak, just be conscious of your decision to remain silent. The operative word here is *conscious*. If you live with others and usually talk, it's wise to let them know that for those ten minutes you won't be talking.

Stretch this out by another ten minutes each week, until you feel comfortable with the part of your morning routine that you do without speaking.

If you are able, during this time you may want to turn off any distractions like radios or phones. From this place you can more profoundly experience silence and its ragged edge.

THE INVISIBLE PATH

Before I left Point Reyes to walk north and around the world, I applied to the University of Montana's graduate program in environmental studies. I applied with some reluctance, because even though I had graduated with an undergraduate degree from Southern Oregon State College in two years, I felt it was a fluke. School is a difficult endeavor for all, but doubly so when you do not speak. The University of Montana's Institute for Environmental Studies responded with some enthusiasm and asked when I wanted to start. When I told them that it would take me two years to walk there from Point Reyes, they were impressed and encouraged me to come.

I left in April 1983, right after Earth Day. In the first year I walked from Point Reyes as far as Port Townsend, Washington, about 1,000 miles, on back roads, highways, trails and old railroad tracks through the mountains. There was a wooden boatbuilding community in Port Townsend, and that was where I wanted to build my first boat, a 17-foot Lawton dory skiff for a friend in Point Reyes, Ingrid Noyes, who had agreed to come and pick the boat up the following spring.

For me, boatbuilding had become a metaphor for life. There was always something to learn. First you had to decide what you were going to use the boat for. Then you had to design or find plans. Once you got the plans, you had to study them and find the tools and the wood and the hardware. Then, after gathering the materials, you had to decide whether you should strike off on your own or listen to more experienced builders. And through it all, you had to solve the problems that arose when you tried to bend and join wood together in rounded shapes.

Before I knew how, why, or what it was to build even the smallest vessel, I had dreamed of building something big, something grand that people would have to take notice of, and in taking notice of the boat they would take notice of me. It was ego driven.

This approach was akin to how I had first approached giving up riding in motorized vehicles. I had thought to impress my neighbors and my community into joining me to change the world, without understanding that the steps I had taken were very small; now I understood that if taken in the spirit of humility, the change that I could accomplish would be much greater, because it would in fact change me.

When I was a boy building boats in my basement, I was building alone. I saw it not as a community effort but as a lone journey, more of a burden than a celebration of life. So it was very fortunate for me that I found not only a teacher and mentor in the form of Bob Darr, but a patron as well; I'd also found my friend Ingrid, who ordered and paid for the boat's planning and construction.

No matter what you know, there is always something new that you can learn if you will only listen. Ask five boatbuilders how to join the same two pieces of wood, and you are likely to get five different answers—and each solution would work.

Life is about journey, the inner journey and the physical journey.

Once the dory skiff was built, I needed to row from Port Townsend across Puget Sound to Whidbey Island, where I could begin walking.

Port Townsend welcomed me in my silence, and I was pleasantly surprised to find that a number of old friends from Point Reyes had moved to the Olympic Peninsula. Along with the openness of the community, this familiarity made me feel at home. Though a thousand miles apart, the two places had many similarities: the vast Pacific Ocean and the mild weather. Port Townsend was located in the rain shadow of the Olympic Mountains, and the weather was a bit drier than that of the Point Reyes Peninsula.

I was informed that it had been windy, cold, and raining for weeks.

"It's usually not like this," said Gabriel as he looked into the gray, cloud-torn sky. On a metal tower at the edge of the bluff overlooking downtown, two orange weather flags wildly flapped a storm warning. The water in the sound seethed.

Gabriel was a friend of nearly 15 years. I'd met him on Tomales Bay before he had moved north with his family to settle in Port Townsend. He had commuted 50 miles each day to his job as a banker in San Francisco. Now he was one of the moving forces behind Bayshore Enterprises, a community outreach program that trained and employed physically and mentally impaired persons. The change seemed to have done him wonders. He was the picture of health and happiness.

"Yoga," he answered matter-of-factly to my tacit inquiry. I listened as he recounted this recent transformation and described how he had become a yoga instructor. My summer walk done, I figured I could use the exercise.

Riding my bike through all the vagaries of weather on the peninsula, I took Gabriel's class for the next month and a half. When the temperature dropped and the lagoon froze, a steady stream of latent and neophyte skaters tried out the ice. Someone brought a box of skates to fit all sizes. My ankle had not yet recovered completely from the long walk, so I decided that yoga was enough. Since walking was my primary way of getting around, I knew I had to be very careful.

In a fashion, I already considered myself a yogi, since the highest tradition of a yogi's search for the beginning of all things is to follow a pathless path. The goal is first to seek the ragged edge and then to discover the divine self. For me, this search often involved a retreat into the seclusion of the Kalmiopsis or another wilderness, whether in the mountains or the wilderness beside the road. With silence and meditation, whether you use a mantra or not, you may slip far enough into the silence to hear the voice of the river. This voice, the water over smooth stones, sounds like laughter, conversation, or eloquent singing.

In the Himalayan tradition, which in large part is an ascetic tradition, the training of a disciple consists of spending 11 months or more in a closed cave. Trainees receive a limited amount of food and liquid on a daily basis. During the ascetic training of Swami Rama, for example, he discovered that by living in silence for that period of time he was able to maintain the deepest states of meditation. During my own training, I found that because my silence had now lasted many years, I could experience the deepest states of meditation at any moment, even at times when I felt so fully engaged in what was happening around me that there seemed to be room for little else.

I had not seen my mother for over eight years when I received a letter saying that she and my aunt, Jean, were coming to visit. "How wonderful," I thought to myself, wondering why everything always seemed to happen at once. It was June when they arrived, after a three-and-a-half-day bus ride across the country.

I knew that they had talked the whole way. Aunt Jean was one of my mother's best friends. She was not my aunt by blood, but it made little difference; she treated me as a favorite nephew, and to me she was a favorite aunt. She was a slight woman, with wispy, gray hair and a voice that seemed a high whisper, playing slow and careful to the ears. Jean and my mother could talk for hours about almost anything and absolutely nothing; it was their vehicle for sharing.

Their last ride reached Port Townsend by the Seattle ferry. I met them at the bus station in town. Last off the bus, the two little old ladies were disheveled from three and a half days on the road. They were still chatting away, and they hardly noticed me enough to smile and say hello.

"Johnny, you look so good," said Jean. "Java, don't Johnny look good?"

"Yeah, he looks good all right." Already my mother was teasing me. She kissed me on the cheek. The smell of two unwashed ladies was overpowering. I pinched my nose and frowned.

"Don't you be turning your nose up at me," my mother joked. "It's been three days we haven't had a chance to wash."

I smiled and patted her gently on the back. My friend Cindy drove them to the house so they could wash and rest after their trip. I rode my bike home and found them sitting peacefully in the living room. They were reading devotional prayer books, a daily habit. My mother looked up, smiled, and returned to her book.

My friend Dick was waiting outside on the porch. He had come over to help me fasten my boat's stem—a long, narrow, curving affair at the front of the boat—to the keel. Later we would fasten the transom at the stern. I had made some errors in my earlier attempts, but now they were made right, and the dory sat waiting for the bottom and the side planking to go on.

"I didn't know you were really building a boat," my mother said. She was clearly impressed with the one I was now putting together on the porch. She spoke some words in sign language, and I was impressed as well.

We took long walks together and talked about everything that was important to her: my father and their relationship, our family, my younger brother Dwayne, and spirituality. My parents had been married for over 40 years, and while listening to my mother I gathered for the first time that their marriage had not always been easy; still, it would go on for another 40 years.

On one of our walks Mom told me that she worried about my brother's marriage and his children.

"And me?" my eyes asked as I pointed at myself and then bit my fingernails. "Do you worry about me?"

We were almost back to the house, and I could see the nearly finished dory behind the railing on the porch. La Java stopped, looked at me, and then looked at the dory. We walked up the stairs to the porch and squeezed past the boat.

"I still pray for you every day, but I worry about you less and less. I know for sure you must be doing God's work, or for sure God is working through you." She hesitated and then looked me in the eye. "All right. You know, to be honest, at first I thought you were crazy, sure enough; but you see, I know you, and what you are doing is bigger than you. That you could stop talking for . . . so many years is enough. But I see how you are with people, and I see how they are with you. I see how you are with yourself. You are different, not as selfish. That's why I am here—and because you are my son."

In India, people practiced silence from time immemorial as a way to achieve transcendence. The oldest scripture in written history, the Hindu Vedas, spoke of this. It was said that Sri Ramana Maharshi initiated disciples by only looking at them or remaining silent. Maharshi often preached that silence was both spiritual instruction at its purest form and the highest form of grace. He believed that a silent guru could purify a seeker's mind simply by being silent.

In silence, yoga and even boatbuilding afforded me an opportunity for deep meditation. Whether I was sitting in a pose or moving thin curls of wood onto the shop floor, I was breathing and reciting—or being—the mantra. Sometimes when I was walking I would have to stop, not from weariness, but to allow myself to catch up to the communion going on within me.

My mother told me that one morning her devotional meditation of the day had been about perseverance. The devotion was about "a man in California, who, after witnessing an oil spill, gave up driving and speaking. Now he is being heard." She had realized the devotion was about me. As she told me this, we became one. When that happens, it is as if you have two bodies and one consciousness, and even the boundaries of the bodies lose their definition.

Listening to my mother, who knew me in a certain way better than anyone, gave me a unique perspective on the journey I was making. It shed light on the direction I was traveling.

"It's the boat," Mom said as she waved her hand in the direction of the porch where the nearly completed dory sat. "I don't think you realize how important building that boat is."

We were sitting in the living room of my rented house overlooking Fort Worden. I briefly looked out onto the sound; an oil tanker, headed to one of the 11 refineries in Puget Sound, was lumbering through the straits.

Mom continued. "I've watched you build imaginary boats all your life—small boats, large boats, and in between, always down in the basement for hours. Then you started reading yachting magazines, and we laughed when you showed us a picture of a motor sailer. Do you remember that?"

I smiled and nodded.

"Now, we don't know nothin' about no yachts, but when we asked you what you wanted to do with that, you answered, 'I'm gonna sail around the world and meet everyone,' because you liked people so much. Honey, we laughed and laughed. Not because you liked people, because that's the way we raised you, but because you thought you had to have the big boat to do it.

"But here I am now reading in my devotion about you and perseverance, and out there on the porch there sits a boat that you are just about finished building, so I got to think there is more to this boatbuilding than just being on the water. Because in my whole life, even though you are my son, I have to say that I've never known anyone like you, to do the things you've done just as natural as taking a drink of water." She reached over, touched my hand, and smiled.

I got up and kissed her on the cheek to thank her for all that she had given me.

Friends came by now and then and took my mother and Aunt Jean for day tours around Port Townsend, but mostly the ladies stayed at home with me, read their devotions, and watching the dory as it took shape. I had now cut the planks from thin fir boards and was riveting them to the sawn frames. My mother and Aunt Jean stayed for a week before they boarded the bus for the ferry to Seattle and the long ride home.

I finished building the dory and named her *Twana*. I rowed her across the waters of Puget Sound toward Whidbey Island. Water covers three-quarters of the planet. Innumerable cultures and religions around the world see water as a symbol of the creation of life. For me, water was one of the motivating factors that had inspired me to make my journey. It was about life. It was about death.

For Sigmund Freud, who founded the school of psychoanalytical psychiatry, the ocean's depths represented the unconscious mind, and the surface represented the conscious mind. When asked to explain what he meant, Freud likened the conscious and unconscious mind to an iceberg. The conscious mind was the iceberg's tip, which usually comprised only one-ninth of the entire iceberg. The remaining eight-ninths—what lay below the surface—represented the unconscious mind. The ragged edge—the interface between consciousness and unconsciousness—lay at the surface itself.

This is where I rowed my boat now: at the melding point of the conscious and the unconscious mind.

Hours passed, and as I rowed, the water, the sky, *Twana,* and I became one; for an instant I was the wind and the sea, wide and deep, rushing to the stony beach where Ingrid waited.

While Ingrid packed the boat onto her truck to return to California, I knew that my trip was far from over; in fact, it had hardly begun. I was on my way to Montana, where a new adventure would indeed be just beginning.

Lesson in Silence: Barriers to Listening
Objective: Identify your own barriers to effective listening

When I first stopped speaking, I realized that for a very long time, I had not been listening to others fully. I listened just enough to think I knew what the other person was going to say, at which time I stopped listening and prepared what I wanted to say in return. In interpersonal communication, it is the responsibility of the listener as much as the responsibility of the speaker to communicate a message. But if you are not a good listener to others, you are likewise not a good listener to yourself and will not be open to new ideas. It will be difficult to hear the silence, or the ragged edge.

Some of the barriers to effective listening are listed below. See if you can add to this list.

1. Calling the subject uninteresting and tuning out.
2. Criticizing the delivery.
3. Listening only for facts—missing the nonverbal communication.
4. Disliking the speaker; disagreeing with his or her views.
5. Tolerating or seeking distractions.

Eliminate these and the other barriers that you have identified, and practice listening.

STUDY SILENCE

When I arrived in Missoula, I stayed in an old school bus that belonged to friends I had made along the way. I enjoyed myself immensely but knew I was putting off the inevitable; and so it was that one day, with some apprehension, I headed for the school. It had been about two years since I'd applied to and been accepted by the University of Montana Environmental Studies Program (EVST). At the time I had applied, I had thought that since my pilgrimage was based so much on concern for the environment and world peace, it would be a good idea to stop and study those subjects along the way. But I'd struggled with inertia.

The problem was that I didn't know where I could get the money for school. I had just enough to repair the snowshoes my friends had sent from California.

I found the EVST office in an old, two-story redbrick building. It was named after Montanan Jeanette Rankin, the first woman member of the U.S. House of Representatives and the only member of congress to vote against U.S. participation in both the First and the Second World Wars.

I stood outside on the steps and felt the warmth of the afternoon sun against my face. The campus was spread out at the base of a mountain, and I watched a slow procession of people making their way along the switchback that leads to a large M embedded in the mountain.

"Uhh . . . you must be John Francis."

I heard the voice stutter.

I turned to nod in its direction.

"We've been expecting you. My name is Tom Roy. I'm the chairman of the EVST department."

We smiled and shook hands.

Once we were inside, he told me how happy he was to see me. Apparently the following day was the last day to register for the fall quarter, and if I had missed the registration I would have had to apply all over again. I pulled two invisible pockets inside out to explain the fact that I did not have tuition to attend school.

"We'll work something out," he said. "Come and see me tomorrow afternoon."

The next day, Tom handed me an envelope with enough money to register for an independent study class. He thought for a moment before suggesting a subject: "Water Studies."

The words slipped out of his mouth thoughtfully; as they did, my body shuddered and I felt slightly light-headed. For the last three months, water and its symbolism had not been far from my mind. If I had had any questions about my journey before, they were now all answered. I knew I would be going to school here.

Tom went on to explain that one credit meant I was an official student. I would have free use of the library and an office that I would be sharing with the other graduate students in the program.

Then Tom said he would ask specific professors if they would allow me to sit in on classes without registering. They would then hold my grades, and, when we figured out how to get the rest of the money for me to go to school, we would officially register for their respective classes, which would allow me to receive the grade I had already earned. I knew that this was not how college was usually paid for. I also knew that the EVST department members were excited that I was there.

This stroke of fortune brought up issues of divine providence, the mantra, and the reality that all that we need is provided for each of us. Even if I had chosen another path—if I had actually felled the Port Orford cedars and was on my way down the Oregon coast with mules and wagons—everything would have been provided for, just as it was now. But along the way, various messengers had helped put me on this invisible path: my friend Chris, who had thought I should use my time walking; Ann, my instructor at SOSC, who had drawn the yellow line on the green chalkboard; an animal lover who had written me a letter pleading for me to reconsider putting a burden on mules; and the deputy sheriff who had run off with my whipsaw.

Now I had committed myself to this new journey, and I knew that by doing this, I was changing not only myself but also the world around me. The idea that I was going to stop in Missoula and attend the university began to sink in. A few days later I wrote to friends in Wyoming, whom I had thought of visiting, had I not stopped in Montana. It did not surprise me when they wrote back and told me they were closing down the community for the winter. It was yet another sign that I was now in the place where I was meant to be.

There are other laws besides inertia.

The first snow had fallen.

Once I began my EVST program, I slipped from a quiet stream of words into a mountain river that moved ideas as it moved boulders in a swift current. Cutting into the banks, the river changed thoughts and direction with the force of countless drops of rain that took the trees, old and young, that had been growing on its shores. I discovered the river's strength.

My first academic endeavor was to identify water resource and management problems in developing countries throughout the world, but especially in Central and Latin America, where I planned to be walking in a few years. I was to put together an initial list of people working on water projects, so that I might visit and work with them as part of my planetwalk. I began to realize that the breadth and depth of my vision greatly depended on the breadth and depth of my own education, both formal and informal.

The nature of environmental studies generally dictated that students be interdisciplinary in their course selections and holistic in their thinking, ready to give up an old belief or be open to a new one in response to new information. I took the traditional environmental courses, which included forest hydrology, toxic substances, resources analysis, man's role in environmental change, and the geography of water resources. In addition, I took courses in the philosophy of ecology, chemical and biological warfare, and war in the environment.

It was after I took war, peace, and Western society that I began to better understand the connections among war, peace, and the environment. And I began to formulate my hypothesis: if people are indeed part of the environment, how we treat ourselves and each other provides our first opportunity to treat the environment in a sustainable way, or even to understand the very nature of sustainability. Therefore, in the multidisciplinary field of environmental studies, we must include human rights, civil rights, economic equity, gender equality, and all the other ways that human beings relate to one another. We as a species would have to end war, oppression, exploitation, and tyranny, because how we treat each other manifests in our physical environment.

When spring approached, my thoughts drifted to the road again, but I had nearly completed my coursework and had already picked a topic for my professional paper: "Pilgrimage and Change: War, Peace, and the Environment." In the meantime, I received the Erasmus Award, a scholarship given to students who would use their studies to ennoble mankind, and this allowed me to continue my studies. By summertime, I had begun working on my paper.

With the Erasmus scholarship I was also guaranteed a teaching assistantship, so I prepared to be the first nonspeaking discussion leader at the university. I had been politely turned down for such an assistantship during my first semester because of my silence, and there was still some concern among the administration that this was not such a good idea. However, my scholarship, administered by the philosophy department, made no distinction as to whether a TA had to speak.

It certainly wasn't the concern of Professor Ron Erickson, whom I was going to be assisting. The class was called the conservation of natural and human resources in Montana. Ron had been the director of the EVST program when I had applied three years earlier, and we had maintained a correspondence as I had made my way north and to Montana. He said he had the highest confidence that our course was going to be a learning experience for all concerned. I did, too, but in my lowest moments I did not share his optimism.

In my section I had 12 students—mostly education majors taking the course because it was required, but also some students from the departments of forestry, music, the humanities, and recreational management. We met once a week to discuss the lectures from the previous three days. For our first meeting I asked my roommate, Sara Miller, to come and interpret my sign language to the class.

Sitting in a circle, we introduced ourselves and said a few words about why we were taking the course and what our plans were. I saved myself until last.

"This is the only time I'll speak to you this way," I explained through Sara.

The students made sideways glances, and their mouths fell open. I felt the shock and disbelief that ran through them, yet I continued signing my introduction. I explained why I did not talk and described the oil spill that had prompted me to walk. When I finished, I answered questions about the lifestyle I had chosen before moving on to the class material.

During the next class I handed out a five-question quiz. After the 15-minute exercise I gathered the class into a circle and began a pantomime in their midst. All eyes were on me as I dragged my hands back and forth through the air.

"What is he doing?" asked one student.

"I'm not sure. I think he's sawing down a tree," said another.

I nodded my head and continued. Now one arm was standing straight upward into the air. I listened to what they said.

"Yes, he is sawing a tree. It's about clear-cutting."

"No, he's using a handsaw, so I think he's communicating something about selective forestry."

"Hey, you can clear-cut with a handsaw!"

Sometimes I did not mean what they were saying—and sometimes I wished that I did—but the learning goes both ways.

"Yeah, but I think this is from our last lecture and more than likely has to do with selective forestry."

At that point my strategy was to step back and let the argument go on. I stepped in only to keep the discussion civil.

At the end of the quarter I received the highest possible teaching assistantship evaluation. When the students were asked to describe their attitudes toward having a silent discussion leader, one answered, "I was shocked. At first, I did not think it was fair that our leader did not talk and all the other groups had ones that did. But all that has changed, and I feel that I have learned a lot more than I would have otherwise."

In the end I felt the same way.

With my advisor, Professor Roger Dunsmore, I began writing my professional paper. I began by describing why I had chosen the path that I was on and why I felt it was important. This was my first opportunity to look at my journey through the looking glass of an academic.

I looked at pilgrimage as it had happened throughout history, and I investigated how other academics, like ethnographer Victor Turner, viewed these journeys. Then I studied the journeys of modern-day pilgrims, like Malcolm X and Mildred Norman Ryder, also known as Peace Pilgrim.

Each pilgrim I studied had something to teach me. Malcolm X was transformed from a racist to a man capable of accepting the brotherhood of all. Mildred Norman Ryder went from caring only about herself to dedicating herself to walking as a prayer for world peace. At the Rose Bowl Parade in 1953, Norman left all claim to her name and property and began her walking pilgrimage. She crossed the United States seven times.

Henry Bugbee, who taught at my university, was particularly inspirational to me. He wrote about the "moment of obligation," which he described as that moment in our experience when we become obligated to a certain action, even though we know it may be an impossible cause.

Bugbee's "moment of obligation" became important to me because it helped me understand my own decisions. Not driving in motorized vehicles may indeed have been a way of addressing oil pollution, but, even more critically, my ceasing to speak had been a critical step in discovering my true self, as well as who I was to become on my journey. Once we understand our true selves, we can more easily dictate our course of action in any and every situation. This is our moment of obligation, which comes out of the experience of our deepest being.

As I worked through my paper, the life goals inspired by my vision quest were becoming clearer. I realized that while it was absolutely necessary for humans to work to save endangered species, to stop the loss of habitat, and to prevent and clean water pollution, it was equally important for us to pursue peace with the same fervor with which we claim to pursue happiness. It is important to understand that peace is not some static, ideal state of perpetual grin in which no one disagrees, but rather it exists as a dynamic thread, a pathless path that moves in and out of fall shadows, of light and sound, of sound and silence—a ragged edge.

My father had never been to Montana before, but he came to Missoula for my graduation. In Oregon he had come with family, but this time he came alone. He was in a mild state of disbelief that I actually had finished a master's degree program. Nevertheless, he was proud of my accomplishment and brought similar sentiments from my mother, who was unable to come because she was teaching. She had gotten her degree in special education after my brother and I had left the house, and she was now teaching in the Philadelphia school system.

"Now, don't get me wrong," Dad started. "Your mother and I are very proud of you. I mean, you have come up here and . . . "—his voice trailed off to a whisper—" . . . gone to school . . . " He looked around to make sure I was listening.

I knew what he was going to say. I wished that he did not have to say it, but he did. "I just don't understand this not talking," he continued. "You have to talk. What are you going to do with a master's degree? What kind of a job are you going to get? You have to drive a car, and you have to talk." He shook his head, laughed, and, looking upward at the mountain, watched the little storm that routinely fell down the cliffs without any rain before disappearing in the desert.

At my mother's request, Dad took photos of me in my graduation cap and gown. The local paper ran a story about me. My father bought a few copies and caught the plane back to Philadelphia. Inside I smiled, as I knew that my father would always be in my life; no matter how difficult it was for him to understand, he would always listen to my truth and speak his own. But I would always know that we had reached a place of mutual respect and love.

In the evening sky
New moon makes a sideways smile
Above the river
July 11, 1986
Salmon, Idaho

A few weeks later, heading south through the Bitterroot Valley on my way across America, I took back roads and train tracks when I could find them. The air was filled with moist smells of green hay and summer rain. I stopped to visit friends and camped beside the road in the evenings. As I limped along, blisters developed on one tender foot and then another.

I continued through the mountains and into Idaho. One night I camped on the edge of the Salmon River in a little island park. I put my swollen ankle into the cool, flowing water and sank it in the soft mud up to my calf. Afterward I packed it in the ice I had bought at a nearby store.

Ten herons rose and paddled lazily through a pale blue sky, almost aimlessly at first, then in unison. They disappeared over a stand of cottonwoods that shot up behind me.

I continued south through Salmon, then Stanley, where the Sawtooth Mountains rose jaggedly into the summer sky. I enjoyed the pleasure of the wilderness that crept close to the side of the road. Once through Sun Valley I reached Hailey and turned east, toward the Arco Desert.

I awoke in some grass between the highway and the railroad tracks. The moon was just a smile, and the morning star an eye. I packed my things and lingered over breakfast in a café. Across the street, a sign on the face of a stone building read in proud electric letters, "Welcome to Arco, the World's First Atomic City."

I was surprised by this information. There did not seem to be much in way of industry around here to warrant a nuclear power plant—just agriculture and tourism. Then the shaded area with the wide pink border began to make sense. It was just east of town: the Idaho National Engineering Laboratory (INEL). I looked more closely at my map and read the small print: "U.S. Atomic Energy Commission Reservation." It looked as if it took up half the Arco Desert, and I had to walk right through it.

I remembered someone mentioning the laboratory as the site of antinuclear demonstrations. However, all I could think about was where I could get water.

The land flattened. Storm clouds moved overhead all day, but the rain fell behind me. I played the banjo as I walked; sweat poured down my face, hiding behind silvered sunglasses. About a hundred white-yellow-and-silver air-conditioned INEL buses carried off-duty workers past me on their way back to town.

The rest area was hidden in the stand of trees that I had watched grow from a low, dark green line on the horizon as I had approached for the last several hours. It had restrooms with hot and cold water, freshly mown grass, and shaded tables.

The previous year, an INEL security team had discovered a cave that the Shoshone-Bannock people had used hundreds of years ago. These peoples' ancestral home extended across the entire length of the Snake River Plain, across the INEL, and north beyond the rugged Bitterroot Mountains. To the southeast their land included the northern fringe of the Great Basin, as well as the bison country of Wyoming and Montana.

When these ancient peoples traveled in family groups from winter and summer villages, some paths took them across the INEL site toward the Big Lost River, one of the waterways that reliably flowed in the spring. The cave contained many items that provided archeologists with insight as to how these early travelers lived, including well-preserved perishables such as rush mats, hides, rabbit fur, and robes.

When I thought of the desert, I thought about the stories of early monastic life, the desert fathers and mothers, and the trials and tribulations of the Christian disciples seeking God. I thought of the desert where most seekers lived as hermits or in small informal groups guided by someone who was more experienced.

In the monastic tradition, monks are looking for a place where there are no distractions, a liminal area like a ragged edge, which exists as a boundary between life and death, between the sacred and the demonic—an escape from the world. Probably most important, they seek a place where they can confront the forces that might keep them from achieving communion with the divine. For me, this boundary also existed as a barrier, both physical and mental, which I had to overcome in order to continue my journey.

There was a part of me that had already experienced the desert in interior stillness and silence, and a part of me still longed for that dark night, where there are no mantras, no images, not even faith—where everything is let go and our dependence on the divine is absolute. So as I prepared to cross the desert, I asked the spirit of the native people and all who had come before to guide me; then I let it all go—all, that is, save for the unexpected.

I struck out across the desert with a gallon jug of water in each hand. I had not gone two miles when a red four-wheel-drive pickup with a kayak on top and New Mexico plates passed me, turned around, came back, and stopped. The woman inside was tanned from the sun, and her steel gray eyes showed curious surprise.

"I didn't expect to see anyone walking along this road," she said. "Do you need a ride?"

I handed her a note, asking if she could place one of my gallon jugs of water ten miles ahead for me.

"Oh, that's the problem." She smiled. She parked her truck and stepped out to visit.

"What is that you're carrying?" she asked. She pointed to the banjo sticking out of my pack. "A tennis racquet?"

I mimed the answer, and in a few minutes we were sitting beside the road while I played "Life's Celebration" on the banjo. The music sounded particularly sweet here in the desert. The morning was still cool, the shadows long, and the sky crystalline blue.

Her name was Karuna, a Sanskrit word used in Hinduism and Buddhism. It stands for compassion or diminishing the suffering of others. This was a remarkable coincidence, since I had been thinking of just such a concept at this time.

As individuals experience enlightenment, they commonly report that because all beings are one, it is natural to extend compassionate action, or Karuna, to everyone. As we help others and aid them in their healing process, all beings benefit. Because of the oneness of all beings, it is understood that Karuna is extended to others not only out of love, but also because it is an entirely logical thing to do. In the same way that you would want to heal your own wounds, you would also want the wounds of others to heal. The Buddhist literature states that Karuna must be accompanied by *prajna,* or wisdom, in order to have the right effect.

Karuna said that she had just finished kayaking 120 miles of the Middle Fork of the Salmon River, and now she was on her way to Jackson, Wyoming, to do some hiking in the Tetons and to visit her sister.

I was happy that someone had stopped. Karuna agreed to carry the two jugs of water for me and to place them at mile markers 290 and 309. After she left I walked a lot lighter, while the INEL busses grumbled by, making up the only rush-hour traffic in the desert.

As I walked through the heat and solitude, sun spirits danced on the horizon and pools of water on the road reflected the sky. There were no clouds, and I never reached the water. The pools were illusions of the high temperature, terrain, and distance.

I thought about my father, a lineman for the Philadelphia Electric Company. He once took me to see the construction of the company's pioneering commercial nuclear power plant in the United States. As we looked over the construction site, my father told me how you could fit in your hand all the fuel needed to produce electricity for an entire city. This was a little exaggerated, perhaps, but as a young boy I had been impressed. In those days, I had no questions; nuclear power plants produced clean, inexpensive energy. Thirty years later, as a man walking across this desert, I questioned all my beliefs.

I drank from my canteen. The water tasted as hot as the air around me. It quickly found its way through my body and evaporated. I hardly had time to sweat.

Another red truck slowed down and stopped. The young man inside stuck his head out the window and called back to me: "Hey, do you want a ride out of this damn desert?"

I shook my head no as I hurried up to where he had parked, at least to thank him.

"Well, if I can't give you a ride, then how about some water, though it's still frozen," he said. He produced a plastic jug whose contents were frozen solid.

I stared at it as if it were an object from the moon, and, once it was in my hands, for one brief moment, I stood on the shore of a frozen tarn beneath the summit of Mount Shasta.

"Hey, are you all right?" His face etched with worry, he looked at me.

I wrote a note asking if he could drive the jug two mile markers up the road.

On a desert road
Sunrise takes the longest time
Blooming like a rose
August 6, 1986
Arco Desert, Idaho

After getting some sleep, I started out again in the early morning when the road was still quiet before the INEL rush. I walked only a few hundred yards before I came to the water that Karuna had left the day before. It was still cool from the desert night. I walked the next five miles and then stopped to rest; I draped my fleece jacket over my pack and some sagebrush to provide some cover, as the sun was already striking hot despite the early hour.

I didn't hurry my walk when I began again. I seemed to be standing on my shadow, unable to project myself out of this desert. It made me feel as I were walking on the edge of existence, step after step, never able to catch up to myself, until finally, as the day drew to a close, I left the Arco Desert behind me. I felt relieved that the ordeal was over, but sorrowful that I could not linger to enjoy the success of the walk.

I was way too tired from the struggle.

When I reached Idaho Falls, the silence still followed me. I found the home of a friend who welcomed me, and I slept, welcoming the dreams of coyotes, hawks, and the desert. And I realized that even in the midst of my everyday life, like the wilderness, the desert would always be close, to offer me its solitude, the fierceness of the sun, and the darkest of night.

Lesson in Silence: Active Listening

Objective: Identifying ways to promote communication

Listening is an active, not passive, skill. It takes a concentrated effort to be an effective listener. People speak at 125 to 150 words per minute; we can listen at a speed of 400 to 750 words per minute. Attention can waiver, and we can tune the speaker in or out. When we tune the speaker out, some valuable information may be lost.

Active listening is used in finding resolution in intractable conflict. With at least 40 ongoing armed conflicts in the world at the time of this writing, it's never been more important to find peace. I'm speaking not just about inner peace, but also about peace among people, communities, and nations.

Active listening forces us to respect one other and to be attentive while avoiding misunderstandings. It also encourages speakers not to be afraid to say what it is they really feel, as they do not fear that they will be attacked.

A good communicator gives and solicits feedback whether he or she is the speaker or the listener. How else can you be sure that what you communicated has been understood? An active listener can aid in communication in a number of ways. See if you can add to the list:

1. Respecting the speaker even if you have a disagreement with his/her views. Active listeners can not only repeat what the speaker has said, but also interpret words into feelings—for example, "This made you feel uncomfortable, happy, or sad."
2. Sincerely listening.
3. Not responding emotionally to emotional words.
4. Not waiting for one's turn to speak, answer, or rebut.
5. Letting go of our prejudices.

Practice these and any other active listening points that you can think of when you are listening to your family and friends. You will bring peace into your world.

Note: We could take this list as an extension of "barriers of listening" by looking at each item in the opposite way.

FEATHERS, OIL, AND SILENCE

I had walked nearly six months and 1,700 miles, from Montana across Idaho and Wyoming to Watertown on the eastern edge of South Dakota, where I stopped to spend the winter. I had found a small apartment and a job at a local print shop. There, over the months, I befriended one of the employees, Amos Spider, a Lakota Sioux. Impressed by my journey and silence, Amos introduced me to his family, and with their help he organized a powwow, or *wachipi,* which would honor our friendship and my planetwalk.

Powwows, which are part of Native American culture, celebrate life, singing, dancing, and friendship. The term "powwow" originates from the Narragansett word meaning "a leader of religious ritual"; over the last few centuries, however, it has come to be accepted as a term for many Native American celebrations—most recently, celebrations with singing and dancing.

I was deeply touched.

Amos contacted Gary Holy Bull, a spiritual leader venerated for his knowledge of traditions and religious rituals, experience with visions, and medicinal powers. He was also a *yuwipi* healer who could perform a special ceremony in which he could call the spirits to help with the healing.

On April 22, Earth Day, just a few days before the powwow, my dad arrived for a visit. It had been almost a year since I had seen him in Montana. He enjoyed coming to visit wherever I stopped, and I enjoyed having the time with him.

The powwow turned into a family affair, with a community potluck of about 30 friends and a dozen dancers who came from the Flandreau Indian School, representing 12 Indian nations. Amos presented me with a friendship quilt with a golden sunburst design made by his mother. Gary Holy Bull sat down to speak with me.

Taking something from around his neck, he said, "I came a long way to this powwow to meet you, and now that I am here, I see that you have touched both white and native people. Your journey is important for all our relations; your message is important. But it will be a long journey. Maybe I will see you when you are done." He handed me a beaded leather medicine pouch of tobacco. "This will protect you on your journey."

This was the second medicine man who had said that my journey was important for all our relations. And I wondered about the synchronicity. I thanked Gary Holy Bull by nodding and holding his hand. He spoke of the four directions and as part of a purification ceremony he smudged me with the smoke from a small bundle of smoldering sage. With cupped hands I waved the sweet smelling smoke into my face over my head and body. Then he asked if I would lead the honor dance around the elementary school auditorium. After the first time around, everyone joined in the dance, with drums beating, feet moving, and singers' voices rising through the ceiling.

After the ceremony my dad came back to my apartment and asked, "How do you do that? How do you walk into a town that you never been in before and bring all these people together without even saying anything? How do you do it? I really want to know."

I looked at him. And in the looking I thought about all the words I would have said—or could have said—about how it is not so much what we say without lips, but what is in our hearts, and how we all long for that kind of straight talk. When we can listen with our hearts, there is nothing that we cannot do together. And how do we listen with our hearts? The answer is with love: talking straight from the heart.

I handed Dad a letter from Barbara Borns, senior student services coordinator for the Institute for Environmental Studies (IES) at the University of Wisconsin-Madison. He read it for a long while. "They want you to get your Ph.D.," he said. "And it looks like they are going to give you money to do it."

I left for Madison a few days later.

I headed south to Sioux Falls and then turned east to cross Minnesota along its southern border, and after 500 miles I reached Madison, Wisconsin. It was the beginning of the summer semester when I arrived. The lunchtime crowd of students and rushing traffic filled the streets. With all the cacophony and confusion, my first thoughts were to leave this place, but silence followed me closely and dwelled amid the spaces between all else, like the inside of a sponge, and I knew that I would stay.

Silence. I wore it like a mantle; it had become part of my skin. It was the place where I found repose, no rush to bandy words, no answering questions with a quick flip of the tongue, no desire even to project an argument. No rush but to listen.

I climbed the steps to Science Hall, maneuvered myself and my pack past the heavy wooden doors, and descended the stairs to the cool underground office that was IES. Beverly Helms, the graduate secretary, greeted me and explained that Barbara Borns had left for a few days of vacation. In the meantime, the department had arranged for me to stay in the apartment of Gary Ray, who was in the land resources program. Gary was also a friend and colleague from my days at the University of Montana. It was good to see him. He made me feel the circuitry and continuity of my journey, and suddenly I felt very tired.

I met Barbara Borns when she came back from vacation, and I was happy to finally put a face to the kind voice of her letters. Then I made my way to the graduate office to see about my fellowship. The graduate school office was located up the hill in Bascom Hall.

I made the climb to find the office of the assistant dean, Akbar Ally. His name was painted in black letters on a rippled, translucent window on a wooden door. Inside, a long wooden counter was stacked with piles of program handouts for prospective students and dreamers. On the other side of the counter were some inner offices and desks where secretaries sat typing and talking on the phones. Occasionally a file drawer opened and closed. Then one of the secretaries noticed me and walked over to the counter.

"Yes, can I help you?"

I pointed to the assistant dean's office.

"Pardon me?"

I pointed again, but this time I made signs for "I want to see," putting two fingers to my eyes and then projecting my hand toward Akbar's office. The secretary looked puzzled for just a moment, and then a light went on; recognition flashed across her face.

"You must be John Francis, and you want to see Akbar Ally, the assistant dean, about the Advanced Opportunity Fellowship."

I was puzzled at how the secretary could know so much from so few signs. Just then Akbar Ally walked in. He was a small man, nattily dressed in a cocoa-brown sport jacket with gray slacks and black shoes. His black hair was salted with gray, and he sported a neatly trimmed mustache and beard. He looked at the secretary and me with a question in his eyes. The secretary stopped him mid-stride.

"Oh, Akbar, this is John Francis from IES. He wishes to see you."

"Okay, okay, yes, yes. Good to meet you." He shook my hand. "Give me a minute." He disappeared into his office. A moment later he was at the door, and the secretary ushered me into his inner sanctum. Sitting down at his desk, he began by asking questions. They started out simply. "So, how did you get here?"

Walking my hands in the air, I showed the ocean pounding against the shore, mountains, hills, and hot desert; sweat dripped from my head; wind and snow blew across the plain. He laughed and began to tell me about the program and the school; then, in the middle of a sentence, he stopped and excused himself. He walked to the outer office, where everything had been strangely quiet for the last few minutes. I heard him talking.

"Yes, I can actually understand him. I can actually understand what he is saying." I heard some commotion, and Akbar returned with a big smile across his face.

"We were all curious as to how you would communicate," he said. "It is definitely a consideration if you were going to get such a prestigious fellowship." In the next few minutes, he assured me that I was getting the fellowship and that I should look for an apartment.

I found a place across from a park that borders Lake Mendota, the largest of the five lakes in and around Madison. It was in a new complex constructed around Nichols Station, an old pumping house that had been used to take water from the lake for city use. I furnished my apartment with a mix of new and used items, given by friends and former IES students or purchased at the university's surplus store at minimal cost. I joined the Hoofers, a university outdoor club, which offers one of the largest sailing programs in the country. I still held the desire that when I did finally reach the East Coast, I would sail across the ocean.

I began my doctoral studies in much the same way as I began my undergraduate degree at SOSC in Oregon. My first class was about what was expected of a doctoral student and the difficulty of writing a dissertation. I knew immediately that I would write about oil spills in the marine environment, because that was the event that had put me on this journey.

It took me two years to complete the coursework and preliminary examinations that fulfilled the partial requirements for a doctoral degree in land resources. Once that was done, I was prepared to research, write, and defend a dissertation. My research topic was an assessment of the costs and legal conventions of managing oil spills from ships in the United States and the Caribbean. It felt like the perfect subject for me, but some of my colleagues frowned on it, as they doubted I would make any money off such a study. After the *Exxon Valdez* spill in March 1989, however, my dissertation took on a new dimension.

When reporters called IES to speak to an "expert" about the environmental catastrophe in Alaska, they learned about my research—and they also learned that I would not answer the phone. Fortunately for all of us, my major professor, John Steinhart, did answer the phone, thus leaving me the luxury to concentrate on my work.

Steinhart had served as an economic advisor in the Nixon White House, and now he held two appointments at the university—economics and geology. He had written *Blowout,* the definitive book on the 1969 oil rig blowout. Many people credit this book, along with *Silent Spring,* for inspiring the environmental movement and the first Earth Day.

At our first meeting in his office, Steinhart asked me to wait outside as he nervously tried to wave away the cigarette smoke cloud that hung in his office. It still reeked of tobacco when he ushered me in and offered me a comfortable chair.

"I'm sorry you had to see that," he moaned, as he made a few waves of his hand in front of his face; a sheepish smile peered through his gray beard and mustache. The top of Steinhart's balding head was shaped like an egg. He quickly slipped a red-and-white pack of cigarettes into one of his desk drawers and said, "I have been trying to kick this damn habit for a long time. But I don't usually smoke in the office. We can go outside and meet if you'd rather."

I hunched my shoulders and smiled politely back at him. Having gone through the same addiction years ago, I felt some empathy.

Steinhart continued. "Everyone is very excited that you are here, and look how I welcome you. Here, at least let's leave the door open."

My face was expressionless, but I was thinking that at least my hero was real. Steinhart went on to welcome me to the institute and to explain why he thought my getting this Ph.D. was so important. "Our committee realized how different you were," he said. "Christ! Who would give up motorized vehicles and walk here? And we thought your message of connectedness was something we all need to hear.

"We are going to work hard to help you, John, and so will you. We don't expect that your message is going to change once you get your degree, but what you are going to find out is that, without those three letters after your name, there will be some of us who wouldn't even listen to you." Steinhart stopped as if he were taking a long drag on an imaginary smoke, took off his glasses, and rubbed the wrinkles on his forehead. "And we are the ones most needing to hear your message. So besides being your major professor, consider me a friend."

And that was how we began.

Most doctoral students feel that their dissertation is their opportunity to study and write about something that is important to them. That is why I wrote about oil, but it is also why I became interested in the dissertation of my friend Nitsa (Ourania) Marcandonatou at the California Institute of Integral Studies (CIIS) in San Francisco.

Nitsa's work was titled "On the Experience of Being Voluntarily Silent for a Period of Four or More Days: A Phenomenological Inquiry." Nitsa told me that her first experience with silence had been a negative one, forced on her by her parents because she stuttered. It was this imposed silence that allowed her to eventually appreciate and see it as a gift.

Through a methodology of written protocols, including self-reflection, interviews, and data analysis, Nitsa was able to illustrate that silence is part of five major religious traditions, as well as psychology. She noted that each religion claims we can transform our state of consciousness through the act of being silent; silence is also a preferred method of purification or an effective prelude to practice:

"These traditions emphasize the importance of awareness of mental processes in order to dissolve ego attachments. Being silent is not only a prerequisite for being present to oneself, which in turn is the preparation for being present to others, but it is a prerequisite for experiencing God, Brahman, Enlightenment, the Great Spirit or the Sanctified Silence."

Nitsa told me that she had always had a disposition toward the sacred, and out of silence came her realization of life, death, and dying. Her vision quest lasted only three days, shy of the traditional four-day Native American journey. She felt that she could have used a fourth day of silence, but she wanted to experiment on her own terms instead.

After Nitsa's three-day vision quest, while she was driving under the San Francisco–Oakland Bay Bridge, she saw fish. This was unremarkable in and of itself, but she reflected on the fact that fish are a traditional symbol for both Christianity and silence. She interpreted her vision as a message that she should go on her own journey in silence.

With her husband and two daughters, Nitsa began her word fast. She said that the first and second days were very difficult, as she went through a kind of withdrawal expressed in fatigue and depression; however, the third and fourth days found her much better able to function within the business of life. While she did feel cut off by and from her family, she nevertheless felt an incredible sense of inner stillness. She intuitively sensed that ultimately everything would unfold in harmony according to a divine plan.

"I also came to recognize and appreciate the wealth of intuitive information that was buried within me," she wrote. "Synchronistic events abound, and I felt that I was living in a slightly different rhythm than those around me."

I could relate to these emotions as I listened to and read Nitsa's words; it was if I were listening to myself describing my own experience. For me, while I had not spoken in many years, I seldom if ever felt cut off or separated from people, even though the wilderness and now the desert were always close My altered state had become just the way life was; yes, it was still remarkable, but just because it was.

In addition, Nitsa's dissertation told me something that I had always suspected: silence is accessible, and must be accessible, to all of us, no matter what our faith or belief. Silence's ragged edge is there before us to touch, whether during the course of our busiest day or in a quiet moment in a park. Silence is always there to take us to a place inside where we all reside in peace.

In her research abstract Nitsa explained that 12 co-researchers—three men and nine women—took part in the study. They all wrote personal descriptions (protocols) of their experiences of being voluntarily silent for a period of four or more days, and Nitsa subsequently interviewed them to achieve a deeper understanding of those experiences.

Based on these interviews, the co-researchers' narrative protocols were distilled to nine final comprehensive constituent themes expressing the totality of the silent experience. Six of these themes were consistent in all 12 subjects:

- experiencing the essence of one's being
- experiencing one's inner life with a heightened sense of awareness
- experiencing more acutely through the senses
- feeling connected and/or unified with various aspects of existence
- feeling a wide range of intense feelings and emotions
- perceiving the experience as ineffable

Three other themes were found to be consistent in 11 out of the 12 subjects:

- experiencing auditory, visual, perceptual, and/or other sensory alterations
- feeling rejuvenated
- perceiving a change in the ontological meaning and/or significance of ideas and nature of personal reality

The subjects characterized their experiences as transpersonal, transcendent, and mystical. Of the 12 co-researchers, 6 spent their silent time meditating at a retreat, monastery, or home, while 6 spent it in nature. Although all nine final comprehensive constituent themes were found to be present in both meditators and naturalists, all six naturalists reported a higher degree of positive interpersonal and intrapersonal integration. While the statistical validity could be questioned because of the small number of co-researchers and the number of final comprehensive themes, that silence in nature as opposed to silence in a monastery or other man-made setting is more or less effective remained an interesting proposition.

There was no natural disaster or news story that inspired the media to descend upon Nitsa for a quote or a sound bite for the evening news, as was the case with my research. Nitsa was instead inspired by the natural kind of frenzy of daily life, that we all experience and can relate to in today's society. For me, this made her work all the more important. With more and more technology eating into our lives, with an ever increasing array of digital gadgets to make life "easier" and to connect us to one another, we have begun searching in ever increasing numbers for that little bit of peace in our lives.

Before I left Madison, my father visited. He was proud and yet dumbfounded that I was able to complete a Ph.D. program. "Your aunt Lucy says I should leave you alone, because you seem to be doing best when you're not talking," he said. Good advice? I'm not sure, but I know he couldn't resist saying before he left, "What are you going to do with a Ph.D.? They're a dime a dozen."

Something had changed this time, however. Behind these sour words, he could not hide the smile that stretched across his face.

I began laughing, and I hunched my shoulders in response. I had no idea what I was going to do with the Ph.D.

I knew, however, that I wanted to get my message across. We need to consider that we all, as a people, are part of the environment that we want to protect. We need to understand that how we treat each other is manifested in the environment around us.

There was a going-away party for me at the local community art center, complete with African drumming and international foods. The music and dancing went on long into the night. It was hard to say good-bye.

My last day in Madison was hectic. Friends arrived at my apartment to say good-bye, and they were immediately enlisted into helping me clean. Across the street in the park, more music blared from the annual pot legalization demonstration. In the cacophony that came through the windows, I wondered how I could possibly be ready to leave in the morning.

I felt like I was being born again, propelled out onto the road with nothing. If I could stay just one more day . . . But I knew that I could not. Besides telling all my friends that I was leaving the next day, I smelled the weather changing from the warm sweetness of summer to the acrid coolness of autumn.

I wanted to reach the East Coast before winter's onslaught.

On a warm Sunday morning, ten of us gathered on the steps of Science Hall to say good-bye. Two friends walked beside me, one rolling his bike for the trip back to town. We stopped near the city limits, and, attempting to wrap their arms around both my backpack and me, they hugged me. They said something about sandhill cranes and how we were going to have a mild winter. After stopping for breakfast, they turned back and headed north across the freeway.

I turned south.

I did not expect that so many people would wave. Some signed, "I love you," applauded, and encouraged me from their cars. It was an indication of our connectedness, of the work we had been able to accomplish in the silence.

Lesson in Silence: Silence
Objective: Making a four-day silent retreat

This exercise is not for everyone, unless you are looking for silence in total immersion. It should be remembered that I planned to stop speaking for only one day, and was so transformed by that one day that I continued for another day, and then another, until 17 years had passed. While this may be extreme, I have met many people who have spent at least a few weeks in unplanned, open-ended silence.

If you feel that you want to try a one- or four-day period of silence, choose a day that is meaningful to you, such as a birthday or another anniversary, to begin. Remember to walk and to keep a journal of paintings, writing, or both.

You might want to refrain from writing or painting on the first day; instead, you can gradually work these forms into your silence.

You can be silent in your community, or, if possible, in a natural place like a wilderness area or a park.

For something more structured, try Vipassana, which means "clear insight into the real characteristics of body and mind"—in other words, seeing things as they really are. Teachers throughout the world teach these silent techniques and lead structured silent retreats in ten-day residential programs during which the participants follow a prescribed code of discipline.

THANKSGIVING: SEVEN YEARS AND A DAY

Gray sky turns to blue
Fields of corn turn to amber
Geese pass overhead
October 2, 1989
Oregon, Wisconsin

As I made my way south from Madison, I felt the season change from summer to fall. For two years I had been locked away studying at the university, and now I felt the season of my life change for me as well. My path, the road, was again in front of me, and this time, along with my pack and banjo, I carried the association of a fellow from one of the great universities. As the fall wind blew and leaves of yellow gold fell around me, I reflected on the transformation and the inner journey, from the day I began walking in California to this day as I left Madison. I continued breathing.

In Oregon, Wisconsin, I stopped in front of the Richelieu Banjo showroom and factory. Through the showroom window I could see an older man kneeling on the floor. His large, bald head and smiling face reminded me of Little Orphan Annie's Daddy Warbucks. He was putting the final touches on a banjo head. When our eyes met through the glass, his smile broadened and he motioned me around to the door.

"Let's see what you have cradled in your arms," he said as he turned my instrument so he could see the writing on the back. "Ahhh, it's a little Stewart. What a sweet banjo. I suppose you can play it if you're going to the trouble of carrying it around."

We spent a few hours visiting and playing banjo music together. To help me on my journey, he offered me a few sets of strings and one of his special banjo heads.

"You know, your banjo head is an odd size," he explained.

I nodded and thanked him. During my time at Madison, I had heard that Mr. Richelieu was a kind and gentle spirit who made and played banjos, and I had wanted desperately to meet him. I was not sure why, except to glean some wisdom, but school, study, and distance had kept us apart until this moment. In his eyes I saw myself, and his offer of strings and a banjo head were symbolic of the unspoken gifts he gave to me.

I walked a little farther to find a place in the grass beside some railroad tracks. The temperature was mild, the sky clear; a million stars sparkled. I let my body melt into the ground, and as I drifted in and out of a deep sleep, I cried silently off and on through the night.

Tears . . . How could this be?

Two years of connectedness, of attachments to individual personalities, falling in and out of love. How could it be otherwise?

That ragged edge of silence comes with a great deal of emotion; it is the deepest part of reality; it's not a linear world, not a story with a beginning and an ending; there is everything, all at once. I let the emotions take over my body—the tears, the pain, the joy, the suffering—all happening right now.

So yes, even though I stood apart, as years of silence gathered close and built up on my skin, tears rolled down my face.

But I also felt a little trepidation about my immediate future. Even as the geese were heading south and a chill in the air urged me on to Illinois, I felt that something was happening just below the surface of my vision, and it worried me in a way to which I was unaccustomed. I had grown used to listening to myself, my feelings, and my emotions, as well as to the world around me. This feeling was not fear. I finally put it off on my concern about the weather. I had left late in the season for walking, and the weather could turn bitter cold before I reached my parents' home in Philadelphia.

I calmed my worries and allowed myself to take the natural world within me. The distinct smell of snow mixed with the aroma of burning fall leaves. I settled down with my portable radio to listen to the World Series. The Giants were playing back in San Francisco; however, instead of hearing baseball, I heard the report of an earthquake at the stadium. The upper deck of the Bay Bridge had collapsed, and I was reminded of how fragile life was and how close homelessness and death really were. It seemed that I was very far away from this place that I called home, but at the same time it was part of the here I lived each day. In the moment of disaster, I felt my understanding of place grow and the interconnectedness of us all become real.

As I progressed across Indiana and caught the scent of more leaves burning, I gloried in the rusty red and yellow autumn colors of the trees. Fewer fields were waiting to be harvested, and more fields now lay empty. The hordes of grasshoppers that rose in small clouds at each footstep in the grass beside the road grew fewer. The temperature dropped.

A cold wind blowing
Through the filigree of trees
Having dropped their leaves
October 18, 1989
Fiat, Indiana

I got to the post office in Bryant, Indiana, in time to pick up my mail, which included a suit of expedition long underwear. Just in time. As I crossed into Ohio late that night, it began to snow.

I looked for a motel but settled for a creek bridge just east of Wabash. I shared the place with two geese, who moved closer as the night wore on. By morning, they were squawking next to my feet. I thought of the deer licking the salt from my face and threw a pebble. They waddled off into a nearby cornfield.

It was still early morning when I squeezed from beneath the shelter of the bridge and trudged through the snow and grass up to the road. The north wind stung my face, and the snow collected on my beard. People looked at me through the flurry in disbelief. A few waved. As I waved back I felt that I was waving to myself, looking from the frosted window of a warm pickup. I stared and thanked myself for being where I was, all at once warm and cold, shaken by an earthquake and standing solidly on the ground.

When I got to Celina, nine miles later, I found a café. Feet wet, I ate and prepared to walk nine miles more to St. Marys. Tom Hoffman, a local newspaper reporter, stopped by the café to interview me. He talked above the afternoon din of customers and Muzak oozing from hidden speakers.

I read about the California earthquake in a day-old newspaper and felt sad. It was an unusual wave of homesickness—not that I wanted to be there, and not that something was missing, but I felt connected to the sadness and pain that I knew Californians felt. Meanwhile, the snow had let up.

In Wapakoneta, I visited the Armstrong Air and Space Museum; its namesake was a native son. The Gemini 6 space capsule was on display, along with space suits, tools, and other memorabilia of flight and space exploration. A planetarium program chronicled the first lunar landing, and the museum broadcast continuous live transmission from the shuttle *Atlantis,* which was then in Earth orbit.

In silence I am on the moon; I am in space and stepping onto other planets, other worlds. In silence everything is possible; my face reflects in the window of the capsule, and I know that I am everywhere at once.

Outside, I looked into the blue sky, shook my head in wonder, and continued slowly over the hills with trees in autumn blaze, past the farms and through the small towns across this new state, Ohio.

Sitting by the lake
Autumn colors reflected
Deep in a blue sky
October 29, 1989
West Lafayette, Ohio

I walked in the dark, on a narrow shoulder. A detour, coupled with weekend traffic, made the walking unpleasant, so I resorted to reflection, remembering when I started and why I was walking, until up ahead a red and orange flashing light told me that the road was closed. All traffic turned left and headed north toward Route 60. I took this as a sign and decided to wait until morning to cross the bridge. It was too dark to cross it without lights.

Finding a place beside the construction in the grass, and happy that no traffic would pass in the night, I lay down to stare up at the sky. I could feel the space between the stars. Unfathomable. For a long moment I held that which could not be understood in my heart and continued to reflect.

Several days later, I crossed the Ohio River into Wheeling, West Virginia.

At the waterfall
The highway is forgotten
In the quiet splash
November 5, 1989
Roney's Point, West Virginia

Wheeling was shoved hard against a mountain. I followed the roads that led to a tunnel, which would cut many mountainous miles off my journey. A maintenance man, working on the side of the road, mimed to me that he had read about me in the paper, but pedestrians were not permitted in the tunnel. He offered to drive me through and then remembered. Instead, I took the alternative route that climbed into the trees and crossed the mountain into Pennsylvania.

Sometimes the benefits of going a different way than you had planned are hidden at first glance. In today's world, in which speed is so valued, sometimes the best way is the slowest way, which meanders quietly through a wilderness just below the boundary of a ragged edge. This is the place where we can reflect and be healed.

The slow climb brought a still, breathing rhythm to my soul and allowed me the mindfulness of the moment, step by step. On the earth lay a variegated carpet of leaves; barely a flutter remained on the branches overhead; the wind seethed, a white noise that dissolved my footsteps into the mountain's voice.

The wind's message was clear, and I felt it in every part of an aching body: Stop. And so I stood motionless, still breathing until the breathing itself became the breeze through the trees with fluttering leaves, and all became one.

Rain wind and thunder
The lightning flashes in streaks
Road spray in my face
November 16, 1989
York, Pennsylvania

As I walked through the villages and towns, I sent postcards ahead to let my parents know my progress. Then, ten days and over 200 miles later, the Appalachian Mountains were behind me.

In Gettysburg, I tried to remember my elementary school field trip more than 30 years earlier—the park rangers, the autumn leaves, and a split-rail fence. The teacher had talked about Abraham Lincoln and how he had ended slavery and given a speech to which no one had applauded. I thought of the thousands of soldiers who had been there, how only a few hundred had had the possibility of hearing Lincoln's words, because in those days there were no public address systems. I read a few plaques attached to the bases of statues and played music through the battlefield, in honor of the dead and dying long ago, as well as for a road crew on a bridge.

There were no more mountains to cross. I sent my heavy under-wear and a sweater to my parents' home in Philadelphia, 100 miles east. With the increase in traffic and the city congestion, I planned to sleep the next four nights, after York, in motels. Luckily, I kept my tent. I used it for two nights more.

My route took me through Amish country, Bird-in-Hand and Intercourse, where black carriages and horses shared the highway with automobiles. I started thinking that I might allow myself to get a buggy and a horse. It was something to consider. Then I remembered the dream of a construction worker I had met in Wisconsin.

We had shared some coffee on the hood of his car.

"I've been wondering about the environment," he said, "and all the dead farms. How could America change so much, so fast?"

I shook my head and took another sip of coffee.

"My wife and I live in an old farmhouse that we thought must have been some farm in its day." He stopped and stared into the sky. "You know, I've a dream of having a horse and wagon that I could take to construction sites, sort of like the Amish of Evansville."

My expression agreed that it was possible.

"I haven't told anyone else about my dream," he said. "Other people would think I'm crazy. I'm not sure you won't; I just have a feeling like I can tell you."

I thought back on a dream of mules and wagons loaded with cedar.

He asked if I wanted to work for a few days on a house he was building. But the geese were heading south, and a chill in the air urged me on.

Closer to Philadelphia, I slept out near the railroad tracks again. The trains were no longer slow, rumbling freights, but high-speed com-muters that swished by with horns blaring.

Two days outside Philadelphia, my father met me on the road. It was surreal to see him on the road like this. I flashed back to the time we had met each other on the road to Inverness in California, when clouds of confusion had appeared to move across the dry, dark landscape of his face. This time, however, there was no confusion. The lines etched across his brow showed simple concern.

He parked his car, and we shook hands. "There is a tavern about a mile down the road," he said. "Let's meet there, and I'll buy you lunch."

I smiled and let him take my pack. I walked with just my banjo slung over my shoulder and played all the way there. I found him at a table in a rustic sandwich shop.

We were quiet in our conversation, minimalistic in word and gesture. He displayed no judgment of me now, only concern for my safety on the road and a deep respect for the journey. I could hear it all in his voice.

In the midst of our visit, a violent wind and rainstorm came up. Trees were blown down, and buildings were damaged. On the route that I was taking, civilization had finally claimed the last open space where I would have felt comfortable sleeping near the road. I eventually settled for a space by the railroad tracks near an abandoned station.

It was rush hour when I finally reached Philadelphia. As I walked along the Schuylkill River and then Wissahickon Creek, I tried to remember that I had been here before. It felt vaguely strange that I had walked here from so far away, so odd to be back in the place where I grew up, the same person yet so different from the boy I had once been.

This strangeness disappeared, however, as I turned onto the street where I was raised and walked up the steps to the door where my parents waited. It was the day before Thanksgiving. I took in the house so filled with ghosts and memories, family and friends who were no longer there, games I had once played, and, in the basement, two sawhorses stretched tight with dreams.

I was filled with gratitude.

There was another hundred miles to walk until I reached the sea, but these were all miles I had known while growing up between the city and our summer home in Cape May, New Jersey. A friend arrived from Madison, and we walked the last few miles together. On January 2, 1990, seven years and one day after beginning my planetwalk at the edge of the Pacific, I touched the waters of the Atlantic at the New Jersey shore, and I knew that I was at the beginning—at the other side of here.

Lesson in Silence: Listening

Objective: To encourage sincerity in listening to one another

"You ask people who have been divorced, and inevitably they will say their spouse didn't listen to them. So now it is a major issue, because we just don't do it, we just don't listen." —Irv Rose, communication consultant

This exercise is meant to be done with a moderator and two or more persons; however, if you come away with the meaning and spirit of the exercise after reading it, you are welcome to go right to the practice of listening.

Break a group into pairs, A and B; then ask A to talk about something that they're really proud of; meanwhile, tell B, the other person, that their task is not to listen. Though they're not allowed to do anything as overt as getting up to leave, they must show by their actions (like text messaging) that they are not listening. Although the moderator should not tell them how much time will be devoted to this exercise, the pairs should be stopped in two minutes. They are then to reverse roles.

Afterward, ask each person how it felt not to be listened to. Invariably, they will speak of their anger and frustration. They will talk about how they felt time dragged on, and about how they felt unimportant and invisible.

After both partners have had a turn, repeat the same exercise, but giving the listener the job of actually paying attention. This time the speaker will invariably feel extremely positive, and he or she will often report how time seemed to fly by.

There are profound feelings associated with being listened to or not being listened to. What is even more profound is what this means about whether we listen to ourselves, or whether we instead take ourselves for granted. The relationship we have with our inner voices is extremely valuable; this relationship allows us access to our inner wisdom.

Along with listening to my inner voices, I also pay attention to my actions. Your actions can tell you more about who you are.

THANK YOU FOR BEING HERE

If your lips would keep from slips,
Five things observe with care:
Of whom you speak, to whom you speak,
And how and when and where.
—Anonymous
April 22, 1990
Washington, D.C.

Keeping silent was a vow I made one year at a time. I was never sure what the criteria for speaking again should be, or if I would ever speak again. When the time came, if the time came, I would know. So each birthday I asked myself, "John, are you going to keep this up? Are you going to keep miming and acting out, walking and not talking?"

In the early years, when my silence was new, I seemed to have a palpable need to revisit my decision. It was virgin territory, this silent landscape, a narrow path through a ragged bramble. It twisted and turned uneasily, up, down, and around surprise and loneliness. I ached with old muscles unused and the growth of new ones. Words piled onto me.

The later years had become more comforting, the silence more familiar, with watercolor views to everywhere. Meaning became rooted in action and lives, movement, the passing of clouds, the clarity of eyes.

Revisiting the vow was the way I kept my decision alive and fresh. It kept the silence an act of choice. It was not like jumping off a tree-swing rope over Stony Creek, something I had done as a child. You knew that once you left that little bare patch of earth high up on the bank, there was no getting back without getting wet or dropping, broken-legged, on the rocky shore. If everything worked right, you just got wet.

Choosing silence seemed like one long, never-ending moment until you looked down from the swing and saw the water. On my 44th birthday, after 17 years of maintaining a vow of silence, I looked down, felt the high arch of invisible rope stretched across time and space, and gave up my last fear because I had a message.

So, on the 20th anniversary of Earth Day, in Washington, D.C., at a hotel across from the Soviet Embassy, I decided to speak to family and friends who had gathered to hear me say my first words. My stomach pushed up inside. After so many years, what would become of me? Would I vanish? Would the internal chatter, the lies, those things that drove me crazy, return?

I was again venturing into the unknown.

The thin steel strings from my old S.S. Stewart banjo were exploding metallic rain at my fingers' touch. I played a tune of a thousand miles and children's smiles, seven years across America, roadside concerts, and old-time festivals. The comfort of habit and the discomfort of change were beginning anew. At the same time, I felt the excitement of a new adventure and journey.

Just one more tune before I spoke: "Life's Celebration," music coming from the road, from the wilderness of silence.

When the music stopped, I stretched my heart and leaped from that quiet place inside. Far out over Stony Creek I soared . . . and let go.

"Thank you for being here."

The words were almost inaudible, the voice unrecognizable.

I turned to see where the words had come from. There was no one standing behind me. I had spoken them. I waited for the lightning to strike, but it did not. I felt the correctness with every inch of my body. No sooner had the first words escaped than I found myself still in silence, the place and the experience of silence still with me.

From the small gathering a gasp arose; then, "Praise the Lord!" The shout went up anonymously. Aunts and cousins murmured to each other around their tables.

I spoke slowly and softly, each word presenting itself to me for brief inspection. I took the words into my being and willed them from the silence into the existence of sound.

"I have chosen Earth Day to begin speaking," I continued, "so that I will remember that now I will be speaking for the environment."

The silence and language felt as if they belonged together, as if they were part of a whole. Creation took place at their intersection, giving us perhaps our closest vision of truth. Believing in that truth, I proposed to the people before me that speech that is not connected to silence is without creative meaning; it may fill the niche of a social process, such as in the case of formal speech or political rhetoric, but it is devoid of inherent meaning.

After the words of the last sentence had come from me, I stopped speaking for a moment and waited.

Catching a glimpse of my mother's watery diamond eyes, I smiled; I hesitated and started speaking again, this time about change and personal responsibility, then about language and myth and how I had come to be on this pilgrimage. I stopped again and looked inside, wide-eyed, at the storyteller.

There is something uncompromisingly honest in the experience of silence. It is from silence that all speech, and therefore all myth, begins. Speech is the myth of that which cannot be spoken. Without speech, there can be no theory; without theory, there can be no answers. When the world of myth and theory confused us, silence was always there, affording us the opportunity not merely to question our assumptions, but to discard them and begin again.

Now, after so many years, I discovered how difficult it was to speak. The words came slowly. I labored through the birth of each one until a full litter was born, and then I watched as they scampered off to live lives of their own. I stopped, thinking that reading might be easier.

People commonly believed that if I did not use my voice, I would lose it. Friends often paraphrased some well-known medical study, although the sources always seemed to elude them, or they thought they remembered seeing someone interviewed on one talk show or another. Many people believed that if I stayed silent long enough I would never be able to speak again, or I would go mad. Others told me that not speaking was ineffective or just plain selfish.

I reached for my master's thesis on the floor beneath my chair and opened it to the introduction. "This quote of Lynton K. Caldwell, an environmentalist, puts into words why I am on this pilgrimage. It is a quote at the beginning of *Living in the Environment* by G. Tyler Miller, the first textbook on the environment that I have read.

" 'The environmental crisis,' " I began slowly, " 'is an outward manifestation of a crisis of mind and spirit.' "

I stopped and breathed deeply. I discovered that reading aloud was even more difficult. Sweat began to bead on my forehead. The thought of continuing settled within me, and I read on, consciously thinking about and forming each word that I saw on the page before me.

" 'There could be no greater misconception of its meaning than to believe it to be concerned only with endangered wildlife, human-made ugliness, and pollution. These are part of it, but more importantly, the crisis is concerned with the kind of creatures we are and what we must become if we are to survive.' "

After a few seconds of silence, applause erupted. It was not a speech like Abraham Lincoln's; I was reading the words of someone else, and I did not have to take a long train ride and wonder if my audience had gotten the message. The message was simple: We are the environment, and on this Earth Day I wanted to redefine what "environment" meant. After 17 years of walking silently across North America and studying environment formally and informally, what I had learned, which I now wanted to share, was simply that we are the environment, and how we treat each other when we meet each other has more to do with our environmental crisis than we realize.

I went around to each table and spoke to everyone individually and in small groups. I enjoyed the rediscovery of the spoken word. I took simple pleasure in saying hello.

My journey of silence had not come to an end. It would always be, and has always been, with me. I had learned a great deal, much of which cannot be learned through speech. My thoughts, my ideas, and my philosophies had grown from a silent world that could not be articulated in words.

The further I moved beyond this ragged edge of silence, the more I realized just how connected we all are—the trees, the sea, every ecology we could ever imagine, and most importantly we, all of us, are connected. It was the same stuff that Nitsa and her co-researchers had found, the same concept that all religions share as the very basis of their being.

When I started talking, my dad, sitting in the audience, let out a cryptic phrase: "That's one," he said, and he held up a finger to signify that, okay, I had started talking, but now I needed to do "two"— to begin using motorized vehicles.

Perhaps. In the future.

Right now, I was thinking more about the message I needed to deliver. This was my new day. I walked out into it.

Lesson in Silence: Listening
Objective: Letting go of our prejudice

Often one's personal interpretations, attitudes, biases, and prejudices lead to ineffective communication; therefore, if we are to be a truly effective listener, we need to accept and manage these attitudes. You only need to look at our society and political parties to realize that we could do a lot better in letting go of our prejudices.

The other day I was at the Higher Grounds coffeehouse with a friend. We were having our cups of coffee and talking about listening without judgment. As we sat in the garden just off a busy street, my friend asked me how I could practice listening fully even after I had ended my silence.

It was a good question.

When I was not speaking, it was almost predetermined that I would listen. I say "almost" because not talking only afforded me the opportunity to listen, to hear the full story of the person speaking to me. There is no guarantee that is our natural inclination, and certainly no promise that this is what will happen. More times than most, we end up getting in the way of ourselves when it comes to holding our judgments at bay.

"But try this exercise," I said. "Imagine that as we are sitting here we are each having a cup of coffee, and I am listening to you speak about some real bit of controversy that I have a strong opinion about."

"I got it," he replied, and anxiously took a gulp of coffee.

"Okay, now here's the deal." I leaned toward him. "I imagine that all that I am as far as ideas go can be put in this coffee cup." Playing along, he feigned a skeptical look over the rim of my cup. "Now, for the sake of hearing you fully, I place my cup with the coffee representing all of my ideas just over here." I slid the cup just a little to the left and out of my easy grasp. "There I am," I say. "I can pick up my ideas and prejudices at any time and have a nice sip, but now I am ready to listen to you about you and maybe hear something new, or in a different way. Maybe you are having a cup of tea and you want to tell me how it tastes. Here is the opportunity to listen."

SIGN LANGUAGE

It is not always a spiritual calling that brings us to the edge of silence. For me it started as a way to avoid arguments, and in the process, a way to learn to listen. But both avoiding arguments and learning to listen were necessary steps on the path to self-discovery.

Buckminster Fuller, the American visionary and architect who invented the geodesic dome and coined the phrase "Spaceship Earth," took a vow of silence for nearly two years after a series of personal crises in the 1920s, including the death of his young daughter and his own thoughts of suicide. "I must really from this point on just stop talking," he declared, "'til I learn what the meaning of meaning is, what do I think and which words do I really wish to use."

Fuller moved his wife, Anne, and infant daughter, Allegra, to a one-room apartment in a Chicago slum, withdrew completely from all friends and social contact, and vowed not to speak again until he really knew what he thought. And then he began to think. His virtual silence was the beginning of what he one day called "a blind date with principle," during which he pondered his purpose in life. Afterward, Fuller resolved to devote himself to the betterment of society.

Maya Angelou is perhaps best known for her amazing poetry and critically acclaimed series of six autobiographies. Less known is the fact that after her mother's boyfriend raped her at the age of seven, and after her attacker's subsequent conviction and murder in prison,

Maya retreated into a five-year voluntary silence. Angelou was sustained and helped to heal by two strong women, her maternal grandmother and Mrs. Bertha Flowers, an educated black woman who instilled in the still silent Angelou a love of poetry.

Angelou's compelling, conversational, eloquent narratives present her personal journey of survival, growth, and self-definition as an African-American woman, with the backdrop of the collective social and political experience of black America in the 20th century. Themes sustained across the series include motherhood, the strength of black women, and being black in a racist society.

In 2006 Angelou was given the Quill Award for her poetry. Her humanitarian efforts have earned her the 1994 Spingarn Medal—the highest award of the NAACP—and the Mother Teresa Award, in 2006.

The lives of both Buckminster Fuller and Maya Angelou were beacons to me. They shed a light and special perspective on silence and discovering the self that often gets buried beneath the noise of day to day.

Perhaps the greatest beacon in my life, however, was Becky Luftig.

Becky was two years old when I stopped speaking. She lived with her brother and parents on the levee road in Point Reyes Station. Like most two-year-olds, she was learning to walk, loved to play, and was always looking to learn new things. What was remarkable about Becky was that she was born deaf. This affected our entire community, which traditionally accepted each new child into our collective family.

So when Becky's parents offered sign language classes, the community learned Signing Exact English, a language that mimics English syntax. It is very different from American Sign Language, which is considered its own language with its own syntax, but her parents wanted her to be mainstreamed. They didn't want her to be sent to a special school somewhere else in the county, but to our local school, with all the children she lived near and would grow up with. Her mom fought the local school board until they finally relented.

In this way Becky became one of my teachers as well. She and her parents were a light to all of us. Even in her silence, she taught us not to go meekly by, but to believe that life, whether we talk or not, was the miracle that was to be lived. By the time she was eight she could not only sign, but also speak and read lips. After high school she was accepted at Gallaudet University, a college for the deaf in Washington, D.C.

When some people learned that I used sign language, they said that was cheating—that if I really wanted to be silent, I wouldn't use any sign language to communicate. Others thought me selfish because, in refusing to speak, I was rejecting the gift that God had given me. Long ago I had learned to always listen to their criticisms, hopefully with new ears. I would smile and nod respectfully. But I had come to understand that there were no rules about how you should be if silence finds you, and this silent time was perhaps an even greater gift for someone who was so talkative and was in great need to learn to listen.

Seven years to walk across North America was a long time, even for settlers who had few roads or bridges to help them on the way. A lot happened to me and to my family as I made my way across the country. By the time I reached the Midwest, I was working on a doctoral degree in environmental studies. One friend, Jim Willse, had left California, moved his family east, and become the editor of the *New York Daily News*. My mother had gone to graduate school at Antioch East and had become a special education teacher in the Philadelphia school system. By the time I set my foot into the Atlantic, my friend George Ludy had died.

But as I made my way from the Jersey Coast to Washington, D.C., on my blue Schwinn ten-speed, the bright eyes and spirit of Becky Luftig filled my thoughts. She had been a little girl, signing a story as fast as she could, when I saw her last. Now she was a young woman and a student at Gallaudet University. I could hardly wait to see her, to see who she had become, and to share who we had become together.

I looked forward to hearing her gasp when she saw me speak for the first time. I wanted to spring it on her as a surprise. Sadly, I heard upon my arrival that I'd just missed her. She had gone to a deaf school in the Philippines mid-semester and was raising money to build on-campus housing so that the students there would have a greater sense of community. Meanwhile, the Gallaudet students were holding demonstrations against the appointment of a hearing president who refused to learn sign language. As a result, I. King Jordan became the first deaf person to be nominated as the school's president, thus symbolizing the rights, the abilities, and the strength of deaf people.

Jordan had also become one of my heroes, because through my years of silence and my learning of sign language I had grown close to the deaf community. I had visited the school a week earlier and had arranged to meet with him. Visiting Jordan at Gallaudet would be a highlight, albeit ironic now that I had ended my silence.

My trusty bike had arrived from Madison, Wisconsin, where I had attended the university. While attending Southern Oregon State College in Ashland, I had begun using the bike for local travel to and from school, but while traveling across the country I had walked. As I was walking across the United States, my friends sent me my bike to use in the next place I would be living.

On my bike, I moved with the flow of downtown traffic through timed green lights. Only a few blocks from the school, I saw a sienna flash from the corner of my eye. As I biked through a P Street intersection, I was struck by a car making a left-hand turn. My face pressed sideways against the windshield. I could see the old woman driver on the other side of the glass, a blank expression on her face. Metal twisted. My bike, and then my body, crumpled to the warm asphalt. As the pain and nausea rose around me in a flooding sea, I pictured the baby robin crushed into the asphalt on that long-ago hot Philadelphia street.

Is this how my pilgrimage was to end, dying on a street in Washington, D.C.? Maybe this was the lightning strike of retribution for beginning to speak after so long. I worried about not having done my daily painting. The pain grew more intense, and each breath required more and more effort. Tears welled up in my eyes, and I began to cry.

Darkness.

"Hey, man, you all right?"

The voice came from a man bending over me. I grimaced. Traffic was at a standstill, and people were shouting things I couldn't hear from far-away across the street. Beside me, the voice was telling me not to worry.

"I seen the whole damn thing." He kept repeating it like a mantra, as if witnessing the event had given him control over life and death, and because of this, I was saved. Slowly my eyes adjusted to see a large, dark face with worried brown eyes, yellowed teeth, and warm, moist breath. It filled my view.

"I seen the whole damn thing," he repeated. "Don't worry; I work for a lawyer."

I have heard about people like this, I thought. They are called ambulance chasers—but he was there before the ambulance had even arrived. The fact that this guy was whispering about money in my ear as I teetered on the edge of death made me think that I was dead or, at the least, hallucinating. I closed my eyes and wondered if the apparition would disappear when I opened them.

By the time the ambulance arrived, I had been moved to the curb, to the consternation of some of the bystanders across the street. The paramedics stabilized my left shoulder and helped me into the ambulance.

It was vaguely familiar, like a small hospital room in off-white and green, with a monitor of some sort and a steel-plate floor with a raised design. I could not remember having been inside an ambulance before, except maybe once on a school trip to a fire station when I was a kid. I did remember the spotted dalmatian that rode with the hook and ladder, and then I thought of my children's book *The Poky Little Puppy*. Only when the paramedics were securing me with heavy wide straps for transport did it dawn on me what was happening.

"Say, where are we going?" I asked, trying not to sound too frantic.

The woman in front of me smiled, stopped, and looked me in the eyes sympathetically.

"We're taking you to the hospital," she said as she continued to fasten me into a seat with the fabric straps. "You know, you've been in an accident."

I nodded my head, and everything moved in slow motion, leaving a comet trail of sparkly light. My thoughts began to race. I tried to assess my condition. Could I walk to the hospital, or would I have to take my first automobile ride in 20 years?

More emergency personnel came in to see me. Howard University Hospital, they said, was about 15 blocks away.

"You know, I think I'll walk," I said nonchalantly, hoping to convince them of the wisdom of my words. There were a few laughs. I quickly followed with an explanation.

"Actually, I don't ride in motorized vehicles." There was silence, and everyone stopped moving. "I haven't ridden in a car for over 20 years." The crew looked at each other and then at me. "In fact, I . . . I . . . didn't speak for over 17 years." The words tumbled out idiotically. Their eyes open as wide as pies. "Yeah, I only just started speaking again yesterday." The moment the words slipped from my mouth, I knew this was going to be a hard sell.

I remembered all those times when people would ask hypothetical questions and make up hypothetical situations to show me how not speaking would lead to some unavoidable tragedy. If only I would speak, they would say, I could explain everything. I would listen to those people and smile. I would often demonstrate in mime what I might do in their invented situations, or I would say that I felt more comfortable dealing with problems as they arose.

But here, now, in this Kafkaesque scene, I was actually speaking, and it looked as if I was going to be carried away in the ambulance against my will.

The paramedics mumbled something to each other under their breath. Then, except for one young man who stayed to watch me, they retreated out the door for a private conference.

The expression on the remaining paramedic's face made me feel that I had only convinced them that I was crazy, and that they would want to take me to St. Elizabeths for psychiatric observation.

"And why don't you ride in cars?" the lone paramedic asked tentatively, as if he did not wish to set off my psychosis. The rest of the crew filed in again. "Do you belong to some kind of religion? Are you afraid of cars?"

"No," I said, and I shook my head slowly. My voice was feeble as I tried to explain about seeing an oil spill in San Francisco Bay, but I couldn't bring my two hands together to form the hull of the two tankers or the collision that had occurred, as I had so often done in my silence, and I had no printed introductions of my life story to hand out. Strangely enough, I increasingly felt like not speaking. I was not sure my answer would be understood.

"You sure it's not some kind of religious thing?" the paramedic queried again.

I waffled an untethered hand back and forth to indicate that what he was saying was not exactly right. The spirit of charades entered the cramped ambulance, and a few guesses bounced around until one paramedic asked if it was like a principle.

"Yeah, it's something like a principle," I agreed. I was a little more relaxed now that the mood was changing from "get the straight-jacket" to "crazy but harmless," and perhaps even "maybe we can let him go."

Behind me, the woman paramedic was undoing a restraint around my waist.

"Principles," she mocked. "Well, honey, if you would just suspend your principles for five minutes, we can drive your butt to the hospital."

"I don't think principles work that way," I explained as I signed the release form one of them handed me. It stated that they had offered assistance and a ride to the hospital, but that I had declined, thus absolving them of any further responsibility.

Outside, a policewoman was waiting to take my statement, and after interviewing a number of witnesses she determined that the accident was the driver's fault. The charge was "failing to yield."

My new attorney friend was more than disappointed that I had refused the ride in the ambulance. "No, man, what are you doing?" he shouted as I stepped from the ambulance. "You've blown it."

Exasperated, he explained under his breath that riding in the ambulance would have meant getting more money when we sued the insurance company. As for me, I was only interested in finding a safe place for my wrecked bike and getting someone to help me move it there on the way to the hospital.

My friend assured me that the law office was on the way and that his boss would let me leave my bike there. The frame was bent, and the front wheel wobbled. On the way, he told me that he was not an attorney but an investigator. I filled him in on the last several years of my life and told him that I had just started speaking, and I didn't ride in cars.

"Hey, man, what kind of shit is that suppose' to be?" He was still annoyed with me for not riding off in the ambulance and securing a hefty commission for the attorney's office.

"Man, you talk crazy," he said. "You must be in some kinda bad shock or somethin'. Why you talk crazy like that? You on somethin'?" He decided he had no reason to believe me, so he did not.

With my left arm in a sling and my friend dragging my blue Schwinn with a crumpled front wheel, we finally reached a row house on North Capitol. Out front, a shabby and faded sign announced that this was the law office of Herman Jones, Esq. The entrance was up some stairs from the street and then down a short flight of concrete steps into a basement.

"You wait here," the investigator said before disappearing.

I waited, chatting casually with the receptionist who occasionally answered the phone while looking admiringly at her long, curved nails. In what seemed like only a few seconds my friend was back. He ushered me up a narrow staircase and into the sprawling office of a senior partner.

The large wooden desk was cluttered with paper. Lining the walls were the obligatory bookshelves loaded with volumes of law books. A picture of Dr. Martin Luther King, Jr., looked dreamily down on us. A humming air conditioner drowned out the sound of the traffic. It barely cooled the air.

Seated in a brown, overstuffed leather chair, Herman Jones, Esq., smiled broadly, offered me his hand, and then asked me to take a seat.

"So, Davis here tells me you been in an accident." Jones nodded at the man who had befriended me and was now standing sheepishly at the door.

"Yes," I replied. I was thankful for the air-conditioning. Even though it was not oppressively hot, I was still sweating from the walk. "But actually, I'm here to see if you'd let me keep my bike here until I can make some other arrangements."

"No problem, no problem." Jones grinned. "Well, you're lucky he was there to see it, because if we have to go to trial he can be a witness." He rubbed his hands together.

I listened politely while staring at a large diamond ring sparkling on his right hand. Jones continued, "At the very least we'll be able to represent you and get you the best settlement."

"I'm thinking that since the woman was ticketed, it wouldn't have to go to trial," I said.

"That's true," he said, "but I want to hear about this walking and not talking business that Davis has been telling me about."

He folded his hands beneath his chin and listened. When I finished, he leaned back in his overstuffed swivel chair and laughed so hard that he spun clear around in a tight circle and sent a pile of important-looking papers to the floor. He kept on laughing until tears welled in his eyes and streamed down his cheeks. Davis looked at us fearfully from the corner.

"Now that's some story. Not that I don't believe you, but you got to admit, that's some story." He put great emphasis on the word "some" and flashed a big, gold-toothed smile. "Is there anyone who could substantiate this story of yours? I mean, you have to admit it's a pretty fantastic tale." He smiled and chuckled to himself some more. Then he waved away Davis, whose expression had turned to sadness and loss. For sure, he was thinking, this guy is crazy, and there would be no commission for bringing him into the office.

I thought for a moment. Rebecca Withers from *National Geographic* magazine, and Shawn Pogatchnik, a reporter from the *Los*

Angeles Times, had covered the event of my ending my silence, and I had met the Washington bureau editor of the *Times* before I had started speaking.

"There was an article in the *Los Angeles Times* yesterday. You could call the editor," I suggested. I offered a number on a scrap of paper. Jones, smiling, declined the offer and dialed Information. He knew all about the scams in which someone offered a phone number to some official place, only for the caller to be connected to an accomplice at some other location.

It really made no difference to me. I was as amused by Mr. Jones as he was by me. When the operator answered, he asked for the *Times*'s number and dialed again.

"Yes, this is Herman A. Jones at the law firm of Jones, Smith, and Franklin. I'm sorry to bother you, but I have a Mr. John Francis here, who was in an accident today and claims . . . oh, you do." The smirk left his face.

"Yes, he's fine . . . Y . . . Yes, sitting right here in my office . . . my address?" He gave his address to the recipient of his call. Then looked at me and asked me where I was going after I left his office. When I told him I was on my way to Howard University Hospital, he repeated the information into the phone.

"No, he insists on walking . . . Oh, he has? That's very unusual, yes. Well, thank you very much." He hung up and turned toward me. Again his face filled with a toothy smile, and he folded his hands behind his head.

"Well, now," he said, "seems as though you were telling the truth. You know, it's a good thing you came to this office because we can really take care of you." Jones swiveled his chair closer to mine. "Just think, if you had been killed in that accident, they would have just put you in the ambulance and driven you away. Same as if you were being buried; they would just put you in a hearse and drive you to the cemetery. We could help you so that won't happen." He leaned closer until I could see the gold of his teeth and feel the warmth of his breath. It reminded me of his investigator, Davis. "We could write a will that would stipulate that in the event of your death you would be carried to the cemetery in a wagon drawn by mules. That would be okay, wouldn't it?" He smiled, and I could see all his teeth.

"Yeah, that's a great idea," I said. I didn't bother to tell him that I had heard all the "what ifs" before. I just agreed and nodded my head. The room seemed to tilt, and a brief moment of gray graininess and nausea rushed over me. I felt my shoulder throb. I was starting to feel the effects of the accident and wanted to get to the hospital, but before Jones let me go he wanted me to meet the attorney who would handle my case if I decided to go with them. It turned out that although Mr. Jones was a lawyer, he was temporarily unable to practice because of some "misunderstanding" with the bar association.

Now I was tired of speaking, and not thoroughly convinced that starting to speak had been the right decision, I retreated to the sanctuary of silence.

I left my damaged bike in the backyard of the office and walked alone the rest of the way to the hospital. In the emergency room, I waited with the other patients. Shawn Pogatchnik, the *Los Angeles Times* reporter, found me there. He had traced my steps from the law office to the hospital to make sure I was all right and had arrived safely. After he left, my body finally succumbed to the trauma of the accident. I began to shake. The room turned again to that grainy grayness and then faded to black.

In next morning's *Los Angeles Times* there was a story about an environmentalist getting hit by a car, refusing to ride in an ambulance, and walking 15 blocks to the hospital.

I never got to see President Jordan, and I never had the opportunity to apologize for missing our meeting. Neither did I get to see my friend Becky, because not long after that, I learned that she had died in an automobile accident on her way to a conference for the deaf in Las Vegas.

I felt a great loss at this. One of my teachers had gone—way too early, and way too young. I made my trek to Becky's college to pay her loss some respect, and there, in a way, I found her, in the very light that shone from the eyes of her friends and peers—those who "spoke" of her spirit in excited signs, who also had been touched by her good works, and by her discovery of silence and self in a noisy world that she could not hear.

Lesson in Silence: Listening Practice
Objective: Listening past disagreement

In a society where disagreements draw the boundaries of our communities, it is difficult to celebrate our differences or to rejoice in our interdependence. But if you are looking to transform the very fabric of our culture, try practicing this next exercise. Now that you have learned that listening sincerely to someone can be a particularly positive experience, even when there is disagreement, you have the power to be transformative.

When you feel confident in your skills, find someone with whom you usually disagree, and ask if he or she would explain to you what it was you were not able to listen to before. Promise to listen.

After spending 17 years in silence I earned the reputation of being a good, if not sympathetic, listener. I became grateful to those who honored me by telling me the things with which I did not agree.

Use all that you have learned about barriers of communication and how we can overcome them by practicing active listening. Find a way to listen to your enemies, and you will find that they are not your enemies, but your partners in finding peace.

light that shone from the eyes of her friends and peers—those who "spoke" of her spirit in excited signs, who also had been touched by her good works, and by her discovery of silence and self in a noisy world that she could not hear.

Lesson in Silence: Listening Practice
Objective: Listening past disagreement

In a society where disagreements draw the boundaries of our communities, it is difficult to celebrate our differences or to rejoice in our interdependence. But if you are looking to transform the very fabric of our culture, try practicing this next exercise. Now that you have learned that listening sincerely to someone can be a particularly positive experience, even when there is disagreement, you have the power to be transformative.

When you feel confident in your skills, find someone with whom you usually disagree, and ask if he or she would explain to you what it was you were not able to listen to before. Promise to listen.

After spending 17 years in silence I earned the reputation of being a good, if not sympathetic, listener. I became grateful to those who honored me by telling me the things with which I did not agree.

Use all that you have learned about barriers of communication and how we can overcome them by practicing active listening. Find a way to listen to your enemies, and you will find that they are not your enemies, but your partners in finding peace.

a will that would stipulate that in the event of your death you would be carried to the cemetery in a wagon drawn by mules. That would be okay, wouldn't it?" He smiled, and I could see all his teeth.

"Yeah, that's a great idea," I said. I didn't bother to tell him that I had heard all the "what ifs" before. I just agreed and nodded my head. The room seemed to tilt, and a brief moment of gray graininess and nausea rushed over me. I felt my shoulder throb. I was starting to feel the effects of the accident and wanted to get to the hospital, but before Jones let me go he wanted me to meet the attorney who would handle my case if I decided to go with them. It turned out that although Mr. Jones was a lawyer, he was temporarily unable to practice because of some "misunderstanding" with the bar association.

Now I was tired of speaking, and not thoroughly convinced that starting to speak had been the right decision, I retreated to the sanctuary of silence.

I left my damaged bike in the backyard of the office and walked alone the rest of the way to the hospital. In the emergency room, I waited with the other patients. Shawn Pogatchnik, the *Los Angeles Times* reporter, found me there. He had traced my steps from the law office to the hospital to make sure I was all right and had arrived safely. After he left, my body finally succumbed to the trauma of the accident. I began to shake. The room turned again to that grainy grayness and then faded to black.

In next morning's *Los Angeles Times* there was a story about an environmentalist getting hit by a car, refusing to ride in an ambulance, and walking 15 blocks to the hospital.

I never got to see President Jordan, and I never had the opportunity to apologize for missing our meeting. Neither did I get to see my friend Becky, because not long after that, I learned that she had died in an automobile accident on her way to a conference for the deaf in Las Vegas.

I felt a great loss at this. One of my teachers had gone—way too early, and way too young. I made my trek to Becky's college to pay her loss some respect, and there, in a way, I found her, in the very

I'M A ROSE

When I first saw Irv Rose, it was fall, and I had been speaking for about five months. But after 17 years of silence, it still clung to me like a friendly sweater. I listened from the ragged edge where I could tell I was smiling, if not at the humor of this elfin spirit before me, then at least at the situation I now found myself in.

I was a project manager and environmental policy analyst for the Oil Pollution Act (OPA) 1990 staff at the U.S. Coast Guard headquarters in Washington, D.C., and I was sitting among a group of fellow product managers as Mr. Rose introduced himself. He was neatly dressed in a dark sport blazer, gray wool trousers, a red-striped tie, and very shiny wing-tip shoes. He had a full head of black hair and a large handlebar moustache to match. He moved with surety and deliberateness at the front of the room.

"I M Rose," he stated with some authority, and pointed to a red rose that was pinned to his lapel. There was some nervous laughter. "No, really, that's my name. Irv M. Rose." Then he repeated, "I. M. Rose."

He said he had used the rose gag to put us at ease, and he had succeeded. We all laughed. I. M. Rose was an instant hit.

He told us that he was here to help us prep for our Two-Minute Briefing, and to generally assist us with communication as well as listening skills. Listening, he said, was the other side of speaking, and without it, no matter how you framed your briefing, all would be for naught.

Listening. I had spent some time learning to listen, so I could have considered myself a kind of expert; however, one of the things that I had learned from my experience was that no matter how much of an expert you think you are, there is always something more to learn. So I smiled and listened, because Mr. Rose was getting set to teach us how to talk. This was a major skill I needed to learn, because, as one of the project managers, I was going to have to brief admirals and legislators.

Irv began right away by telling us about a survey of the ten things that people fear most, death and public speaking being among the choices. His question to us was where death lay relative to public speaking. He looked out over the class. No one had an answer.

"Okay. Let me give you a clue. Death is at number four. Anything . . . ?"

There were no sounds in the room. Then I raised my hand.

"Number five?" I asked tentatively. After nearly six months of practice my voice was still quiet, and I had to think about what I was going to say before the words came out. Maybe that was a good thing, but I was no orator, and fear of public speaking was right up there with being afraid of bears; I was positive that fear of bears must be in the top four.

"Good guess, but number one was the right answer," countered Irv.

We all looked at each other and could understand why. It seems as if we all act as if we've just taken a vow of silence when pressed to stand and talk. Often our insecurity makes us feel vulnerable, likely to fail, and with all eyes on us we feel exposed to harsh judgment. Another reason is that many of us lack the skills to prepare and deliver a speech.

Oddly enough, I felt very confident in my ability to deliver a silent presentation, using mime and music; I had always thought that if I could use words, things would be much easier. For the most part I discovered this to be true, particularly when I spoke about the business of oil spills and writing federal regulations. When I moved on to another subject, however, the silence intruded on my words. If I were in a group conversation, I simply stopped speaking and listened from the edge. God knows how I would behave when standing before a group of Coast Guard admirals.

To begin, Irv asked us to prepare a two-minute personal introduction over the next five minutes. Once we were done, each of us had to get up and deliver the briefing to the rest of the class.

The attorneys were the best at presentations, though Irv critiqued even them for using jargon—words that were often meaningless except in a specialized group, like "wanting to work on the reg negs," which meant the "regulatory negotiations." We civilian managers and analysts avoided jargon, but we fidgeted with keys, paced, or balanced on one foot and then the other.

"I . . . umm, am from Texas . . . umm, and . . . uh . . . came here to . . . umm, work on, aah . . . policy," said a young analyst from an environmental nonprofit. Then she started over.

Irv stopped me midway. Yes, I knew I was guilty of the "umm" word, and I had indeed fidgeted with my keys, but I was the only one he had stopped midstream.

"Wait a minute, Mr. Francis. You're not supposed to make up a fictitious introduction; these are supposed to be true. Are you telling us that you walked here from California and didn't speak for 17 years?"

I nodded yes, and someone else chimed in affectionately. "Yeah, Doctor John is the strange one."

"I just never heard of anything like that," said Irv. "Please go on; I'm sorry for the interruption."

I stammered through the rest of my introduction.

When the exercise was over, we were surprised how little we had known about each other—and, now, how much we did know. Irv said the next exercise was going to be about something that we were doing at work. We would work in pairs and choose which of us to present. As audience members, we would act as a group of admirals and U.S. representatives. This time we would be videotaping and critiquing our work.

With lawyers and some public officials on the staff, the idea of videotaping sent murmurs though the class, but it was not about the fear of our spirits being captured in a little black box; it was about privacy and what was going to be done with the film. At this point we were not working on classified material, but since it was in the development stage it was not available to be released to the public. Irv assured us that the film was solely for our training and would be erased once we were through. I thought our concern was much more about vanity than about Coast Guard policy.

After each presentation we viewed the video and were asked what we thought. For the most part we all felt that the presenters did well. Speakers, before they started, took out the coins from their pockets, stood erect, lost most of their hums and ums, and generally stayed on topic. We each began with a brief intro, got into the topic, and ended with a short recap.

Probably the biggest problem that we faced was trying to give just enough information for complex regulations, some of which crossed the line for information overload. An example of this was with the briefing on the regulations that were going to require double hull construction on all new tankers over a certain tonnage. First the presenter described the regulations, and then he commented on where the material was in the regulatory process and when the final regulation might be finished. He quoted some costs of the construction, how much oil could be saved from spills, the cost of the oil, and the projected administrative cost to the government.

We all thought that it was a good briefing, considering how much we knew he had left out.

"That you felt that everyone did well, even when the presenter felt they were terrible, shows us a very important point," Irv commented. He waited for emphasis and then spoke slowly. "You are your own worst critic.

"Were you nervous up there while you were talking?" he asked one of the presenters.

She confessed that for the first 30 seconds she had been terrified. But when we looked at the video, he pointed out that neither the camera nor the group could pick up on any of her anxiety. That stuff was all inside. In fact, Irv went on to explain, everyone in this room wanted each member to succeed, so if there was something that you didn't quite get right you could be sure that this group was going to let it slide; what's more, he said, that's pretty much how all audiences will be.

"Maybe at the Rotary Club," someone blurted out, "but not on Capitol Hill." A laugh went through the room, and Irv acquiesced the point.

All I could think of was that when I had stood in front of my family, friends, and the media on Earth Day, I'd been scared to death, but no one had seen me sweat. Likewise, I could remember how nervous I'd been about defending my dissertation, only to find that the committee was so stunned that I could actually speak that I felt that perhaps I didn't have to do much more than that to earn my Ph.D.

When Irv put the videotape on me, I found that, even though the class liked my presentation, I could see all the pimples. It was painful to watch myself, as I could see the mistakes over and over. Nonetheless, it was extremely helpful.

Irv had taught us to be more conscious of what our bodies were doing when we spoke: were we switching from one foot to the other, fumbling with keys or change in our pockets, or using the "umm" expression at the end of each sentence or at the beginning of the next? He explained how to use notes and said that picking out a friendly face in the audience to talk to would help us focus. But most important, he gave us the confidence to do the two-minute briefing.

"Tell them what you are going to tell them. Tell 'em again, and then tell them once more, all in two minutes."

A short time later I was called to brief an admiral about an oil tanker inspection I was supposed to process in Philadelphia. As I was still not using motorized vehicles for my personal transportation, I had agreed to use a bike for any travel up to 300 miles from headquarters; for greater distances I could send someone, and if I absolutely had to be present, we would use video conferencing.

On this day my supervisor, Norm Lemley, grabbed my arm and hauled me into the cafeteria for lunch. He surveyed the crowd, a mix of civilians, officers, and regular sailors in uniform.

"Over here." Tray in hand, he nudged me with his elbow, and I followed a circuitous path through people and tables until we found ourselves standing in front of Adm. Gene Henn.

Admiral Henn was the vice commandant in charge of the OPA 90 staff. He was a very likable, approachable person, but he was still an admiral, and they are notorious for not having time for idle chatter. The communication workshop only served to drive home the point. I was sure Lemley was not about to engage in idle chatter.

"Good afternoon, Admiral. Mind if Dr. Francis and I join you for lunch?"

"Not at all, Norm. Have a seat."

"Thank you." We sat down and began unloading the contents of our trays onto the table. Norm said, "I think we'll be ready for the next regulatory negotiation meeting this week." The "reg neg," as it is often called, is an innovative program in which the stakeholders in a specific regulation meet before a judge and negotiate all the points of interest prior to the regulation's ratification. Once the parties agree and documents are signed, all parties give up the right to challenge the regulation in court. In this instance the stakeholders consisted of the oil industry and environmental groups. According to Irv, "reg neg" is just the kind of jargon that is a barrier to communication, and the U.S. Coast Guard is filled with them.

"Next week John is going up to Philadelphia for a tanker inspection." Norm slipped this in between bites of a fried fish sandwich. Admiral Henn stopped eating his own meal and looked at me.

"Oh, really. How are you going to get there, John?"

I stared back at him blankly, and for the moment all words left me. Automatically, as if I had never started speaking, I mimed the rotating pedals of a bicycle with my two hands; I had turned to silence in times of stress just like riding a bike. I had no desire to speak, only to listen and to be still, while all of life and its importance swirled around me. Here, even as Dr. Francis, project manager and environmental analyst for the U.S. Coast Guard, I could feel the ragged edge of silence, and find peace.

"You're going to ride your bike?" asked Admiral Henn.

Coming back from the edge, I nodded yes.

"Commander Diaz is going with him," added Lemley.

"That's good. Be careful."

We took a few more bites of our lunch before we excused ourselves from the table. A smile settled on Lemley's face as we exited. "There," he said. "We've fully briefed the admiral."

Back in the OPA 90 staff office, the secretary began making all the necessary calls to plan our trip. The oil company was concerned that I was riding a bike to the oil port in Philadelphia.

"He just doesn't ride in motorized vehicles since witnessing an oil spill in California," the secretary said into the phone. She paused and listened to the response. "Well, yes, he's been featured on CBS TV, but I don't think that *60 Minutes* will be showing up, although they might."

She turned to me and asked me to promise that *60 Minutes* would not show up. "They're worried that there might be an oil spill while you're there," she reported. "They said they're sending their vice president of safety to meet you."

It took one and a half days for Commander Diaz and me to reach Philadelphia. On the way, my breathing became my mantra. It was a road I had ridden before, the geography familiar. It was the same ride I had made the previous year, after I had defended my dissertation on oil spills and received my doctorate.

Back then I had pedaled through traffic on busy District streets, my breathing in sync with the nearly level landscape, and I had been mindful of the traffic passing close to my left side and turning in front of me. I had ridden for hours before that was behind me.

In Baltimore, gospel music mixed with Sunday morning preaching that all poured out of the Baptist churches on North Avenue, sometimes over loudspeakers. The city's Sunday streets eventually gave way to suburban sprawl and then to small towns and the rolling hills of the Maryland countryside. My rate of breathing matched the elevations and steepness of each hill. At Conowingo Dam Park I stopped for lunch. On the west side of the Conowingo Dam and adjacent to the Susquehanna River, it was a recreation area that the Philadelphia Electric Company had developed for employees and the public. My father had since retired from the company, but my brother still worked at one of the coal-fired generation stations a little farther on. That made me feel a little like being home.

The tanker was docked at the Sun Oil terminal, not far from the international airport. I remembered stories my father told me about cleaning the storage tanks at Sun Oil. It was dangerous work. One spark could cause the most catastrophic explosion. He had kept the job only a few weeks before signing on with the Philadelphia Electric Company as a lineman.

When we arrived at the terminal, Richard Halluska and Tiffany Rau of OMI, the owners of the tanker, met us at the dock. Richard was of medium build with a neat mustache, and he wore a brown sport jacket and an orange safety helmet. Tiffany was tall and slender, and she wore wearing khaki slacks, a windbreaker, and a safety helmet. Along with the OMI crew, a Coast Guard sailor was there to do the inspection. Before the inspection, however, we sat in the main cabin and sipped hot coffee. After the preliminary introductions, Tiffany asked about the bike ride from Washington.

"It was great!" I said. "We made it in a day and a half, and we had good weather." I looked at Commander Diaz, who nodded in agreement.

With his hands folded beneath his chin, Richard looked at me. "I heard you don't ride in motorized vehicles as a protest or something. I hope you don't mind me asking, but you seem so . . . uh . . . normal."

"No, I don't mind," I responded. "I'm glad you asked. It's true that I gave up riding in motorized vehicles after witnessing an oil spill in California, but I wouldn't say it's a protest. I actually believe that all of us who use oil have some responsibility for all of the pollution it causes, even the spills, and not just the oil companies or the people who transport oil."

Richard looked at Tiffany, and they both looked back at me; in unison, they asked, "What does that mean?"

"It's just like I said: If you're using oil to get around, then you share in the responsibility for any spill that occurs; we're all demanding more oil cheaper and faster, and in the process some of it spills."

"So what you're suggesting is a sort of shared responsibility?"

"Yes, exactly." Everyone in the cabin was listening. I continued: "Don't get me wrong, I think that oil transport companies have the greater responsibility when we're talking about oil spills from ships, just not all of it. But for the record, my research has found that most of the oil that finds its way into the marine environment comes from automobile crankcase disposal."

"Well, you're the first environmentalist that I've heard talk like this," Richard replied. At his words, the lines of tension etched in his face relaxed, and a wave of relief washed over our small group.

I said, "I think I'd like to refer to myself as an environmental practitioner instead of an environmentalist. I know it may just be a matter of semantics, but "practitioner" implies becoming, and doing something in order to improve. In the end I think it's about learning how to live better on the earth."

"I couldn't agree with you more," said Richard. "Frankly, we were a little nervous when we heard that one of the people who was going to be regulating our industry was bicycling here from Washington to do a tanker inspection because he'd seen an oil spill and didn't want to contribute to the pollution. We're relieved to find that you're someone who can see both sides and who we can talk with."

Sitting beside me, Commander Diaz was laughing. "He's pretty much an anomaly up at headquarters as well."

As I heard myself say these things, I could not help but remember when I first had experienced the oil spill near the Golden Gate Bridge. I'd been angry, and not in a place where I would have listened or accepted any responsibility. Now, sitting in the dining room aboard this oil tanker, I realized that many things had changed: Yes, there was a growing awareness of environment, but the most profound changes had occurred in me. I had learned to listen. And I promised myself to practice this the rest of my life.

On the bicycle ride back to Washington, my breathing was my mantra. But even in reverse, and on a different day, the hills remain the same, dependent on the elevations and the steepness of the rise, the breathing, and what passed through my mind sometimes changed, like the weather.

Lesson in Silence: Taking Responsibility
Objective: Living on the ragged edge of silence

As I have discovered about walking, the planet, the earth, begs us to walk on her as everything begs us to listen. Not only do we need to actively listen to ourselves and to each other, but we also need to listen to all things.

By now you have read lots of words and have practiced several exercises. Hopefully you have learned to be still and to listen. Take this skill out into the world and listen to creation; above all, listen to yourself and to your fellow humans. Each day, make this your practice. Listen to and trust yourself. Do not be afraid of what you hear. When your mind is still, listen also to what is not said; that is the silence, and without it there can be no meaning.

EPILOGUE: WRITING FROM SILENCE

I can't say enough about the importance of keeping a journal from beginning to end, as it can be a reflection and artifact of our journeys through life. At the very least it creates a time for us to sit and reflect on the wonders of the day. Painting, music, and photography can also aid us in our search for the moment. Early on, Ben Kimmelman taught me the value of keeping a journal, before I stopped speaking, right into the days of keeping silent. Keeping a journal is still a very important part of my journey.

I revisited not speaking once again in summer 2010 while living in the summer home of my youth in Cape May, New Jersey. This was the home that my parents resided in after retirement, and the abode where they both eventually died, first my mother, then my father.

I moved here with my wife Martha and our two boys, Sam and Luke. We arrived in Cape May on New Year's Eve 2009, in time for the most severe snowstorm in memory. We stayed in a rental unit while our home was being repaired, and finally, in May, we were able to move into our house while repairs were still under way.

In the early summer Martha and the boys went to visit her mom in Lawrence, Kansas, leaving me to write and deal with the construction, during which time I began these four days of silence. I am happy to be able to share them with you through my journal.

For these journal entries, paintings were done in a separate book, while the written entries were typed directly into a computer.

For comparison I have included actual samples of my journal entries from when I first started to write within silence, beginning October 9, 1973. Each offers an expression of a full day, something that would be easy for me to carry on my walking journey, something that could become a practice. They are not edited and are seen in their entirety.

There are many styles of journals, illustrated with pen and ink and watercolor; there are research journals, calendar journals, and scrapbook journals; they can include photographs, poetry, unedited notes, or heavily edited prose. So experiment and find the one that suits you best. Don't be afraid to change styles as you go along.

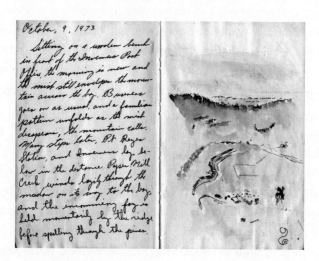

October 9, 1973
Sitting on a wooden bench in front of the Inverness Post Office, the morning is new and the mist still envelops the mountain across the bay. Business goes on as usual, and a familiar pattern unfolds as the mist disappears, the mountain calls. Many steps later, Point Reyes Station, and Inverness lay below in the distance. Paper Mill Creek winds lazily through the meadow on its way to the bay, and the incoming fog is held momentarily by the ridge before spilling through the pines.

Beyond stone dirt road
Ocean and sky touching blue
As the dragonflies

July 20, 2010
West Cape May, NJ
Waking into silence, not a word to say except to sit a moment on the side of my bed with eyes closed. I am remembering that I am not to speak today. At first it seems like such a chore, my head filling with all the work I have to do and the "what ifs?" that tend to get in the way.

My body is a little tender at 64 years, moves me through a light workout, a personal Yoga. Down on the floor I am stretching, sitting, twisting, and all the time breathing. And when I am finished I feel better. It's something I don't do every day, but enough.

When I am dressed, I find my banjo and fill my daypack with my pen and paints. Out on the road I am walking; the sun is already high, the weather hot. A breeze is blowing from the sea as I walk toward the beach. This is a familiar place, this not talking, and this particular road side, the fields already planted, filled with something green in long rows. Inside there is still the mantra, not so much as being spoken, but more as being acknowledged at each breath. In all these years, through the talking, the motorized travel it has never left me, except when it becomes "the silence."

There are a few cars that pass me, more than a few bikes with people on their way to town or the beach. I find a low livestock gate and clamber through the empty spaces into the Cape May Migratory Bird Refuge. I sit in the shade and look. After a while, I begin to draw, then paint. Looking down the road, some folks approach me with spotting scopes on tripods. They smile and wave, as if they understand already that I am not talking. I am surrounded by poison ivy and tall green grasses that are waving in the breeze, dandelions, yellow gold and the white blossoms of yarrow and Queen Ann's Lace.

On the way home I unsling the banjo and play a favorite tune, in a new way, improvising as I walk along the road. The banjo speaks even if it is not heard. When it is seen people wave. By the time I am home to begin my chores, I know again life as a gift. It feels right to be here, appropriate to write of silence from this place.

In the middle of the afternoon I heard a knock downstairs. Our contractor, Jack Desmond, arrived with his partner and the load of hard wood flooring that was to be installed during the week. They expected me not to be speaking and I didn't disappoint them. They themselves spoke only a few words.

Jack's partner unloaded the truck and with some difficulty stripped off the plastic protective wrapping. I took out my utility tool with its small sharp knife, and the wrapping easily fell away. Jack shooed me back upstairs to continue writing.

Some emails came in and there were some messages on the phone. I listened but there was no need to answer any. Yesterday Martha worried what would happen if there was an emergency. This silence thing was all right but I had a family now. I had to remind her about the time my mother called my cousin Shep because my father was on death's doorstep.

I wrote until it was time to ride my bike down town to go shopping. All I needed was ice. The coffee shop was closed tight. I took my time. After dinner, the sunset and the night sky were filled with fireflies, thunder and lightning.

October 10, 1973
The air is clean and the sky is clear save for a few high puffs of clouds. On the bay, the tide moves in and the hillsides have begun to sprout

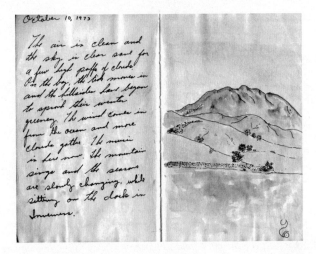

their winter greenery. The wind comes in from the ocean and more clouds gather. The music is here now. The mountain sings and the season are slowly changing, while sitting on the dock in Inverness.

Listen to the birds
And the voices of the sea
Look into blue sky

July 21, 2010
West Cape May, NJ
I am up earlier today, looking forward to take a walk after taking a shower and stretching. Sometimes I call it yoga, because there are some poses that I use that are, but many poses are exercise and stretches that have just come to me in practice over the years. I feel better when I do this morning routine. I think it is good for my body as well.

It is cloudy when I begin my walk to the bird refuge. I have my banjo in my hand, almost an afterthought as I left the house. I was playing something that I used to play all the time. Unlike Life's Celebration it is slow and methodical at a bit of a ragtime beat. But I want to play it, to hear it again and have it take me to that place. Every time I think I will play Celebration, I force myself back. I don't remember its name, only that I wrote it when I did not speak.

I walk past the farmer's field playing, my head down looking at the roadside white line, noting the texture of the asphalt. It is quiet, only a few cars pass. On the main road at the edge of the refuge, there is traffic. I cross to the left side of the road facing the oncoming cars. My music has stopped and the banjo is again slung over my right shoulder, mute. Bicycles pass and then across from me there is a woman running. As she passes she turns around and shouts.

"My son plays the banjo."

"Then your future is secure and you will be blessed for a thousand years," is what I want to say. But no words come from my mouth; I settle for a large smile and a "thumbs up." In that moment I think about my youngest son, Luke. At 3 he loves the banjo, and has his own that he plays with his own great style. I am reminded of my family, separated today by many miles and mountains though not as if we are apart.

Humor always finds its way on the ragged edge of silence. I feel best when it is not at the expense of others. Banjo players are continually sharing self-deprecating jokes among themselves, so I find myself laughing at times but not out loud.

Once inside the refuge a woman birdwatcher asks if I am going to serenade the birds? I answer with two fingers that could mean "just a little." I know that I am really here to listen to the birds, and the sound of the sea, my feet crunching on the stone dirt road. I follow it over the dune. I sit, I watch and I listen.

Along the beach the Piping Plover, a small endangered bird's nesting area is roped off in an attempt to keep their eggs safe, if not from *predation at least from the rest of us. At the far end at Cape May Point is the lighthouse. I've climbed it many times to look far to sea, dreaming a sailing dream. I often wanted to be a lighthouse keeper. The idea of living alone in such bleak and beautiful places intrigued me.*

At the end of the Point is the old convent, where nuns still visit for the summer. The sisters of Saint Joseph a Philadelphia based order have been coming to this retreat for over 100 years. From here I think it's haunted with a hundred ghosts.

But now I can hear the birds call, a piercing song of a Redwing Blackbird, along with the honking of the dark Brant Geese, laid onto the deep texture of the sea.

Heading back home and out of the refuge, I play that tune whose name I can't remember. I walk slowly and think about a friend who just died. The email came in the afternoon to say he died in the morning doing the thing that he loved. He helped disabled kids ride horses, his partner at his side.

It made me think of the times I had seen death's familiar face on the road in California, in the jungles in South America . . .

As I think about my friend who has died, I think of his partner and how she must feel. She had known me before; during and after the 17 years I did not speak. I know that she knows I am present with her without words. Still this death has put into focus what I would like to offer from this place, that is how to live.

In a way, the four days of silence is somehow the same and also much different than seventeen years of silent open-endedness, when there had been no set time to end. In fact, back then I had no knowledge if I would ever start speaking again. After five years, inertia took over; "a body in motion keeps on wanting to move" or in this instance remain silent. So the quality on the edge of silence at this time was perhaps different, but how?

July 21, 2010, 5:00 p.m.
Our contractor came again, this time bringing more materials for the floor. The workers would be putting down the floor in the morning

along with doing some other work. He wondered if the noise would bother me. I hunched my shoulders and brought in the trashcans. It was recyclables today.

In the afternoon I took a bike ride through the neighborhood, and stopped at a neighbor's house. They were in the middle of their own remodeling and construction. I did not have to explain my silence. I didn't feel that I needed to speak. The electrician was just leaving. His wife had just had a heart attack and he was on his way to the hospital over in Delaware. His helper took my hand, very comfortable with my silence. He said he remembered me from when he was in the sixth grade and I visited the West Cape May School.

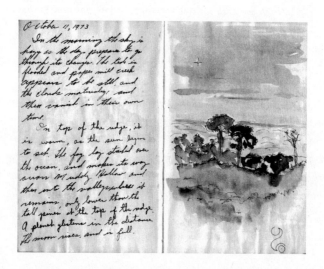

October 11, 1973
In the morning the sky is hazy as the day prepares to go through its changes. The tide is flooded and paper mill creek appears to be still, and the clouds materialize, and then vanish in their own time.

On top of the ridge, it is warm, as the sun begins to set. The fog lay stretched over the ocean, and makes its way across Muddy Hollow and then into the valleys where it remains, only lower than the tall pines at the top of the ridge. A planet glistens in the distance. The moon rises, and is full.

Off hot city streets
Sitting where cool garden grows
Claiming higher ground

July 22, 2010
West Cape May, NJ

I felt myself waking into this miracle and I am grateful for the silence, and the miracle that rises from it in vibrations and all its many forms. I am surprised that it has taken me so long to come back to this place, to be in the space where I am the listener, and I can listen. So when I opened my eyes this morning, still dragging the gossamers of the morning, I was listening. I heard my breath, the bedclothes against my head and body . . . the ceiling fans. I felt the gentle breeze they make.

I sat on the side of the bed with my eyes closed in meditation. What was it that I felt? Gratefulness. Grateful for the silence and the expression of life of which it was a part. I didn't remember gratitude being on Nitsa's list, but knowing her as a friend, I am sure she felt that as her being radiated love, and how could that be without being grateful. But already I am contemplating change and counting days and the differences in the changes that are happening today.

When I didn't use motorized vehicles, I quickly discovered how much of the world still relied on motorized vehicles and adjusted accordingly.

At the Inverness Post Office, I received my first lesson. After giving up using motorized vehicles, I thought I should let some family know. So I wrote a long letter and was standing in line to buy some stamps. The postmistress saw me and whispered something to the other employee who immediately disappeared out the back door. A few minutes later he returned with a satchel, with the words Pony Express written in big letters. When I got to the counter, she took my letter, and, after putting it in the satchel, she hung it on the wall.

"We're sure you don't want your mail riding in the plane with the rest of the mail, but we're just not sure when the next pony is gonna get into town."

You can imagine that with most grocery stores and restaurants that the food wasn't grown in the back or didn't get there in a mule driven wagon. The point is that purity of motive or intention is often the best that we can do at any given time. In fact I did send the letters via air and bought whatever I needed from the local store.

It was barely 7 in the morning when I heard someone downstairs. I climbed down the spiral staircase. It was Tony, our carpenter, already at work fixing the doorway into the back of the house. We both smiled at one another and nodded.

"I heard what you are up to John," he said in an unusually soft voice. He extended his hand and I extended mine. Of course he meant he knew I was being silent, because we had already met. He had been

working at the house for nearly two months and I had given him and the crew each a copy of my book, Planetwalker: 22 Years of Walk-ing. 17 Years of Silence. *He went on to explain what he was doing and I left him to his work and returned upstairs to continue my day.*

I did a good morning workout, grabbed my pack and filled it with my paints, some books and my computer. Today I wanted to walk to "Higher Grounds" the coffee house in West Cape May with an out-door garden. It was the only local coffee house that was open all year around, so it doubled as a community gathering place as well.

As I walked out the door, I turned on my cell phone. It buzzed in my hand and made loud noises, so I know I had voice mails and a text mes-sage. I chuckled silently at how I had become so attached. But just the same I was not in any hurry to find out who called or why. I could wait to find that out later. Just in the way I thought about receiving messages made me feel as if I had become a different person.

I walked out into the morning. It is earlier than the day before. I played the banjo right away, Celebration of Life, picking out the melody, repeating chords the same but differently in time, as I walk up the Avenue. On our side of the road there are houses; on the other there are fewer homes that are spaced between fecund and vacant fields. The corn was almost head high, and dark green leaves spilled from each stalk like waterfalls. There are no golden tassels yet, something to look for. In our garden the dozen or so stalks of corn had fallen prey to the appetite of Raccaloons which is what Luke called Raccoons at three.

The banjo plays softly and something is changing. When I reach Higher Grounds, the coffee house, I sat myself up on a cushioned bench across from the blue birdhouse, facing the sidewalk and the street. The wren family that occupied the house earlier had left a few weeks ago and there were no new tenants. I sipped on Ice green tea while the Beatles reminded us through the speakers that Love was all we needed. I thought I was going to read or write, but I was more interested in watching and listening to the people who did come and sit in the garden and had meetings and worked on laptop computers than doing any work myself. So I set myself to do a painting.

After I started talking and after I walked the length of South America, one day I just stopped. I needed a break from the compulsion. So it was that I now returned to that space, where creativity was given substance and form. I painted what was in front of me from the miracle that I awoke in today and contemplated the silence from which everything arises and everything will return. In transformation, still coming from the silence that pervades, the wood birdhouse, painted blue, the cast iron fence, the flowers and the trees in front of me but also a part of the inner landscape that is me.

Maybe this is part of an altered state experience, though I remembered that on the first day I felt intoxicated. It was odd in a way, because at the time I wanted to deny what I was feeling, and felt as if I wanted to hide it. The feeling lasted only the first day. It is interesting that the co-researchers in Nitsa's study also felt what they have described as an altered state of consciousness, where reality took on other non-ordinary dimensions.

On the way home I played my familiar tune on the banjo, repeating a melody, repeating chords, until a different tune uncovered itself in the rhythm, changing and transforming to something new. My eyes moistened, then dried in the warm breeze from the sea.

When I got home the place was filled with workers, putting in the wood floor, and laying tile in the bathroom. Symbolically another form of transformation is taking place in the house that could represent my family or me.

I retreated upstairs to write. They had all gone for the day and only Tony banged in planks of floor. He said he wanted to work late and take off early the next day. I hooked up the trailer to my bike and rode over to get a Pizza for dinner. When I got back Tony was still there banging away. We shared a slice of pizza and I went upstairs to finish dinner and continue writing.

At the knock on the door I answered in soft voice, but loud enough to send a chill up my spine "yeah?" If Tony had heard me he acted as if he didn't. The probable mechanism for that would be something like denial but not quite. Since he was now used to not hearing me speak, he actually did not consciously hear the word. Me, on the other hand, I heard the word very well. I opened the door and he said he was going to be leaving, that he would see me tomorrow. I nodded and waved goodbye, and he left.

In the evening it is quiet except for the sound of the ceiling fans and feeling the cool breeze across my face. Outside from the balcony I hear the crickets and the ocean's not so distant voice. The fireflies glow soft bioluminescence, the moon growing silver white and the flash of the lighthouse light as it makes its circle in the dark.

Today I was able to let myself answer email and text messages. I answered only a few of each.

October 12, 1973

Morning comes and the air is cold and fresh. The bay appears as a smooth glass, mirroring all above it, in its depths. The tide has started to ebb, as a fresh breeze moves across the water and small ripples become waves and move to, and away from the shore.

As time passes, the sun sets. The moon once more, accompanied by a planet rises out of the north-east casting its reflection onto the bay. Silver moon dance, all is a shimmer.

> *Crawling on the shore*
> *From a million years ago*
> *Stories of the past*

July 23, 2010
Higbee's Beach,
West Cape May, NJ
I woke up at dawn. I had only slept for a few hours. Downstairs I could hear the workmen hammering, continuing to lay down the floor. I stayed upstairs and did the lightest of practice, but bowing with my eyes closed, a modified salutation to the sun, I nearly touched my toes. That made me smile. When I got down stairs, the full crew was at work.

The porch was done and they had moved things from the dining room and kitchen. I could see progress.

I used to look at houses as little boxes that we lived in waiting to die.

This day felt like a different day to me, as in not the same routine. It wasn't going to be a morning painting. I had started too late for that, and I wanted to ride my bike and play my concert banjo that my friends had gotten together to give me when I lived in California. It was a Gibson long neck Pete Seeger model. It was the new tune that was still with me from yesterday that I wanted to hear on the big banjo. It had its own voice that was deep and resonant, much different from the higher sound of the small S.S. Stuart, fiddle banjo, which was the easiest to carry, and itself over 100 years old.

I spent a few minutes cleaning my desk in the office; soon enough I would be back working there and I would want the space in order as much as possible. My office is in the room at the front of the house, along with the main entrance. After that I took the Gibson into the living room, passing through the crew that was working, and on to the back porch. Their radio was blaring some rock anthem as I walked through, but when they saw the banjo and understood I was going to play they turned it off.

I started slowly, slipping the corduroy fabric outer case lining and then the latches and lifted the top. It spoke softly as the red velvet lining moved across some string, "Thrumm," it said in greeting. And as I picked it up it spoke again, touched by a light morning breeze. Yes, it has been too long, but I am here now. I cradled the instrument in my arms.

My friend who owned a music store gave me the Gibson when it became apparent that I was serious about playing the banjo. I already had a rental to learn banjo that was made in Japan, a Conqueror that did well enough for me. I had read somewhere that the quality of the instrument wouldn't keep a good musician from making music, but my friends said they wanted me to have an instrument that was worthy of the music that they were hearing me play. They said it would be my concert banjo. An instrument I could play when I settled down for the winter, one that I wouldn't have to tie broken strings together.

It wasn't that I was so poor that I couldn't afford to buy strings for my banjo, as much as it was fact I was on the road on in the wilderness when strings broke, I would just square knot tie the string back together.

So as I cradled my Gibson in my arms, thought of all the others who have held her as tenderly and of my friends and the wonderful gift they gave me, and then I touched the strings. The music rolled from my fingers, the five steel strings, until something new, in a voice that was very old and resonant filled the back porch and the yard. I think I played an hour, but during these days of silence time had become less reasonable. I wake in the morning, and then the afternoon is gone, and as I begin an evening ritual midnight is already here.

When I finished playing and took the banjo back into the house, the crew said how they hadn't wanted me to stop playing, but already the radio was on and they were keeping time with the swinging hammer and the whine of the electric saw to yet another rock anthem.

I didn't know where I was going, except I had played the morning music and my pant leg was tied up. I grabbed my pack with my paints and walked out the door to the bike and turned away from the bird refuge, away from downtown and the Point and lighthouse. I turned toward Higbee's Beach.

The ride is on Bayshore Blvd, past the expensive houses of Cape May Estates, but Cape May is an island, and no matter which way you walk or ride your bike, you will come to the water; this water is the canal that separates Cape May from the mainland. Besides this beach there is a dune forest, none of it developed; it's a beautiful long solitary walk toward the Delaware Bay.

There are lots of boats passing, leaving and returning to the marinas; if I wave, the people wave back as if we know each other. I walk along looking at the colored stones that are sticking in the sand, and further on is the ferry terminal; a large white ferry boat is waiting for its turn to back out into the bay for the trip to Lewes, Delaware.

It is a place for horseshoe crabs to come ashore. They are remnants from another age and haven't changed much in over 250 million years. They are like looking at living fossils. I remember them as a kid when I was growing up in Cape May; I hadn't seen them anywhere else.

I walked slowly, not in a hurry, to just sit and do my painting for the day. For the walk back I went through the dune forest, knowing that in the morning, I am going to speak again. I wonder how I will be. Will there be something new out of something old?

I ride the bike home the way I came and smell the warm green breeze of freshly cut grass. More planks are on the floor. The bathroom tiles are done. I give Frank a Planetwalker *book. He reads the cover, and moves away from the radial saw.*

"What, seventeen Years?" It is a question, so I nod.

"I'm glad you gave him your book," Brian, his partner says. "He thought you didn't like him cause you didn't talk to him."

I sent an email to Joyce letting her know that I will end my silence tomorrow and will call. It crosses my mind that I should fly there but she says it isn't necessary. As I ride the bike to the market for toilet paper and laundry detergent I feel overwhelmed by life, but at the same time there is a stillness in which I am waiting. I stop at Higher Grounds; it should be closed but Katie is still there so even with the closed sign on the door she takes in customers. For a while I sit in the garden sipping iced Earl Grey tea and watch two young girls in conversation. I am thinking about speaking and not speaking. There was a list of folks I had to talk to.

As I am sitting there I realize that even though I know I am speaking tomorrow, it is Friday and I have been thinking it was Monday; the days have been confused, except for my watch and journal.

At home Tony has already left, and Brian and Frank are just about finished; they are cleaning up. As I begin writing I look at the computer screen and bright blue light arcs across my field of vision, something I can't explain. It is very old, and all my words are gone.

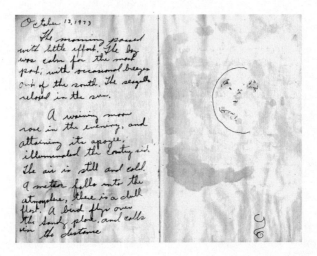

October 13, 1973

The morning passed with little effort. The bay was calm for the most part, with occasional breezes out of the south. The seagulls relaxed in the sun.

A waning moon rose in the evening, and attaining its apogee, illuminated the countryside. The air is still and cold. A meteor falls into the atmosphere, there is a dull flash. A bird flies over the Sandy place, and calls in the distance.

In evening's stillness
My heart is waiting to beat
My voice waits to speak

July 24, 2010
West Cape May, NJ

When I look at both sets of journals, the words and paintings that I do today compared to the earlier ones that I did, I find that the early journals have a simplicity and purity of the earlier time. And they are reflective of that time. At that time, I lived the simplest "Walden" life, either on the road or in a small cabin in the wood. It was a simple practice born in and of itself. They are what they are. In that place I was writing more from silence and less from its ragged edge.

On the other hand, my recent journals are more expansive and inclusive; as a meditation they are also reflective of my life, busy with things going on in a worldview that dips in and out of silence only as a matter of habit, as the business of life gathers close and crowds the wilderness and the desert. It is here that the ragged edge of silence can be found. Here, I feel my mind overwhelmed, but even in the deluge, there is still the practice of sitting, painting, and writing.

The importance of this to us is that even in our ordinary lives, fractured as they might be with going to the store, repairing our homes, making the bed, raising a family, and all the countless activities that go into pursuing happiness and the business of living life, there is the opportunity to find meaning, to find ourselves and some peace in the world, on the ragged edge.

In the house where my parents lived and died, I can touch them both. When my mother said, "If you were happy you really wouldn't have to say so," it was so very telling of how she looked at and understood silence and my place within it. My dad, who followed me across the country, never gave up, never let go, not with his love, nor with his advice: "You have to ride in cars and talk."

My father was right about what I was going to have to do if I were going to fulfill my vision. I was going to have to ride in cars and talk. And maybe in all our lives, or at least in some of us, this is going to hold true. But first, I think one of the most important things we need to do is to take a walk and listen, and to find the ragged edge of silence; then, from that place, peace will come.

Lesson in Silence: Journey

Objective: To find your path and share it with us

Father Robert Kennedy, a Jesuit priest, was a young man when his order sent him to study religions in Japan. In his studies he found Buddhism, and after many years his Buddhist teachers gave him the title of roshi, an honorific title denoting an "old teacher" or "elder master." After ending my last four-day silence I visited with him at St. Peter's College in Jersey City, New Jersey, where he teaches Japanese and ecumenical theology. We laughed a lot and sat in silence. When it was time to leave, he gave me this koan:

> A young monk was walking along the road with his teacher. After they had gone on awhile in silence, the monk turned to his teacher and asked, "Roshi, what is the path to enlightenment?" With a stick the teacher drew a line in the road. They continued on in silence.

No one can really tell you how to find your path. We all start with a blank page. But if you have done any of these exercises, you have already begun.

ACKNOWLEDGMENTS

I would first like to thank my friend, sister and colleague in silence, Nitsa (Ourania) Marcandonatou, who shared with me her own research and experiences. Nitsa's encouragement and generosity is equal to my own desire to make silence assessable to everyone. Also I am grateful to Father Robert Kennedy, for improving my understanding of silence and the use of koans in the Buddhist tradition. I am still on that path. Equally I give my sincerest thanks to Irv Rose for his teachings in communications, listening, and the two-minute briefing.

I especially thank my editor, Ken Bingham, without whose tireless work, enlightened perspective, and painstaking detail to what words were needed to be included in my explanation of silence this book would never have been completed in the allotted time. I am indebted as well to Ruth Chamblee and Lisa Thomas at the National Geographic Society book division, who were unwavering in their faith and encouragement.

Finally I want to thank Katie Panamarenko, and all the workers of the Higher Grounds coffeehouse and café, for providing a warm and welcoming atmosphere for all the writers, artists, and community members of West Cape May, New Jersey. And last but not least I want to thank my wife, Martha, Samuel, and Luke for making a home where love, music, laughter, and silence exist between all our words.